T0369031

SKIN IN THE GAME

Journey of a Mother and her Marine Son

Peggy Logue

Order this book online at www.trafford.com
or email orders@trafford.com

Most Trafford titles are also available at major online book retailers.

Printed in Victoria, BC, Canada.

ISBN: 978-1-4269-2433-0 (sc)
ISBN: 978-1-4269-2434-7 (dj)

Library of Congress Control Number: 2009914223

Our mission is to efficiently provide the world's finest, most comprehensive book publishing service, enabling every author to experience success. To find out how to publish your book, your way, and have it available worldwide, visit us online at www.trafford.com

Trafford rev. 1/22/2010

 www.trafford.com

North America & international
toll-free: 1 888 232 4444 (USA & Canada)
phone: 250 383 6864 ♦ fax: 812 355 4082

For my son, Cpl. Michael J. Logue U.S.M.C. He and his brother Marines served combat in Iraq in 2005, with bravery and compassion.
Thank you, Lima 3/25th for what you did and who you are. You are remembered as an important part of American history in the 21st century.

FALLEN BROTHERS of LIMA COMPANY 3/25TH:

LCpl Timothy Michael Bell, 22
LCpl Eric James Bernholtz, 23
LCpl Nicholas William Baart Bloem, 20
LCpl Michael Joseph Cifuentes, 25
LCpl Wesley Graham Davids, 20
Cpl Dustin Alan Derga, 24
Pfc Christopher Robert Dixon, 18
LCpl Christopher Jenkins Dyer, 19
LCpl Nicholas Brandon Erdy, 21
LCpl Grant Bruce Fraser, 22
SSgt Anthony Lee Goodwin, 33
LCpl Jonathan Walter Grant, 23
LCpl Jourdan Lin Grez, 24
Sgt. Justin Fenton Hoffman, 27
SSgt. Kendall Howard Ivy, 28
Sgt. David Kenneth John Kreuter, 26
LCpl Christopher Paul Lyons, 24
LCpl Aaron Howard Reed, 21
LCpl Edward August (Augie) SchroederII, 23
LCpl William Brett Wightman, 22
Cpl Andre Lewis Williams, 23
Sgt. David Neil Wimberg, 24
HM3 Travis Levy Youngblood, 26

SEMPER FI

*If we divide into two camps -- even
into violent and the non-violent -- and
stand in one camp while attacking the
other, the world will never have peace.
We will always blame and condemn those
we feel are responsible for wars and social
injustice, without recognizing the degree of
violence within ourselves. We must work on
ourselves and also with those we condemn if
we want to have a real impact.*

-Ayya Khema, "Be An Island"

FOREWARD

Peggy Logue's *Skin In The Game: Journey of a Mother and her Marine Son* tells the poignant story of one military family's very personal experience with the Iraq war. But Peggy's words and experiences as a mother sending her son off to a war in which she and her husband did not believe, reflect and give witness to the heart and the hurt of so many military families who opposed the U.S. invasion of Iraq or at some point concluded that the war in Iraq was wrong. Peggy's tears are our tears, her fears our fears. By speaking out and sharing her heart, Peggy has exposed so many details that made up – and make up – our raw, anguished journeys. But beyond echoing the experiences and the hearts of military families, Peggy's heartbreaking yet uplifting narrative provides the vast majority of people in this country who have no skin in the game with a rare and stark reflection of the months, weeks, days, hours and moments of our trauma as the nation was sent off to war in Iraq. As military families we understand better than most that it wasn't really the nation who was sent to war – it was our loved ones, and our hearts went with them.

At this writing, in fall of 2009, it has been more than seven years since my own stepson deployed with the 24th Marine Expeditionary Unit, first to Kosovo, on his way to Iraq. That was the fall of 2002, when the drumbeats for war in Iraq were getting deafening. While George W. Bush, his administration and the majority in Congress were crying "We've got to go to war!" we noticed that none of them were really going anywhere, nor were their loved ones. In November, 2002 my husband Charley Richardson, myself and a father whose son was about to deploy to Kuwait decided to form an organization of military families speaking out to try to prevent an invasion of Iraq. We called the organization Military Families Speak Out (MFSO), and hoped to organize and build the voice of military families opposing the invasion – families who had a great stake in the debate, a strong need to speak out, and a special voice that could make a difference. Peggy's early chapters took me back to a time before that. In August, 2002, the weekend before our son was to ship out, Charley and I went to Camp Lejeune in North Carolina to see if we would be allowed to be with him before he shipped out. As it turned out, we were able to spirit him away to spend twenty-four hours on Okracoke Island. How does a family say good-bye to a loved one being sent off to a war that shouldn't be fought? As military families, so many of us did just that. *"There is nothing we can do to stop this or change this. Is this our last good-bye?"* Peggy's narrative has captured moments like these in ways that touch nerves and hearts for those who experienced them, and made palpable the powerlessness, the pain and anguish for those who have not.

Unfortunately, the original goal of Military Families Speak Out – to prevent an invasion of Iraq – was not realized. MFSO grew from the original two families to about 200 military families at the time of "shock and awe" on March 19, 2003; to over 4,000 military and Gold Star families (families whose loved ones died as a result of the war) in 2009. Peggy's narrative focuses on a time period in 2005 when more was being uncovered about the mistruths and lies that led us into this war, more people in this country were questioning the reasons and need for the war, but the fierce battles raged on. Her son's unit, once called "Lucky Lima," was well-known to many military families who were daily and sometimes hourly tracking the casualties of this war. Lima Company, 3rd Battalion of the 25th Marines, a unit of 160, was to lose 23 of their own in their seven-month deployment in 2005.

Throughout her narrative, Peggy gives voice to the crazy cadence of our lives as military families with loved ones deployed. She describes commonplace events that take on new meanings. When the phone rings, we jump: is it our loved one calling from Iraq, or someone with much more sinister news about explosions and life-threatening wounds? That knock on the door – will we open it to see officers in dress blues with news we dread the most? One MFSO member left work every day and drove around or went to the mall until she knew her husband was home – she couldn't bear the thought of being alone if such messengers were going to arrive. But those without *skin in the game* know little or none of this – of our strangely tattered lives

Peggy also illustrates the particular dilemmas of military families who honor and support our loved ones but condemn the war they were sent to fight. Peggy speaks of struggling with how a newspaper's readers would view her as the result of her quote in an article that questioned the war in Iraq. *"Will they then accuse me of not supporting my son? How painful. How dead wrong."* In fact, it has been voices like Peggy's that have helped disconnect "support for the troops" from "support for the war," and teach the American people – and our politicians – that the most supportive thing they can do for our troops, once deployed to an unjust and unjustifiable war, is to end that war, bring our troops home quickly and safely, make sure they get the care that they need and deserve when they return, and never again let them be recklessly sent off to another war.

During her son's deployment, Peggy was introduced to and joined Military Families Speak Out, and became active locally in the "Bring Them Home Now" bus tour that carried military and Gold Star families, Iraq War Veterans and Veterans of other eras on a speaking tour from near Bush's ranch in Crawford, Texas to Washington, D.C. in September of 2005. She housed the families and Veterans when the tour came through Ohio, participated in meetings in Congressional offices, and spoke at community forums where she was able to share, as she put it, *"the terror that I live with."* Peggy commented about this experience, *"I am finally doing something rather than sitting at home on the computer or watching and waiting for news from Iraq. It feels so good to be taking action."* Peggy echoes the sentiments of so many MFSO members, for whom the organization has been both a vehicle for taking action, and for finding kindred souls who walk in our shoes.

Periodically in the narrative, Peggy notes that the pain and anguish she feels about the war in Iraq is tied to her son and other troops being put in harm's way, in "kill or be killed" situations; but is also tied to the understanding that others are being harmed – the Iraqi people who are caught daily in the war's cross-fire. She exposes the often hidden but very real human toll, the burden of a war being carried out in all of our names, for which we all have responsibility.

The bittersweet ending of Peggy's narrative reflects another cycle of events that this war has unfolded. Those of us who have been lucky enough to welcome loved ones home and hold them again in our arms, are familiar with well-meaning questions from friends and relatives such as, "Isn't it wonderful to have your loved one home safe and sound?" Unfortunately, many of us don't know that our loved ones are or will be safe or sound – they have been exposed to physical and psychological traumas as well as agents such as depleted uranium that could put them at risk for decades to come. Peggy wrote, *"I thought with Mike home my grief would end and all would be well. And all would be normal. But the truth is it takes years to get back to some sense of normalcy and wellness......It is hard to pick up the pieces of war."* Returned Veterans and their families are struggling every day trying to pick up these pieces. The casualties of the war in Iraq did not all come home in flag-draped coffins. Months or years after returning from combat, Veterans living with the psychological injuries of war have taken their own lives; the suicide rate among returned Veterans keeps climbing. Other types of violence have appeared in homes and relationships; the divorce rate has skyrocketed. All the tears of this war will never be wiped away.

Peggy leaves us with a challenge, and it is a timely challenge indeed. Her personal narrative gently but powerfully raises the weightiest of questions about war: *"Those of us trying to heal from our experiences of this war may never completely heal until war in Iraq is over, and maybe not until all war is over."* In fall of 2009, most people in the United States seem to believe that the war in Iraq is all but over. Yet troops are still being deployed there, and the toll of troop deaths this year has averaged two deaths per week in some months, to almost one death each day in other months. Iraq has become the hidden war, switching places with the once-forgotten war in Afghanistan which is now back on the front pages. 2009 has been the deadliest year for U.S. troops in Afghanistan; in October the death rate averaged almost two troops per day. At this writing, the President is struggling to chart a course for what many deem a quagmire. Polls indicate that more and more Americans are questioning a course that continues the U.S. military occupation of Afghanistan. Once again, the voices of military families are coming to the fore, as families who have *skin in the game* are speaking out. They are helping to re-frame problems and call into question what has been conventional wisdom. While political leaders have maintained that "Funding these wars is funding our troops," military and Gold Star families have countered, "Funding these wars is killing our troops – and the people of Iraq and Afghanistan." Peggy's remarkable book will inform those who are, or should be, grappling with both the immediate and the long-term questions of foreign policy, of war and peace. For those who haven't had a loved one serving in these current conflicts, it offers a window to explore the world of military families and learn from their experiences. And for many military families, those with skin in the game, Peggy's book will help validate feeling and experiences and pave a way to connection so that families can take comfort, and take action. Together we will not feel so alone; collectively we can make a difference.

In Peace and Solidarity,
Nancy Lessin
Co-founder, Military Families Speak Out (www.mfso.org)

PREFACE

After prolonged and heated discussions with the Marine recruiter guaranteeing that Mike has the freedom to change his plans, Jerry signs a waiver for Mike, then seventeen, to join the U.S. Marine Corps. It is one month before Mike's 18th birthday. He will become part of Lima Company 3/25th Marines in Columbus, Ohio.

June 2004, two days after graduating for high school, Mike is in Boot Camp at Parris Island. He completes training in late August and is a day late starting college at Ohio University. Overnight Mike goes from being a boot camp Marine to a college student.

This story begins in late January, 2005 when Jerry and I find out that Mike will receive orders to go to Iraq.

Nine months after graduating from high school and nineteen years old, Mike is sent to Iraq with the 3/25th Lima Company Marines. Something we are not prepared for nor planned for as we are told Ohio Marines have not been involved in combat since there are "not enough leaders in this Reserve Unit."

I keep a journal of my thoughts and feelings, my emails and responses, news articles, and anything that crosses my path dealing with our Marines and the war while Mike is deployed. I record it all for him and for us. I live this war day by day and some days, minute by minute.

Now it is a book that reflects my journey as I try to deal with my sons' decision to become a Marine at a time our country is at war. I speak only for myself as I face the hardest time of my life. I do not intend to be a political voice for anyone. I am a mother, a mama bear, wanting desperately to protect her child. I share my rage and fear sometimes wildly because this is how I feel.

I am aware of the mothers and families who lost everything. I am deeply humbled by their grace. Some of those families support the war and I hope I do not offend them as I speak my thoughts against war.

These Lima Company Marines endured a very intensive combat history and performed as the noble young men they are. They are of the tradition of warriors, showing bravery, courage and compassion.

The families also showed an amazing courage. Our lives are never to be the same.

I honor and respect my Marine son and all those who serve and want to make a better life for others.

Semper Fi.

ACKNOWLEDGEMENTS

First I acknowledge the 3/25th Marines of Columbus Ohio for their service and their courage and integrity.

Helping me through the writing of this book has been my writers group, especially Linda Martin, Barb Rohrer and Suellyn Shupe. They read with me each meeting and often cried with me. More than anything they encouraged me and stayed with me as I worked to get it finished. They knew it could be done.

I am also thankful for all those who I quote in the book. The family and friends who wrote beautiful uplifting words to help us during this difficult time. And for the journalist and politicians and anti-war protestors who stepped out to speak against this war when speaking out was considered unpatriotic.

My husband, Jerry has always been my best and first supporter. He has read and re-read this book so many times. It has been hard for him because it refreshes the memories over and over. But he has good insights and with his gentle spirit has made suggestions that made my writing better. I am grateful for his love and support.

I am also thankful for the support and encouragement of my Marine son who lived this journey and has a larger story to share but holds it in his heart. He is a committed Marine who chose to serve in the spirit of a true warrior. Mike's help in guiding some of the events and his insights make my story more accurate and more meaningful.

ABBREVIATIONS

AAV – Assault Amphibious Vehicle (Trac)
AO- Area of Operation
CO – Commanding Officer
IED – Improvised Explosive Device
Humvee – High Mobility Multi-Wheeled Vehicle
I&I – Inspector and Instructor (Active duty officer who runs drill center)
Kabar – personal knife used for close combat
KIA – Killed in Action
LCpl – Lance Corporal
Medevac – Medical Evacuation
MRE – Meal Ready to Eat
NJP – Non-judicial Punishment
RPG – Rocket Propelled Grenade
SAPI plate – Small Arms Protective Insert (ceramic plate in pockets or flak jacket)
SOI – School of Infantry
WIA – Wounded in Action

Table of Contents

INTRODUCTION

"What?"

"He's going to Iraq," First Sergeant Halbig repeats while distracted by some other important responsibility found in his papers scattered on his desk. Jerry and I sit numbed and speechless.

"Why weren't we told? When was this decision made? Does Mike know?" The questions blurt out of my instantly parched mouth and trembling voice.

"No, Mike doesn't know yet," he answers while still fidgeting with papers.

"When do you tell him?" I push through feeling that my heart may explode.

"When he gets back from SOI," Sergeant Halbig casually responds.

"But no! How will he get ready?" I question in panic.

"Everything he needs is in his sea bag," is the quick and confident reply.

"No! How...how...?" My voice tries to find words that ask

how I deal with this news. How do I deal with this? What do I do? How did this happen? Mike wasn't supposed to go to Iraq. So I say "how does he get ready?" But I am asking for much more.

Sgt. Halbig totally misses the meaning of my questions. He looks at me quizzically. He must be saying to himself, "What?" He appears confused by my questions. I know this is "business as usual" for him. But it is not for me. This is frightening. It is like receiving a death sentence. "You have two weeks to live," kind of death sentence.

Sergeant Halbig attempting to show interest and understanding just says, "I'm sorry, we just follow orders. These decisions are made 'up the chain.'"

Jerry and I feel like we have fallen through a hole and a trap door shuts and locks. There is nothing we can do. Mike, "property of the United States Government" is going to Iraq. I tell Sgt. Halbig that I will call Mike that night. He shrugs an "okay" and then we flood him with questions that he either refuses to answer or can't because he is "just following orders." We remind him of the promises made to Mike and the contract he signed stating that he would be in the Delayed Entry Program, would go to college and learn to fly for the Marines. Sergeant Halbig can't find it since they have "just moved into our offices." Mike's paper work is "here somewhere." Besides, there is some "loop-hole that voids the contract," especially if "we are at war." The conversation is more and more frustrating and our immediate concern is to tell Mike and to go see him.

We leave the Drill Center in Columbus feeling like we have picked up the weight from Atlas, stuffed it into our back packs and heaved it onto our shoulders. And our heads bend to the ground. Now what? What do we do?

Jerry and I can barely speak. We each deal with the shock in our own way. Jerry is a good problem solver and I can sense his mind reeling with thoughts about what to do. I am feeling overwhelmed and hopeless.

"We should go see him tomorrow," I interject into Jerry's pensiveness.

"He may not be allowed visitors," Jerry responds not wanting to make a quick decision.

"We need to see him," I insist. I sound forceful and feel frightened.

"We'll think it through and see what Mike wants."

"They said he wasn't going. How can they change their minds? Do they think we are just pawns and they can move us around at their will?" I begin to cry.

We become silent and continue our drive home lost in our shock. That evening we call Mike.

"Honey, Sgt Halbig says you are going to Iraq."

Silence.

"Mike?"

"Yeah, I hear you." After another thoughtful pause he says, "I've been expecting it… Might as well go and get it over with."

"I am so sorry, Honey. None of us expected this."

"I know, Mom, it will be okay."

"He says you'll go to Twenty-Nine Palms right after School Of Infantry. You should be able to catch up on the training. The deployment to Iraq would be in early March."

Silence.

"Mike, we would like to come and see you."

"This is my only free weekend before training ends."

"Okay, great. We'll pack up and leave early tomorrow."

"I'll have Saturday and Sunday liberty. Maybe we can go to the beach."

We talk longer but our words attempt to cover the devastation we are feeling, total surprise, and total helplessness.

Jerry and I were told we didn't need to come to the Family Readiness meeting in December in Columbus before the Unit left for Twenty-Nine Palms, California, because Mike is "not going to Iraq." At this meeting the families were told the plan for the Unit and what they should expect and how to prepare themselves and their Marine. Now we have to figure out how to prepare for this and play catch up. And do it alone. And so does Mike.

The next morning we drive to North Carolina to visit with Mike at Camp LeJeune. It is cold and rainy, dark and windy the whole weekend, the weather mirroring our feelings. Mike shows us around the base. We share some meals, our thoughts and some laughter. Then, we leave.

When we return home Jerry and I call Sgt. Halbig and ask him if we can have some time with Mike when he completes SOI before he is sent to Twenty-Nine Palms. At first he refuses and acts like we are being unreasonable. Several days later we call again and are told Mike will have a few days before leaving to join his Unit in California. I don't know if this is to comfort us or just a convenient decision based on air flight availability.

Here we are now, looking for Iraq on the world map and looking squarely into her face. This was never supposed to happen. We are promised, and Mike is promised that as a Marine in the Delayed Entry Program, he will be able to go to college, and learn to fly.

I flash back to the thoughts and feelings I have when Mike first tells me he wants to become a Marine. My thoughts are panicked:

What about peace? "Giving peace a chance?" What about sitting down and talking, and listening? Respecting others? Respecting their culture and way of life? What about a peaceful solution to problems? What about love, creation, life? Have you thought about the Peace Corps? And what about your ideals, virtue, values? What have I taught you? My mind reels in anxiety as thoughts fall over each other trying to be expressed in urgency, like trying to singly stamp out a forest fire.

And…How can you go off to somewhere and kill people? Isn't this what the military does? What about killing people? Can you really point a gun at someone and fire? Can you take another life? What does killing feel like? What will it do to you?

Isn't it you who prayed with me a thanksgiving prayer as we cut the branches to carve a path through our woods? Isn't it you who prayed a gentle prayer while holding the fledgling bird that fell from her nest? I grieve to think that what you know about life and its sacredness might get brushed aside as you face violence and destruction. I grieve for your lost innocence, for your soul.

These thoughts came before Boot Camp and before the deployment.

And now Mike is being sent away and may face physical harm but will indeed face spiritual harm and we can do nothing to stop it. We are naïve when he asks us for our signatures at seventeen to become a Marine. We are made promises that we trust. And Mike is filled with dreams of being a warrior.

Jerry and I have learned so much and want to share this experience with others. It has taken more than four years since the return of Lima 3/25th to be able to write this. It has not been easy. I could not face it at first and would rather not have gone here as often as I have had to.

There is a force behind me I can't explain. A friend in my writer's group through her tears said that when I said to them "I feel pushed by a wind" she saw Lima Company fallen Marines standing behind me.

Maybe it is for them that this story is written. I feel it is a story for mothers, fathers, families and spouses who have the honor and terror of having a warrior in their life.

I know Mike is a Marine for noble even idealistic reasons. He sees himself in service for his country. He wants to serve, to give back. He has no real enemies. He has had to learn to see another as the enemy. He wants to help people.

I share how we feel while Mike is away in war. Jerry and I

want people to know that those in uniform are *real* flesh and blood, treasured by those who they call family and friend. The injuries are to *real* people, the deaths cannot be reversed. Lives are sacrificed and families are hurt and many suffer. And it is all so final. The sadness is on all sides. We cannot grieve for the American Marines and Soldiers and their families without also grieving for the many innocent Iraqis who have lost their lives and their loved ones.

Jerry and I know and fear that Mike may lose his innocence as the ideals that motivate him will pale and be replaced by war. And my pain, my deep pain is about what will happen to Mike spiritually. I know we can fix a broken leg. We can mend a shattered skull but we have not mastered the art of healing the soul.

Not long ago Mike said he is "just beginning to feel normal." We can say the same. We are just beginning to feel "normal." But it is a "new normal." We will never be the same. Because of this war "normal" has a different meaning. Maybe it is because we don't cry as often that makes us feel more normal. But the pain of war lingers in our lives. Our souls are scarred. I believe many from this war carry scars of the soul as well as of the body.

Our great nation is a vessel of compassion for many in the world who suffer. Our warriors are the ones who represent us as we reach out to help others. We need to train them for this kind of service with honorable goals. We must give to the world our compassion. This is what makes us different and a great nation. We do not want to be a nation of destruction.

I want to say to those who lost their sons, fathers, and husbands; I do not want to offend you by anything I write. I do not think your Marine or Soldier died in vain. I wish there were another way.

Jerry and I want those who still have someone in combat to know that though it is a small number involved in war they are not alone. And although we still succumb to the tears, the anxiety, the fear, the injured spirits that we experienced four years ago…we are surviving.

Some who read this will say it is their story because they have experienced many of the same things. I know this because every time we see or hear about another Marine or soldier KIA (killed in action) or see another WIA (wounded in action) or see a homecoming, we feel those same feelings we had when 3/25ᵗʰ Lima Company was in Iraq. Once you experience having a Marine or Soldier in combat you will always feel connected to others experiencing the same. Those of us who are trying to heal from our experiences of this war may never completely heal until the war in Iraq is over and maybe not until all war is over.

Jerry and I have been married for thirty-four years. I have seen Jerry cry only in the last three years.

I begin the journey of our life as a family involved in a war far away and yet as close as our next breath. We are part of the one percent of the American people who are paying deeply for this war. We have "skin in the game".

CHAPTER 1

Into the Dark Night

It is February, 2005 and Jerry and I go to Las Vegas for the first time. Not for fun, winning or losing. We are going to soak up time with our nineteen year old son who is on a forty-eight hour liberty before being deployed to a different desert in another country, Iraq.

Marine families aware of the forty-eight hour liberty are discouraged to come to Las Vegas because they have "already said their good-byes" in January in Columbus. Good-byes are difficult and there is the attempt by the Marine staff to minimize that anguish.

The 3/25th Division Marines left Columbus in January to spend three months in Twenty-Nine Palms, California training for their deployment in Iraq. Mike is not part of that order, is behind in training and instead is sent to Camp LeJeune in North Carolina for SOI (School of Infantry).His orders are then changed. He is going to Iraq. We go to Las Vegas to spend time with Mike and to say our good-byes.

Jerry and I, Crista(Mike's sister), and cousin, Darren fly to Las Vegas and check into our motel. The Marines are coming from California by bus. We will meet them in the lower level of the Tropicana Resort and Casino. We gather with many other families waiting for their Marine. Those who do want to see their loved ones once more and are willing to suffer the good-byes again. We know that for some this will be a final good-bye. We don't know or think about whom that may be. We wait and wait. We walk. We talk. We feel anxious.

Finally we catch a glimpse of the first bus turning the corner followed then by bus after bus. The Marines dressed in their "desert cammies" swinging their back packs over the heads depart the bus. They take a large view sweep with their eyes but head right inside knowing they aren't going anywhere until dismissed.

We look straining to find Mike, hoping for a quick touch. In their uniform dress the Marines all look the same. And you can only see the bridge of their nose and their chin. But you think you will recognize your son.

"There he is," I shout, only to see "no it isn't." Buses empty and Marines walk by but where is Mike? Then while stretching and straining and desperately searching not seeing the tree for the forest, Mike appears right in my face. I don't see him approach. I am looking too hard. A quick hello and a hug and he joins in formation with five hundred other Marines.

The Marines receive their instructions, are told to have a good time and are dismissed.

Now, we have some time with Mike alone. There is a sense of confusion for each of us. What to say? How to be strong? How to say good-bye?

First on Mike's mind is food. We settle on a restaurant, order a meal and begin to relax and enjoy our time. Darren teaches us to play his favorite slot, *Texas Tea*. After a short while,

Mike comes to me red in the face, frustrated and embarrassed. He says he has won twelve dollars and went to cash it in and the lady calls security on him and says he shouldn't be here.

"What?" I say.

"She says I shouldn't be here." Mike responds. I get up and go to the cashier.

"Please tell me what this is all about," I demand, feeling like a mama bear protecting her cub. I know my son is going to war. I don't think there is anything or anyone who will question what he is doing this night. I never thought about his age. My God! He is going to war.

"According to Nevada Gambling Regulations he is not allowed on the casino floor. I cannot pay him any money. He needs to leave," she says.

"But he is here with the Marines. They are going to Iraq. This is their liberty. What are they supposed to do?" I quip.

"I don't know Ma'am. I can only do my job. I called the supervisor. She will be here soon. You can talk to her." She looked away not able to allow herself to get involved with my grief.

Mike steps back. He doesn't know what to think and is more concerned about being in trouble with the Marines.

The supervisor comes forward and the clerk tells her the problem. She then turns to me and re-iterates the Nevada Gambling Regulation that forbids anyone under twenty-one from being on the casino floor.

"We didn't know that. Or didn't even think of it," I say to her. "There are five hundred Marines in Las Vegas tonight and most of them are under twenty-one. They are on liberty before going to Iraq. What are they supposed to do?"

I am nervous and frustrated and feeling confused. How can this be? It seems so petty. Mike is heading off to a foreign land with a rifle in his hand and she wants to tell me about Nevada Gambling Regulations? Get real! Don't you get it? My son is going to war! I think these thoughts but can't speak them. I am hurt. I am hurt that he has to go to Iraq, hurt that we have to experience any of this. Hurt for our young men. Hurt for the innocent Iraqis. Hurt.

I look at the supervisor, young and unaware of war and say, "I understand your position and I am glad there are gambling regulations but this is different. These young men are going to war. Some of them will not come home. We are asking them to sacrifice their lives and yet we won't let them collect twelve dollars from a slot machine? Isn't there something wrong here?"

My face feels hot and red and I feel the releasing of the swelling tidal wave of tears that are rising and ready to break over her. She begins to sense my frustration and my grief as I let go the pent up tears I carry while seeing my son go to war. I cry, feel embarrassed and apologize. It isn't her fault Mike is going to Iraq.

She gives me the twelve dollars, explains that Mike can walk around the casino but cannot be on the casino floor and offers to buy us all dinner at the casino buffet. I take a few deep stammering breaths and attempt to pull myself together. I don't want Mike to see me crying. I thank her. We leave the casino floor.

That evening we enjoy a buffet we wouldn't have paid for ourselves and later talk about how ridiculous it seems to be man enough to fight a war but not old enough to play a slot machine with your family.

The time goes quickly. Crista and Darren fly back to Cincinnati. Jerry and I stay until Mike leaves. We rent a car and take Mike away from the city and head towards the mountains. A cold snap has come in and the road is closed because of ice and snow. Mike seems nervous. We are too. We come back to the city and go to Mike's room.

I have a gift for him and it seems like the time to give it to him. He is sitting on the opposite bed and I face him. I hold out my hand with a medallion I bought for him to wear in Iraq.

I ordered it from a catalogue. It is a wheel with the religious symbol of all the different faiths represented on each spoke. I don't know if Mike will catch the meaning but it feels like the right thing to give him. He will be wearing it all the time. It represents all faiths. All people. All on the same wheel. People. All one. And in a quiet moment by myself I think, if he were to be captured, maybe his captors will see this wheel of faith, recognize their symbol, and spare his life.

"Mike," I say as I give it to him, "I know you are aware of the sacredness of all people. I want this to help you keep that awareness. You may need to defend yourself and your brothers and I understand that and I want you to. I don't want you to get hurt. But remember also that life is sacred." I hug him. As he hugs me I can sense his confusion about this moment. What will he be ordered to do? He is too big to cry and yet his eyes are moist and red.

We leave his room and head to the casino where the Marines will soon depart for California. The casino is going full blast upstairs and down here, five hundred Marines are listening intently as they are given orders and waiting for their next command. Things move slowly in the military. This is something you find out quickly. It is as though there is something going on behind the scenes and at any given moment, sooner or later, an order comes down and the response is immediate. In the meantime waiting is the order.

Several Marines approach Jerry and me and tell us they will watch out for Mike. "Don't worry", one says, "we will take good care of him." Mike has only been with the Unit for a month. He is "the new kid on the block." I appreciate those words of comfort. But there is nothing that will take the ache of fear away.

The busses file in and the Marines begin the move to load up. In formation once again the order is to say a final good-bye and prepare to board the busses. Hugs again. Hold the tears. One of Mike's final words to us is, "I feel a little behind in training, but they say I'll catch up quick." I assure him he will. What am I to say? There is nothing we can do to stop this or change this. I have to encourage him. But I feel my insides drop as he voices his concern. My God! He doesn't feel adequately prepared. But he is going anyway.

The busses load. Bodies moving inside. Putting stuff away, getting comfortable and waiting for the signal that all are on board and ready to go. And so the busses begin pulling away. We follow Mike's bus down the drive as far as we can. Our eyes on him. His on ours. The lights of Las Vegas are glaring, blocking the stars shining over our heads. And then the traffic light turns green and away he goes into the dark night. And we also into the dark night.

CHAPTER 2

Wordless Times

The next morning, Jerry and I leave Las Vegas and head to Arizona. We think seeing the Grand Canyon may help us cope during these next few days knowing that Mike is heading to Iraq. It will be awhile before we will hear from him and spending time surrounded by the awesomeness of nature may calm our nerves and feed our spirits. We know the military will make plans to leave the country secretly so as not to give the enemy an easy target. We also know they will be leaving soon. Our trip to the Grand Canyon is a nurturing break and a distraction from the tension that has claim on our lives.

We stay in Williams, Arizona, a small town not far from the Grand Canyon and drive back to Las Vegas the following day and then fly home. We go immediately to the kennel to pick up our dog, Snoopy. He is so happy to see us and is jumping and barking and clawing his way all over us inside the car when the cell phone rings. It is Mike. The Marines are in Shannon, Ireland and he tells us they will be in Kuwait by evening. It is hard to hear him and hard to concentrate as Snoopy desperately tries to get our full attention. It is such a frantic scene. Mike can hear Snoopy and it makes him laugh. We all laugh. Then a pause and silence takes over as again a loss for words sweeps over me. My heart sinks and I want to encourage and support Mike.

I have wordless times. Saying good-bye to my son going to war is one of them.

Settled now at home we know there are friends and family who want to be kept informed about Mike and his deployment. A larger plan evolves. We not only want people to be informed we want them to be involved. There is not one person we know that can escape this plan. We construct an email list on the computer that we call "Mike's Marine List." The goal is to keep Mike and the war in their consciousness. There is nothing more important to us. Our son is to become like their son. They will know and will experience this war as we attempt to keep them informed. And anyone who speaks to us or relates with us has to know that nothing else in our lives means anything to us until our son comes home. We are desperate to protect him. We keep him in the forefront of our life. We hope that the power of the community supporting us will somehow protect Mike. Call it the power of prayer. We want everyone to know and we want everyone to help. We don't want anyone to dismiss this. Nor forget it. We are warriors for Mike. It never leaves our consciousness.

We want all to know that flesh and blood in war; "skin in the game," changes everything about your life. It allows a certain power to speak out because there is so much to lose. Jerry and I know we are like many other people. If Mike was not in Iraq, we would probably be as apathetic as the next person. And this is shameful. But, Mike is in Iraq. Our mission and our need is to be aware and to keep others aware.

We begin implementing Mike's Marine List quickly after getting the phone call from Shannon Ireland.

March 4, 2005: Two- hundred and eleven days to go.

Hello Friends and Family,
Michael is in Iraq. He called yesterday from Shannon, Ireland. He said he would be in Kuwait by evening. He will be sent to the western province, Al Anbar in Iraq. There are three possible sites where he may be stationed.
We had a great time in Las Vegas, although bittersweet. Sad and beautiful as we watched and were with all the loved ones saying good-bye to their Marine, all five hundred of them.
We have a calendar hanging with the countdown. Two-hundred and eleven days to go. If they keep their promise Mike will be home.
Semper Fi. (Always Faithful)
Love
Peggy & Jerry

We know we need to get organized about sending mail and packages to Mike. The Marines set up a family support group facilitated by what is called *Key Volunteer Network*. This group facilitates monthly gatherings and is the contact between the Marine staff and the families. They have the answers or can get answers.

I contact Isolde, the Volunteer coordinator and ask how to send packages and if we should send water. Her son is Mike's platoon leader and I think she might know more so I ask, I plead "Isolde, do you know where they are?"

Oh Peggy, I wish I knew where they are. Guy gave me three possibilities before he left but they were not given their exact assignments until they were on the plane and I have not heard from him since. All I know is that they are somewhere near the Syrian border.

I understand that the Post Office provides boxes free of charge with a flat rate regardless of weight. I do not list every darn item in the box but use generic terms like personal hygiene items, snacks, reading material etc. No water bottles are needed. They have their camel backs.

Then, in a follow-up email to Isolde I say that maybe she has experienced this before since her son has been a Marine for awhile. I tell her that sometimes we just cry and I want to know how other families are coping. I ask her, "Are we just wimps?"

Peggy,

No, you are not wimps. Trust me, most of the families have their ups and downs and times when they just cry. Then we pick ourselves up again and go on.

While my son has been in the Corps for almost twelve years now, and has done peace keeping in Bosnia, drug trafficking in South America, and other deployments. He has done nothing like Iraq. Actually this will be his first combat ribbon he is earning. He'll soon be running out of room on his chest with all the medals he has earned. He is very focused and won't allow inattentiveness since lives are on the line. So, he'll be tough on his Marines, but it is only for the good and safety of the Platoon.

I try not to dwell on where he is, but believe me, there are times tears just roll down my cheeks. I am really not afraid, but smart enough to recognize the danger our Marines are in on a daily basis. Not knowing where they are and what they are doing, and not hearing from him is the hardest thing to cope with. How I long to just get a note that I can carry close to my heart, or hear his voice, even for a minute. I really miss him.

So, I do understand how you feel. I always say to everyone who questions their emotions, it's okay to cry. Do it. Most of all take time to write often because that shows our love in a tangible way. I am not writing deep and wondrous things in every letter. I just talk with him. Chit chat about little daily things. Describe the birds feeding at the feeder on a snowy Sunday morning. I reckon I paint pictures from home in words.

Hang in there. If you ever need to talk, I am here.

Lovingly, (Isolde)

CHAPTER 3

Letters From Iraq

We finally receive word that our Marines are in Al Anbar Province at Haditha Dam. We look this up on the map taped to Mike's closet door and then go to the computer to see what we can find out about the region. The dam is the second largest hydroelectric contributor to the power system in Iraq. "It was built with help from Azerbaijan, construction beginning in 1978 and completed in 1986. The dam currently acts as the headquarters for a Marine Battalion that is charged with securing the Haditha area."(Wikipedia).

Al Anbar is the largest province in Iraq by area and shares borders with Syria, Jordan, and Saudi Arabia. It has one of the lowest population densities and is overwhelmingly Sunni Muslim.

Now we have a sense of where on this earth Mike is. We study and study the map looking for hints as to what he might see. We know that Haditha Dam is somewhere on the Euphrates River. His first letters aren't encouraging.

"3/05/05

Hey Mom and Dad,

I'm at this darn place. I'm doing good. We are temporarily sleeping in a hall way. It is about five hundred steps down from the top. It's a haul with all the gear and two sea bags. So far to get here we've loaded planes and unloaded, loaded and unloaded helicopters. It's good to finally be in our AO (Area of Operation). It's a good mission. We should be able to do a lot for the country. Please don't talk to people about where I am or what I am doing, because it goes around, and the information is made public. So don't tell the paper because the bad guys can read the newspapers too. Then they find out our Unit's location and everything about our families too. So please don't say any specifics to anyone. It's hard I know but just say I'm in Iraq and I'll tell you all about it when I'm home.

Anyways, this is a nasty hallway. It smells like sulfur, very strong. It's poorly lit and the water leaks from pipes. It was built by the Russians.

How are you guys?

Send me food. I'm hungry. The chow's not very good.

I love you. Be safe. Mike"

"We should be able to do a lot for the country," Mike says. Jerry and I hear Mike's desire to help and his willingness to serve. We also hear his fear of the "bad guys" finding out where the Marines are and "everything about our families." We read innocence in this first letter.

"3/07/05

Hey Mom and Dad,

How are you guys doing? I'm great.

We should start getting busier here. We have work to do for our own living conditions. I said I could weld so I might do some of that on our vehicles to improve them.

I miss the family but the experience from this is amazing. Hopefully I'll get mail soon and get to call.

Love you. Mike"

"3/08/05

Hey Mom and Dad,

Also, would you send baby wipes and toilet paper, a bottle of anti bacterial soap and tooth brush, a role of packing tape then I can send a camera back to you. Can you send some chips, cheddar cheese dip, tuna, canned spam, Vienna Sausage, artichokes, pita bread, canned cheese, Ramen Noodles, Easy Mac. We have a micro wave. Also, power bars, snacks, peanuts, pistachios, some dried fruit and candy bars.

Thank you. I'll greatly appreciate it.

Love you. Talk to you soon. Mike"

The food list makes us laugh. It almost sounds like he is away at college. But knowing he isn't, getting his requests met becomes an important goal. We inform Mike's Marine list of all of his requests. And the generosity of support grows. Mike starts receiving packages and is very appreciative.

So far. So good. We begin to think that maybe this won't be so bad.

CHAPTER 4

"No Need to Know"???

March 26, 2005: One- hundred and eighty-nine days to go.

All,

One of our Marines from Weapons Platoon was seriously injured recently. He was first flown to Germany and arrived at the Bethesda Maryland Navy Hospital yesterday afternoon. His parents are with him. I do not have any information as to the extent or nature of Chad's injuries and perhaps this is a situation that could be categorized as "no need to know." For those who would like to send a card or letter I am sending his address. It would be appropriate for us to let him know he is loved by us. Thank you. (Isolde)

The bubble begins its burst. We clearly understand now that the Key Volunteer Network is a life line to our Marines.

I email Trice, the mother of another Marine in Mikes Unit. I met Trice at one of the support group meetings held in Cincinnati. She is as troubled as I about the war. Her son,

Kevin is part of 3/25th Marines but has been assigned to Kilo Company and is at a different area in Iraq training Iraqis. Jerry and I are developing a whole new group of friends as we need to share stories and information with other parents and families of serving Marines.

Trice, did you get the email from Isolde about the injured Marine? Scary. Have you heard from Kevin? Do you ever just cry? (Peggy)

Peggy, yes I got the message from Isolde. I will send Chad a card and pray for quick recovery. And yes, I do have times that I just cry. Wednesday I heard on the news that an Ohio Marine was killed in the line of duty near Tikrit. His name was LCpl. Kevin Smith from Springfield. When I heard "LCpl. Kevin" my mind went to a place I didn't think it could. I cried so hard for his family, what he must have gone through and that I didn't know where my son was. I didn't know if this guy was one of our guys or not at the time. I wanted to make one thousand phone calls to find out, but I didn't. My Kevin called yesterday morning. I felt so bad we weren't home. But it was such a relief to hear his voice on voice mail. (Trice)

When the Marines are at their base they have access to computers and can email home. They also have a phone system called Segovia. In my first email to Mike I told him we are organizing our packaging supplies and that his bedroom has become our central depot. I also told him that on top of our refrigerator we have a clock set to Iraq time. So we always know in what time of day he is living. We look at that clock as frequently as we do our own.

March 27, 2005: One- hundred and eight-eight days to go.

"Hey Mom,
I have finally figured out what is going on. Now I know how to use a computer and the phone system. How is everybody? I talked

to Darren. He is sending me a camera. That will be awesome. In a couple of days I will be out of contact again. I am doing good. A little tired. I received a few packages already. Could you send me typed addresses so I can send thank you notes to people? I'll try to call around 7:00 am Easter.

We were cleaning up a guy's house the other day. He had mortar fuses thrown all over the place. There were about three hundred scattered on the ground. I told Sgt. Z they were like Easter eggs. He took a picture of me with my arms full. I'll try to send it to you.

This country is so dirty. There is trash everywhere. It is disgusting the way these people live. It was like this before we came over. I've been nice to them and try to show a lot of support but they are all back stabbers. I really do mean that. There may be a few that are trustworthy. You may ask them about bad guys and they say, "What? I don't understand." Or they will say there are no bad guys. They all speak fairly good English. But when questioned they act like they don't understand. And we can catch them in their lies. One day we were driving down a road where IEDs (improvised explosive devices) are placed. We started questioning a few men on the road. A religious leader came down and spoke on their behalf. He said, "I am your friend. You can trust me. If I see anything I will tell you." So we had to let them go. Later that evening we were driving down that road one hundred meters and the streetlights go off and an IED booms. My vehicle was already past the blast site. We were all fine but a Marine in the 3rd vehicle caught shrapnel in the neck and head. He is going to be fine and was sent home for rehab.

Just trying to describe some of what we face. Hope I don't scare you, Mom. Don't worry. I am doing fine. You don't need to protect me from harm. I can do it for the both of us now.

Love you and Dad and Sis and Bro.

Feel free to forward my story to the family and friends and also thank them all for their support.

Love you."

Mike has been in Iraq for less than a month and he is questioning the trustworthiness of the people he came to help. He came, as he said in his first letter home, with hope to, "do a lot for the country." Now he speaks negatively about them and I think he feels more vulnerable.

With the first casualty, we no longer feel they are safe. No longer feel all is well. No longer feel everything is under control. The bubble has cracked open and tests our sense of reality. Nothing is taken for granted in war. All is at stake. All is vulnerable. And, yes, there is a need to know.

CHAPTER 5

Warriors for Peace

While American Christians celebrate Easter Sunday, Lima Company is about to end their first month of tour in Iraq. They have experienced their first injury and now taste the danger of their situation. We receive an email from Mike saying that they have finally moved into their rooms. He describes it as small quarters but better than the hallway he has been sleeping in five hundred feet below. He tells us he will be going out for ten days and we won't hear from him.

March 28: One- hundred and eighty-seven days to go.

A message from Darren on email:
I've had the pleasure of talking to Mike on Instant Messenger two nights in a row now. He gets a half hour each morning to get on the computer and clean his equipment. Yesterday it was his rifle,

today it was his mortar. He told me he hasn't had to use the mortar yet, and I didn't ask about the rifle. His morning schedule seems to coincide well with my late night schedule. Hopefully we will get to talk more, soon.

Obviously danger faces him almost every day. In conversations with him, he shows the poise of someone twice his age. This has been typical of Mike since he was a kid. He does his job and believes that his fate is in the hands of God. Please keep praying for him and ask God to continue to protect his fate."

(Darren)

"Hey Mom! How's everyone? My platoon left today. I found out about ten minutes before they left that I wouldn't be going. I am upset. I wanted to go. Well, I'll relax and probably meet up with them tomorrow. I'm all right. I miss the family. Talk to you later. Love ya."

Mike, I miss you so much. Take care of yourself. Let me respond to your words, "You don't need to protect me from harm. I can do it for both of us now." You may be able to protect yourself from harm but I am a MOM and I will continue to worry and pray until I see your wonderful smile and feel your strong arms around me again. I love you.

I do worry. I continue to email Mike's Marine List with information and thoughts. One of the items I send in March is a quote from Deepak Chopra on how to practice peace.

Sunday: Practice BEING FOR PEACE
Monday: Practice THINKING FOR PEACE
Tuesday   : Practice FEELING FOR PEACE
Wednesday: Practice SPEAKING FOR PEACE
Thursday: Practice ACTING FOR PEACE
Friday: Practice CREATING FOR PEACE
Saturday: Practice SHARING FOR PEACE.

CHAPTER 6

Blue Star Flags

Jerry is reading and studying about Iraq and the culture so that he can better understand where Mike is and what he might experience. He responds to an email Mike sent about the Iraqis and how they seem to live. Jerry tries to help Mike understand the history of the Iraqis and their tribalism.

Mike, I've pulled an email of yours because there are a few thoughts I would like to share. Al Anbar Province is mostly inhabited by Sunni Muslims. They were in power for about twenty or thirty years. Saddam is a Sunni. Now they are out of power. Less than ten per cent voted in the election in January. They make up about twenty per cent of the population.

Al Anbar is a province where many insurgents operate. You must know that as you experience it. Northern Iraq is populated by the Kurds with about twenty per cent of the population. Baghdad and the rest of Iraq are pretty well populated by the Shite Muslims.

The Sunnis don't like the Shites but they also don't like anyone who picks a fight with their Muslim brothers. It gets very complicated. The Iraqi people live in a different culture and their tribal traditions and customs go back hundreds of years, long before the Romans and the Greeks. The Sunni have lost power and they don't know you or any of your brothers-in-arms. So they don't trust you. They really don't know who the bad guys are.

It is very hard for you to trust them even if you have the best of intentions. Be careful. Be on your guard but try to respect other humans. We cannot solve their problems in a short time. Hopefully the Iraqi National Security Forces will be able to take over your work in the near future. Just recently sixty-four Sunni clerics told their followers to join the national security forces and begin to help.

As for the dirt and filth you see there, fortunately, we live in one of the most sanitary and richest countries in the world. What would our town look like if we did not have sewers or garbage pick-up? Have you ever seen the inner city of Cincinnati? My first job in Warren County was litter prevention coordinator. You would be surprised at the number of illegal dump sites we found and cleaned up.

Be patient. Keep focused. Thanks for listening to your dad ramble.

I am proud of you and what you are trying to do. It takes heart, guts, wisdom and much more.

Just love you so much.

Dad

By the middle of April we become aware that there will be stretches of time when we do not hear from Mike. It is scary because we know he is on a mission and we have a sense these missions are very dangerous. The vulnerability of our Marines and the seriousness of this war colors every aspect of our lives.

We receive a call from Mike at 5:30pm April 12th. They are back at the dam and are preparing to leave in a day or so. Mike signs up for use of the phone five hours previous. Then he waits two hours in line to use it. He asks us for food.

"It isn't very good here. We got to go to Al Asad (the air base) and I got a good meal there. Boy. The guys there have it made. They have lots of good food. And work out rooms and air conditioning."

I ask him if it is pretty where he is. He says there is water behind them and they can look out and see the city lights from the dam.

When Mike returned from this last mission three packages awaited him. There is no room for them so he sleeps with the packages and his clothes on his bed.

April 17th We get an email from him.

"Hey, I'll try to call soon, Mom. But if I don't would you send me the x-box. I also need bedding for a single and a towel and washcloth and body wash. Love you. I'll talk to you later."

April 19th another email.

"Hey, Mom, I'm doing good. I miss you all. I was thinking about the Boundary Waters too. It's getting hot here. I got a newer humvee. It is a hardback with armor. I sit inside something now compared to the bed of a truck. We gotta go. Love you so much."

April 21st another email.

"Hey, Mom, yesterday we were a quick reaction force. We had to leave the dam. Today we came to re-supply and will be out for ten or twelve days. I only have forty-five minutes. I gotta' go. Love u . Bye."

Darren set up a web site for Mike, www.mikelogue.com. We up-load pictures that Mike sends home. People can send him messages and read interesting articles that come across the web.

I send Mike emails every day. I try not to make them long. But I try to keep him in the loop about home, stories from home.

There is a Family Day meeting in Columbus and we make Blue Star Flags to hang in our windows. This practice started during WWII. I had not heard of this before. The family of the serving soldier or Marine hangs the flag in their window until the loved one returns home. We hung our flag and then began to notice other Blue Star Flags hanging in windows. Now we know why.

And the Gold Star Flag means that a loved one was killed in action.

CHAPTER 7

Operation Matador

Some women friends and I plan a get-away for a few days just after Mother's Day. I go, knowing that I can get home in about three hours. We are enjoying our walks and talks together and sharing meals, although I always feel a little distracted. But, I realize how much I need to be in a serene natural setting with my friends.

Tuesday morning I am out by a lake enjoying quiet meditation when one of my friends calls to me. "There is a call from Jerry," she says.

Jerry tells me that our Marines have taken some injuries. The details are very sketchy. Jerry does his best to stay calm and keep me calm as I struggle to get information he doesn't have. I am in shock and fear overcomes me. I need to get home.

My friends circle me with love and prayers. Do I wait and see what information comes? Do I leave? Quickly, we decide I need to go home. We pack up our things and begin the three hour return trip.

My mind races with dreaded thoughts. I am against this war and sick about Mike having to be there and now there is the possibility that he is hurt. I feel bad that Jerry is home by himself to hear this news and to deal with it alone. I can't wait to be home.

Jerry sends an email to Isolde.

Isolde, the Chicago Tribune carried a story today titled, Marines Surprised by Insurgents. Major Steve Lawson is quoted. Another web site www.icasualties.org reports a casualty for 3/25th Lima Co. from Columbus. What have you heard?

Peggy is out of town until Wednesday.

Keeping our Marines in prayer. (Jerry)

Jerry, Lima Co. has ten injuries. Those are well under control. Unfortunately we have had our first KIA. Dustin Derga has been killed. His dad is dealing incredibly well with it and plans on attending every future Family Day, including homecoming.

It's been a tough two days. Know that I care but need to follow guidelines. Much love. (Isolde)

After I am home and talk with Jerry to see what he knows I send an email to Trice. Her response follows:

Peggy, I had not heard the news about the Marines/Sailors being killed. Thanks for keeping me informed. I'm wondering about Kilo Co. because Kevin is with them and they have had it pretty rough lately. But I don't think they are at Haditha.

I had such a rough day today. I didn't get much sleep last night because right before going to bed I heard that a Marine was killed just west of Baghdad. I knew in my heart that Kevin was okay, but the news did not say exactly where or what battalion he was from. I just knew a family was having a much worse night than I was having because of their loss. On so little sleep I went to my step-daughter's graduation. Kevin should have graduated with her today. One of the speakers was the father of the young man that died last month in the fire at Miami University. The father accepted his son's diploma. His speech had such an impact on me. I had not cried as hard as I have today since that family day in December, the one you missed because you didn't even know Mike would be going to Iraq. I really felt the sacrifice Kevin is making delaying his graduation. When I talked to him last week he seemed upset about being behind all of his friends, including his step-sister and his fiancé. I made light of his concerns at the time but today I realized what he was going through and missing out of. I do know that Kevin is gratified by the work that he is doing by training the Iraqi National Guard and that makes me feel very proud of him.

Okay, maybe this is way too much rambling and self pity, but I needed to get it out. Anyway, next Mother's Day will be much happier for both of us. Our sons will be home and getting on with their lives. I hope the rest of the week brings nothing but good news. (Trice)

Jerry and I search and search for more news about what is happening to our Marines. We go to www.icasualties.org web site. It lists the KIA soldiers, Marines etc. It doesn't give names until the family is notified. But you will see how many are killed and where it happened. We picked up a news story on the computer from CNN.

On Wednesday night, a U.S. Assault Amphibian Vehicle struck an explosive device in Qaim, the border town about 320 kilometers west of Bagdad where the assault began Saturday, said U.S. military spokesman Capt. Jeffrey Pool said. Two Marines were killed and 14 wounded, he said.

The U.S. military has confirmed five Marines killed in all. However, The Washington Post, which has a journalist embedded with the offensive, put the figure at seven in a Thursday report.

Six of the dead came from a single squad, which also has 15 wounded, according to the Post.

In one battle early in the offensive, foreign fighters holed up in a house in nearby Obeidi killed two Marines and wounded five, the report said. In another attachment, an explosive device detonated under their vehicle, killing four Marines and wounding 10, it said.

The article identified the squad as one of three belonging to 1st Platoon of Lima Company, 3rd Battalion, 25th Regiment.

"They used to call it Lucky Lima," the Post quoted Maj. Steve Lawson, the commander of the company, as saying of the badly hit squad. "That turned around and bit us."

The offensive involving more than 1000 Marines, soldiers and sailors is one of the biggest in Iraq since Fallujah was taken from militants six months ago.

We know some are hurt. We know some are killed. We are frightened. I quote a friend who says to me: *I thank you for the courage to send things in the midst of terror. You must feel so wild inside with all this. It is impossible to know what to say about this horrible situation and your beloved so involved. I guess I can pray for an end to the madness, and that somehow, someday Mike is transformed out of this experience of horror into love.*

I rush off a note to Isolde:

We got a CNN report off the internet about the killing of two Marines and wounding 14. Quote... "Krickmeyer quoted the 1st platoon's commander saying at least 60% of his troops have either been killed or wounded in this week's fighting. The report said that the troops were part of Marines 1st Platoon Lima Company 3/25 reserve unit based in Columbus." Isolde, Please let us know what is going on. Thanks.

Dear Peggy,

Please don't overreact to reports. Yes. We have had some casualties and injuries but nothing I can report as of this time. Since you have not received a phone call, you can be sure your son is okay. Much will be reported tomorrow. Hang in there. (Isolde)

"Hang in there." Hang in there? How do I do that? My son may be lying dead in a war zone or badly wounded and I can't find out, and I am to "hang in there." All the parent buttons kick in and Jerry and I are frantic and desperate for news that Mike is safe. The emails start flying from family to family digging for information and comfort that ours is not one of the KIA. All of us trying to get information we need to calm our fears. This is one of those emails from the mother of another Marine.

The "terrifying" article we discussed yesterday is in today's Plain Dealer. It's titled "Battle, Bomb Wipe out Lucky Lima Marines". The reporter did re-word a few things and changed the title of the article. The facts may not be wrong but they are somewhat misleading. She doesn't explain that four of those who were KIA were from an attachment. Obviously that doesn't make it any easier on us since those Marines were fighting right alongside our Marines and we are one big family. But I think it is scary that we can read details that graphic in a newspaper before all families have been notified and when we haven't heard anything official from our command. Every one of the Marines in Al Anbar Province needs extra prayers right now as they continue Operation Matador. You're all helping me cope with the day to day struggles of this deployment and I'm grateful for all of you and so glad you keep in touch. I'm proud to be part of the Marine Corps family. Thank you. Semper Fi! (Mother of a Marine)

The Toledo station WTOL published a report on line on May 13th 2005 6:01 am.

The military has confirmed five Marine deaths so far and says about 100 insurgents have been killed in the operation (Operation Matador). One of the largest U.S. offensives since Fallujah was reclaimed from militants. Chief Warrant Officer Orrin Bowman, the site commander for the Columbus based company confirmed Thursday that the company was participating in the operation and had taken casualties. He declined to say how many from the Marine reserve unit has been killed or release any names.

Jerry and I read these articles and feel numb. What's happening there? Is Mike okay? Where is he? What did he see? What did he do? Is he safe? Who has been killed? Do we know them? How are the parents and the family? No. No. Wait. Wait. How does this work? What did they say about how you will be notified? We struggle with memories of procedure. Oh, the energy of terror.

The above article continued to report on two earlier deaths that week.

The military has identified two Ohio Marines with the 3rd Battalion, 25 Regiment who have died in Iraq since Sunday. Lance CPL. Wesley G. Davids, 20, of Dublin was killed in an explosion in Karabilah on Wednesday and Cpl. Dustin Derga, 24, of Columbus was killed by small arms fire in Ubaydi on Sunday, according to the Department of Defense.

In the meantime, my sister sends us an invitation to come to a concert her city has planned to celebrate the Golden Years (1955-2005). Part of the celebration is to be a tribute to our Armed Forces. *Our presentation includes these beautiful pieces that will sound absolutely gorgeous with our 300 voice choir and orchestra: "Salute to the Armed Forces" honoring the Army, the Navy, the Air Force, the Coast Guard, and the United States Marines. This piece includes "Caissons Go Rolling Along", "Anchors Away," "Semper Paratus "(Coast Guard Hymn), "The U.S. Air Force" and especially in our hearts, in honor of our brave and courageous son, brother, nephew and cousin, PFC Michael J. Logue, the "Marine Corps Hymn."*

It would be good to attend this celebration but by now we fear leaving home.

May 15, 2005: One-hundred and thirty-nine days to go.

Family and Friends,

At 10:00 pm Friday night the Marine staff in Columbus called a Family Meeting. Jerry and I were surprised to see how many families were able to respond and come. The Derga and the Dixon families, who lost their sons, were there.

You may have heard that Operation Matador is over. There

were nine Marines killed and fifty-four injuries. Of the nine KIA, four were from Lima Company. We are not sure of the condition of the injured. They tell us there are four categories of injures from not serious to very serious.

No news is good news they say. Since we haven't had any news about Mike we can assume he is okay. The Sgt. who makes the calls was at the Family Meeting Saturday and he said he made all the calls.

Chaplains and counselors were present making their services available to us. We could hear tears. A young woman who we met in Las Vegas at the departure was sitting behind us. Her husband had called her. He was one of the injured. He had to jump out of a window and his flak jacket got caught and he landed on his face. He has back injuries. Another mother was crying uncontrollably. We approached her. She told us that her son and Dustin Derga were buddies. Her son watched Dustin go down.

We talked to other parents and families who search the web day and night looking for news, looking for assurance. We learned of other web sites like IraqiNews.com. We found we were not the only ones afraid to leave our homes.

During that meeting one family received a call from their son from 2nd platoon who said that his platoon was on their way back to the Dam. We could hear the sigh of relief cross the room as we surmised that they would all be heading back to the Dam. Maybe they are safe and maybe we would get a call.

Mike is in a dangerous place, seeing things he could never have imagined or prepared for.

We are thankful for your prayers and support. They lift us. Like a net that keeps us standing.

Yesterday one of the Sergeants said "their job isn't finished. Their deployment isn't over."

Update:

Mike called Lindsay at noon today from a satellite phone the squad was passing around. They had just come from a service for the nine KIA Marines. He said there were about forty-six injured.

He sounded "tired and down," she said. She couldn't get the whole story but Mike was there in the midst of it all. Said he wishes he could come home and just talk and tell us what has happened. Then he said he had to do some laundry that night. Oh, how we wish he could just come home.

Peggy & Jerry

Keeping friends and family informed and keeping Mike's presence in Iraq in their minds through my email list is working. I receive email responses after Operation Matador. They are important to our sense of hope as the power of prayer is life sustaining. What follows are some of those responses from Mike's Marine List.

We rejoice with you and we cry with you. And we really pray with you and for you. We are not crazy and we pray that our leaders are a little bit on the sane side too. (friend)

Five more months. Every week/hour is agonizing. I'm praying for him. (Nephew)

I have followed the news of Operation Matador knowing that Mike must be there. I was so glad to hear that it was over and that you hadn't heard anything. I know that this is not the end and that your life will be on hold for many months. I am so aware of how consuming this is for you. Please know that my thoughts are constantly with you. (friend)

Thanks for the update. Thank God for protecting Mike. We are worried for you. We think about you always. We cry for you. We pray for you. We feel your pain as much as that is possible. Carrying the Logue family in our hearts and prayers with love and pride. (Sister)

What a nightmare. You can't script it. You can't hold your breath for five months. So what to do? Don't sit by the phone. (friend)

I can't begin to imagine what you all must be going through. I try to read your messages and I get chocked up and tears pop out. Please know that you and your family and Mike are in my heart and prayers. (friend)

Gosh! What a relief. I'm sure there were some tears of joy and gratitude there. We are holding him in the Light each day. Blessings on him and all of you. (friend)

You guys are doing great. What a wonderful peaceful family. I have always admired that in your family. Our thoughts and prayers are with PFC Logue and your family. What can anyone say at these times? (Brother)

CHAPTER 8

Close Call or Miracle

By the middle of May Jerry and I make sure one of us is always home and the TV is turned on to a news channel. Because of the time difference we know that Mike is beginning his day as ours' is ending. A few hours of sleep and one of us is up on the computer hoping to get an instant message, find an email or just surfing the web for news from Iraq.

Today we get a call from Mike. He is still in Al Quaim.

I send this email to my list about the phone call.

May 16, 2005: One- hundred and thirty-eight days to go.

Family and Friends,

We just talked to Mike. He is still in Al Quaim. He said they will be there a few more days. He sounded subdued.

He told us about the AAV (Assault Amphibious Vehicle –

trac) that hit an IED killing six Marines and wounding many. His mortar team was in that trac until the convoy stopped and they were told to come to the trac behind this one. They then were following and watched as the trac they just vacated exploded some thirty seconds later. He said there was nothing they could do. The fire was too intense.

I asked him repeatedly if he is okay. He said he is.

He wanted to know how we are. We assured him that we are all fine and feeling a lot of support from family and friends.

What can I say?

Peace.

Responses to the email:

I am so glad you were finally able to hear Mike's voice. I'm sure he is feeling down right now. How awful to be watching something like that and to feel helpless to do anything to help your buddies. I am asking God to heal their hearts and their bodies and blanket them with love. (friend)

I saw a program that spoke about Post Traumatic Stress Syndrome in men back from Iraq. They said that the sooner it is treated the easier it is to deal with. During this war they have therapists available to the people in the war fields. I hope Mike will take advantage of that opportunity even if he doesn't feel it necessary at this time. I continue to embrace Mike and all of you in light and energy. (friend)

We heard from Shad yesterday and today. He's doing fine, although he said there are several of the guys that are really struggling emotionally. He said the memorial service they had for those who lost their lives was very difficult, but necessary for them. His platoon hadn't gotten transportation back to the Dam yet. I'm not sure if that is the case for all of Lima Co.

We attended the calling and funeral today for Dustin Derga, a great turnout along with a great response by the town of Pickerington. An emotional day for all of us. Unfortunately there are two or three more funerals this week. (father of another Marine)

The conversation with Mike sends chills throughout my

body. What a close call. He is seconds from being blown up. Is this a coincidence? The story of why he wasn't in that AAV at that moment makes sense but a deeper story resides somewhere in my soul.

Mike's platoon leader Gunny Delgado does not want his men in AAVs. He calls these tracs, "coffins on wheels." Gunny keeps his platoon out of them as much as possible. I clarify that with him when they return home. Instead, they travel in humvees.

On this day Mike is put in a trac with 1st platoon to make room in his trac for snipers who are traveling with them. This operation does not accommodate humvees. At a point where they are about to head for the night position, the convoy stops to wait for another platoon to join them. During this pause Gunny Delgado sends the snipers to their own trac and has Mike and his other men come back to his trac. He wants his men together.

They begin "rolling" and thirty seconds later Mike and Gunny Delgado see a fireball. It is the trac of 1st platoon

A Navy Doctor with 3/25th Marines wrote about this explosion.

The AAV had continued to burn for over twelve hours, cooking off its ammunition. Afterward there were the charred remains of four Marines still in the vehicle. Once removed they had to be sent to Al Asad for identification, and we still do not know their names by bedtime. My heart goes out to the poor guys that had to take the bodies of their friends out of that vehicle. [1]

We receive this email from Mike after he returns to the Dam.

"Hey Mom and Dad, I'm at the Dam. I'm good but dirty. I got a lot of packages. I don't need anything else just a controller and

---

1   "Sword in The Lion's Den: Navy Doc with 3/25 Marines in Iraq, by Captain Glenn F. Thibault, MD, p.119,Publish America,2008, Baltimore.

movies or games. We will be leaving again in a few days. Hopefully, not for too long. Let everyone know that I am busy and haven't been able to write them. But I really appreciate their support. I have to go clean my rifle. Love you. Bye."

Mike, you will be okay. You are strong. Just keep bringing strength and power from somewhere deep inside you. It is so great to get all your messages. Love Dad

Hey Babe, So good to hear from you. We think of you every waking moment. We trust you are and will be safe. Crista was so glad to hear from you. She shared as much as she could remember from your conversation. She was sniffling a little bit and I asked her if she was okay. She said yes she was just happy to hear your voice but it was hard to say goodbye. That sums up how we feel. We love to hear from you but it is hard to say goodbye. And so there are tears once our phone disconnects. Love you, Mom

I reflect on what is happening. I wonder how many "close calls" Mike or any of them might have. How does that feel? It makes me question how it is that Mike avoided this tragedy. Is there power in prayer? Are the prayers of my family and friends for Mike giving him protection? Who knows why some live and some die. What influenced Gunny to bring his men together at that time? Are there answers or just questions? Was this a close call? Or was this a miracle?

I mourn for those young men in that trac. And weep for their families.

CHAPTER 9

Why?

Marine families search for and share information of the injured. Trice receives a message from Greg Cifuentes. He is one of our Cincinnati fathers whose son, Michael is a friend to her son Kevin. Greg's email follows.

We finally heard from Michael and I hope you have heard from Kevin. Below is an email that Michael sent. We also heard that 3rd platoon, Michael's platoon, had many injuries from last week's battle, but we have yet to confirm that info. At least we know that the ten are okay, although Michael confirmed that they are on high alert status right now. I imagine that they are like ten hornets trapped in a glass jar. I hope someone doesn't drop the jar.

Keeping you in my prayers. (Greg)

Greg shares his son Michael's email. We learned that "Segovia" is the phone system. When there are injuries or casualties the system shuts down to keep wrong or harmful information from coming in or going out of the base. It is shut down to protect the Marines and their families. Michael Cifuentes'email:

Hey everyone. Segovia's been shut down for several reasons for the past week, so this is the first time I've had a chance to let you know I'm okay, as well as the nine others from Lima here. I'm sure you've heard Lima's taken some WIA and KIA and that's all I'm going to say about it.

Other than that, we are doing fairly well here. Obviously, I can't say too much about anything to y'all. But that's the way it goes. I miss you all and am looking forward to the end of the crap here. We all hate this place.

I love you and pray for you all every night. (Michael)

Jerry and I try to stay up on who is injured, where they are receiving treatment and how they and their families are doing. We send cards and correspond by email to families offering support and help. It is hard to know what to say. We have a sense of angst while ours is safe, still in harm's way and can be the next "recovering."

May 20, 2005: One- hundred and thirty-four days to go.

Family and Friends,

Crista, John, and Lindsay got a phone call from Mike. Uncle Bob, cousins Darren and Adam chatted with him on instant messenger. What relief this is to hear his voice. He wants to come home. But says he is doing okay. He is so thankful for all the packages and now has plenty, and keeps them under his bed or shares with other Marines. He would like to thank each of you. He said they will be heading out in a day or so. When he doesn't call or email, we know he is out. There is much that doesn't make the news.

This experience has helped us relearn the power of prayer, healing energy and support, and concern and compassion from and for others. It seems someone else's pain awakens the ability in others to heal.

We ask for prayerful support for the un-named casualties here and in Iraq.

That same day I email Mike telling him about the Marines that we heard are injured and how they are recovering. I ask him if he knows Carl Schnieder and Michael Cifuentes.

"Hey, I know Cifuentes. He first showed me around when I reported in in September. Is he alright? Where is he? And Schnieder was on that "trac." (AAV)

Anyway, I am fine. We are leaving in a few days for about seven to eleven days. How's the fam? Love you."

An update on Carl Schneider is passed around. His parents are part of our Cincinnati group. This email is from Carl's mother.

We are on day seven down here in Texas. Carl is getting better bit by bit. Good news, his skin grafts took with a ninety-nine success rate. He is off the ventilator but has contracted a small case of pneumonia. We are told that that is common. He still has a hard time speaking and as of yet has not said anything about the explosion. However we are hearing horrific stories from other Marines. He has been up and yesterday walked twenty-five steps. He is still in ICU because he is not eating enough. We want to thank everyone for their prayers, not just for Carl but for all the wounded. This place is heartbreaking but the faith shown by all the soldiers and their families is inspirational. Good news, two of the Marines caught in the explosion are going to be heading home within a few weeks. There are three Marines as far as we know from Operation Matador still in ICU. Keep up the prayers for all please. Thanks again for the concern of all our Marine parents and families and know that we are keeping your sons in our prayers.

Jerry and I are feeling the heartbreak of the parents dealing with their injured Marines. How fragile life is. How tough life is.

These beautiful young men have scars for life physically and emotionally. They will never be the same and their scars will always remind them and their loved ones of this time. While feeling concern for the wounded I also feel the fear of more heartbreak and this leads me to write my feelings to Mike's Marine list.

May 22, 2005: One- hundred and thirty-two days to go.

Family and Friends,

We haven't heard from Mike for a few days so we know he is on another mission. He called us from the Dam and by his third day back sounded pretty good. He said their trucks were ready and he knew they would be going out soon. He would try to call again but if not it would be ten or more days before they got back.

While at the Dam he showered, took his turn cleaning their room, fried his x-box because he didn't have the right plug for 220 and spent time on the phone and computer. He tells me the routine, "shit, shower, shave is often interrupted by incoming mortars." There is never down time. No time to relax.

On Saturday they had a memorial for the fallen Marines.

Jerry and I succumb to tears as we realize what some parents must be feeling now and what our son might be feeling as he sees some of his buddies being memorialized. And I feel angry and hurt and I ask "WHY?"

Why are we there? What are we doing? Who is guilty for the death of these young men? And who takes responsibility for the many that are seriously injured and will carry scars for the rest of their life? And realize that very little attention is given by the media to the fallen. This is the first war that we have not been able to see the fallen return home.

Are we Americans in a state of denial? So we can stay happy and feel safe? Meanwhile our heroes are unnoticed. Might seeing them return, coffin after coffin awaken us to the reality of war and maybe lead us to begin to ask questions? Or would getting news about the injured, engage us and make us feel?

What about the power of prayer? If we knew how many, if we could see them come home and follow their stories, wouldn't we pray for them and their families? Wouldn't the families feel our comfort and support? Wouldn't a compassionate people respond to the pain of those in the burn unit? Those who need anti-depressants? Those who can't sleep?

Or would this make us change a little about the way we are doing our life? And is that what we fear? Change? Sacrifice?

You are my audience to express my grief, my frustration. So far, Mike has been safe from anything physical. But I pray for his emotional self, his soul-self. I pray for all the men and women and their families.

To know a mother who now sees her healthy young son suffering burns all over his body with memories he will never heal. Or to be the one who receives the flag from his draped coffin. I have to ask WHY?

Responses follow:

Your pain is in my mind. My heart hurts for you. My eyes cry tears for you and for the families that I do not know and for the young men and women in a country that is archaic, not knowing who is for you or against you. People who want change must stand up for what they believe. They must be the ones to fight for their freedom. Just as we Americans must stand up and say enough Mr. President. Bring our young men and women home. The Iraqis must fight each other and we need to get out and not side with the losers or winners. We have helped put into power the very same that we have removed. I wish I could hug you. Know that my heart is with you as my tears flow over my cheeks for your despair. Mike will return. (friend)

It's hard to say anything that is worth it when it comes to lives lost... There is a good chance that this effort may prevent the next IED from being planted, RPG fired, etc. which could save future lives. I have it easy. I was probably snoozing on the bus when Mike was trying to save the Marines in that burning track. Since I am not there I try not to quarterback the steps and missions they plan. (nephew)

Thank you for sharing your fears and grief with me. I weep whenever I read your notes and my heart is so touched. (friend)

I too must ask why. I am not able to watch some of the programs that show the horrors of war. It is too real and too close. I would rather be thousands of miles from the scene and pretend that nothing is going on. But you and Jerry make it real. Denial is an easy place to escape to. Mike as well as both of you is in my prayers daily. I know the power of prayer. (friend)

Still keeping Mike and all the young people over there in our prayers. Was looking out over the snow-capped San Juan peaks and Mike came to mind. Just fervently believe that is what he should be looking at. Not some dusty desert towns filled with hostile residents. The mountains are an easy place to pray so I prayed for Mike and all of you. (friend)

When I read these messages my heart aches for you and for Mike and all the others who must experience the war firsthand. I am convinced that if mothers were making the decisions concerning war and peace we would find a way to lasting peace. Perhaps all of you moms with children involved should march on Washington DC. (Friend)

Angie and I cry out WHY with you. (friend)

CHAPTER 10

Thank You

Mike asks that I forward a thank you note to my list.

May 25, 2005: One- hundred and twenty- nine days to go.

"Family and Friends,
I wish I could individually thank and speak to all of you. To accomplish that now would be impossible because there has been so much support for me and my platoon. Everyone here and I thank you for the packages that comfort us and your prayers that are protecting us. I appreciate all that has been done. It's overwhelming on my end to see all of the support.

As you know I am in Haditha. We are getting rid of the bad guys. That's about all I can say. We are doing an awesome job here. We are known across Iraq for our accomplishments. Other Units pull to have us help. We just want to finish up our jobs and safely return home. That's what we pray for. Everyone wants to be with their family and friends. We are all proud to be doing our job. We love it. It's what we are trained for.

Love.

Michael"

I feel the sincerity in Mike as he writes this thank you. He is moved by the generosity of people. And he has no intimation that people are moved by what he is doing. He is a proud Marine. He knows he is the "best." He knows others want him fighting alongside. He has no doubt they are doing an "awesome job." In his idealism, I also read his innocence.

I get responses to Mike's thank you.

Peg and Jerry,

Could hardly contain emotions when I read Mike's thank you. What a blessing Mike is. I know that we are so very proud of him. And I know that Mom and Dad would be also. At this point I consider him unique in the family. I know deep within you guys are so very proud of him. Mike does not owe any thanks to what little we can do for him. We owe him admiration and so much love for what he is doing for us and his brothers in combat. We shall maintain Mike's vigil with you with all of our love and prayers. Thank you for keeping us up to date. We love you all and we so love our PFC Michael. (brother Bob)

Well, I am always thinking about you. I hope you are more up than down. I just can't imagine. I wish I had some words to give you like not to worry too much because it is out of your control and he's a strong warrior. He's okay until we hear otherwise. Or he'll be okay. But reality is that he is your son and you are going to suffer and you are going to worry and you are going to want him home safely. Those vibes of protection and peace are going out to him, the others and to you. It just has to be so hard and I am so sorry you have to go through this. He is trying to help others and that is admirable. I find that crying helps out too. (friend)

Hate reading that stuff but one needs to know. Can't imagine how difficult it is for you. The mess was created before Mike got there and there is almost no way to correct it except to speak the language of the insurgents which is violence. If I had a couple of wishes it would be that we hadn't gone there in the first place. But since that is a wasted wish my second would be that we weren't there alone. I believe we would carry more weight if the UN was behind it. Maybe they would back off then. (friend)

This weekend as we honor the great men and women who bravely served in the military forces I wanted to take a moment to thank you as parents for raising such an amazing young man. I tell my son Josh (who is only 5) about how your son is so brave and how because of people like him we are safe where we live. It is very difficult to explain things like war to young children and even we adults don't understand it. We are praying for Mike and for you. Thanks for your courage and strength as you wait for his safe return. He is a hero to all of us and you are heroes to me. (Daughter of a friend)

Chapter 11

Operation New Market

May comes to an end and the Marines are engaged in their ninth mission since their arrival in Iraq. The other missions were: Operation River Bridge, Operation Treasure Hunt, Operation Outer Banks I, Operation Outer Banks II, Operation Grand Central Station, Operation Birthday, Operation Outer Banks III, Operation Matador and now Operation New Market. Quoting a sergeant, "These Marines are earning their uniforms not just wearing them." Mike agrees. This is how he feels.

June 1, 2005: One- hundred and twenty-two days to go.

I send an email to Mike.

Haven't heard from you so I believe you are out on another mission. Hope you are okay. We know when you come home that you don't necessarily want to live at home with us. Don't feel bad about that. We expect you might want to be on your own. But we are here when you need *us. We can even keep beer in the fridge. Hope to hear from you soon. Love you. (Mom)*

"Hey Parents. How are you doing? I'm fine. I am ready for the time to start flying by. So hopefully it hurries up. I hope I can mail some pictures out soon. I don't know how long we are here for. Talk to you later. Love you."

"Hey. I'm at the Dam for a couple of days. Tomorrow a general is coming here for breakfast and to meet Lima Company and talk with us. That will be interesting. I'll be getting up for that in about four hours. My shoulder has bursitis, nothing serious. We had time off at the dam or at least a slower pace for a couple of days so I had it looked at. It's my left shoulder. It is weak and painful during rotation up and to the rear. I went into a house and got tripped up into a steel door with it. Nothing to brag about. I basically fell so don't go telling everyone I'm injured. Just so you know. Love you. Mike"

My nephew sent an email saying that he and Mike were on instant messenger.

He sounds as though he is doing well. I asked if he was going on a mission any time soon and he said nothing big for a week. He told me he has a DVD player but no DVDS. I would like to get him a bunch and wanted to know if you knew what his favorite movies were. Hope all is well. (Nephew)

Another note from Mike.

"Hey Mom and Dad, I'm running out of time. Sorry. Can you send some Hellman's Mayonnaise and IDK (I don't know) but maybe bread could make it here so I can make a good tuna sandwich. And pickle relish and mustard. Small stuff. Love you. Mike"

CHAPTER 12

Happy Mother's Day

June 9, 2005: One- hundred and fourteen days to go.

Family and Friends,

We got a call from Mike yesterday. He was really tickled about everyone trying to get him fixed up with a tuna sandwich. Thanks for all your suggestions.

They have been going out on day missions. A doctor visited with them and went through the symptoms of fatigue. In the ten or more that he listed Mike said, "We knew we had all of them. Just walking up a flight of stairs we were exhausted."

So, being away from the routine of little sleep, or no sleep or can't sleep, to getting some regular sleep, they are beginning to feel better.

He said they are doing some training while not on a mission. The other day they did something he didn't want to do.. They went out on the lake above the Dam and while the boat was doing, he thought 50 knots, they practiced "man overboard." This was with their boots on, and wearing their "desert cammies" and flak jackets. He went in twice. He said, "The water tasted nasty I know it sounds pathetic but it was like a day at the beach. At least I can say I swam in the Euphrates twice."

He doesn't know when the next big mission will be but they are all happy to be resting up.

He has blown the fan that we sent him and the x-box. They seem to have trouble with electricity. We will have more pictures on his web site soon. He has sent three cameras home and a video that Darren will get posted on Mike's web site.

Thank you for all your prayers and support for all the young men and women who truly are giving up the comfortable American lifestyle where it is so easy to get a tuna sandwich, go for a swim on a real beach and enjoy air conditioning. We have so much. Don't we? Blessings.

Love Peace. (Peggy & Jerry)

Trice was planning to host the next Cincinnati support group. She sent this email.

Peggy and Jerry, I am waiting to get a few more responses back to decide whether to have our Cincinnati meeting on the 26th. I'll let you know in a few days. I hope June will be a quieter month for our guys than May was. What does Mike say the weapons platoon has been doing? I hope he has remained safe. Has he sent more pictures? Kevin wrote us and said he moved into a new barracks. He is rooming with five other guys. He didn't say if he is still in Hit… I was hoping to have our meeting this month to find out what other parents were hearing from their sons. I sent Carl Schneider a Marine quilt that I made for him while he is recuperating. His mom says he is staying in the guest building with her now and will see a surgeon again on Wednesday. I think about what he and so many others are going through constantly. Making the quilt for him was my mental therapy for getting through the days after Lima Companies casualties. Take care. (Trice)

An email letter was sent updating us on Carl Schneider's condition.

Thanks for the continued good thoughts. As far as an update on Carl, here it goes. He has some areas that are doing great. His donor sites on his thighs, his left hand and both arms are healing wonderfully. He still has a paralyzed left vocal cord. They will talk about options when his swelling goes down (a few more weeks). He now has a wound vac on his right hand. He had four exposed tendons plus the grafts that didn't take on his ring and little finger. This thing vacuum packs his hand and sucks out disgusting ooze and gunk and facilitates healing. He hates it. He has to lug it with him and it hurts like the dickens because they splint his hand and then suck all the air out to keep them in place.

He says the pain is bad. I finally got him to stop being such a Marine and admit it hurt and take a pain pill. Today they took it off to check it and he said it was the most god awful pain he has ever felt (which I guess it would be with all the raw exposed nerve). However he is doing better and this thing is actually working. We are hoping that within the next two weeks he will have enough granulation on these areas to be able to do another skin graft. My guess is that we will be down here until mid July. But we keep praying that it will be sooner that we can bring him home. We are keeping all of the guys in our prayers. Thanks (Brigid)

I read the email from Brigid Schneider and I marvel at her composure. I would be outraged and angry. I would yell and scream and feel so devastated. But, maybe I wouldn't. Perhaps the daily -ness of taking care of an injured child from war leaves you silent and full of grace. Perhaps.

One of the items on the wish list of what to send the Marines is cards that they could then send back to their mothers for Mother's Day and the same for Father's day. One of our families sent mother's day cards and sometime in the middle of June I received Mike's Mother's Day card. The card had a butterfly a sunset and a field of grasses. It said, *"Wishing you a beautiful day of happiness. Have a wonderful Mother's Day. Thinking of you."*

Mike added his own note.

"Mom, I love you. Happy Mother's Day. You deserve it. You and Dad have done a great job with us. Thank you, Mom. I'll talk to you when I can.

Love you. The 'most loved'.

Your son, Michael".

A Mother's Day card from my son far away in a desert country in battle and knowing how dangerous it is and how young he is, I can't begin to say how meaningful that card is and how dear. How good and normal it must feel for him to be able to send a card to his mother for Mother's Day. He signed it the "most loved" because that is the title he has in the family. Although they each know Jerry and I love them dearly, they have given titles to each other. Crista is the "best child." John is the "favorite" and Mike the "most loved." I am not sure I like labeling but they came up with it and so it is.

And so in June I celebrate Mother's Day.

CHAPTER 13

Operation Spear

The day begins with frightening news.

(KTEN Online News Friday, June 17, 2005 - 9:36:18 AM Iraq: Operation Spear, AP) Operation Spear started in the pre-dawn hours today. Officials say about a thousand US Marines and Iraq soldiers are in Anbar province, hunting for militants. The province along the Syrian border is where the military says it killed about 40 militants in an operation last week. One general calls the 380 mile long Syrian border Iraq's 'worst problem' in terms of keeping out foreign fighters bent on causing destruction.

The Marines have lost eleven men and two sailors in incidents around Anbar in the past week.

Again, the alarms are going off in my mind as I search for more news.

Baghdad (Reuters U.S. jets drop 500lb bombs in Iraq Operation by Luke Baker) U.S. F-16 fighter planes dropped a series of 500lb bombs on insurgent targets in western Iraq overnight as the U.S. military launched a heavy offensive against rebels near the Syrian border... The air power was in support of Operation Spear, the third major offensive U.S. forces have launched in western Iraq in the past six weeks with the aim of crushing insurgent activity in the Euphrates valley which stretches northwest to Syria...Iraqi troops and U.S. tank and amphibious assault units were involved, said Captain Jeffrey Pool of the U.S. Marines. About 1000 troops were taking part in all...The leader in Qaim of the Muslim Clerics Association, a leading voice for the once-dominant Sunni Arab minority, said he was calling for businesses to remain closed and residents to stay in their homes after weekly Friday prayers in protest at U.S. action he said was endangering civilians... "The U.S. forces are escalating the situation and we will declare a general strike after Friday prayers," the Association's Mudhafar al-Ani said...

It was unclear how much resistance U.S. forces were meeting..."

We aren't told if our Marines are part of the 1000 in Operation Spear but we have to assume they are because it is in Al Anbar province and that is where they are. Now we wait and wonder and pray and search the news all day and email and phone other Marine families. *What have you heard? Do you think they are there? Why don't they tell us? God, I hope they are all okay. Call me if you hear anything.*

We get an email from Isolde about a program on Fox News Network.

"War Stories with Oliver North" will feature bravery and devotion to duty that were exhibited by your Marines and Sailors during Operation Matador. Interviews and footage of the operation are part of the special programming. Thought you may be interested in watching it. Semper Fidelis. (Isolde)

While searching for news about our Marines I find an article entitled *"Bush Wounded by Anger over War"*. *(Times online, June 19, 2005 by Tony Allen-Mills Washington) Increasing American concern about the conduct of the war in Iraq has forced President George W. Bush to sideline some of his domestic priorities in favor of a new public relations drive to bolster confidence in the coalition effort...*

The president's move follows complaints in his own party that the public has been misled about the coalition's difficulties in Iraq. Almost 100 Americans and several hundred Iraqis have died since the beginning of last month despite a claim by Dick Cheney, the vice- president that the insurgency was in its "last throes.",...

There have also been complaints in military circles that the president has recently been more concerned with his proposed reforms to the US pension system..."He's out in the sticks talking about a social security problem that might occur in 2047, and meanwhile the boys in Iraq are getting killed and injured every day", said one officer. "Don't you find that a little odd?"...

In his weekly radio address yesterday, Bush called the war a "vital test" for American security and said there would be no question of a withdrawal...

US forces yesterday launched their second offensive in western Iraq in as many days, aimed at clearing insurgents from the Euphrates river valley. Operation Dagger (Spear), involving 1000 US Marines and soldiers was concentrated in a hostile, deserted area west of Bagdad.

Yet such thrusts have failed significantly to dent insurgent activity, and coalition commanders acknowledged last week they had been unpleasantly surprised by the terrorists' ability to modify their tactics in response to US military might...

"We always accentuated the positive and never prepared the public for the worst," complained Lindsey Graham, a South Carolina senator." People are dying in larger numbers than we thought and the insurgency seems to be growing stronger, not weaker."

Frustration builds as I read the articles about the war and the administration that ordered the war. I feel desperate and helpless to protect my son. I don't want the president or anyone to think he is expendable. He is not. We cannot second guess when we send our young off to war. We better know what we are doing. I am not convinced we do. I am not convinced we have any moral right to be there. And in many articles and reports I read, it sounds as if we are truly unprepared for what is to be faced in Iraq. And that is irresponsible and shameful. How can we hand a mother a folded flag and know we didn't do our part to protect her son. All of the Marines and Soldiers are at risk and it better not be due to lack of awareness or preparation by our leaders. Some of ours have already lost their lives and many others are wounded, and I am feeling a deep emerging anger.

Confirmation comes that the 3/25th Marines are indeed involved in Operation Spear. One of the mothers got an email from her son saying that they had captured fifty terrorists and took no battle-related casualties during the operation. The email ended with "Sleep tight tonight!"

Mike finally returns to the Dam and is able to make a phone call. I send the information out to Mike's Marine List. I also share a story about meeting two injured Marines in a restaurant in Cincinnati.

June 24, 2005: Ninety-nine days to go.

Family and Friends,

Operation Spear ended a few days ago and the Marines are back at Haditha Dam.

Mike called yesterday. He is fine. It was 1:00am Iraq time. His sleep pattern is erratic. He said he will be there for a few days so we will hear from him again. Then he said they will be going out for two to three weeks.

He has received the DVDS you all sent and he says thank you. He says the computers are so slow he has a hard time getting all his messages because they have a time limit on the computer. He would like to thank all of you.

I told him to check out his web site, www.mikelogue.com. He chuckled. But if you haven't checked it out, please do.

Jerry and I were having dinner at a restaurant in Cincinnati. To our amazement two of the injured Marines from Operation Matador came in. They have been home since the beginning of June but face surgery and therapy for healing. They were with one of the women in our Cincinnati support group whose husband is in Iraq. She just had a baby. We talked for awhile before they were seated. I felt compelled to tell our waiter that there were two heroes in the restaurant. I shared the story of Operation Matador with him. I told him these two Marines ought to at least be given a free meal. He spoke to the manager who then spoke to the Marines.

When we were leaving we went over to their table and visited with them again. I found my hands automatically touching all over one of the Marines, his back and shoulders, neck and head. I felt an intimacy with him and he seemed to understand. I was trying to touch my son.

I told them how thankful we were to see them and said Mike would be so happy to know that we saw them and to report how they are doing. The Marine who I caressed looked up and said, "Please tell Mike and the other Marines that we are thinking of them and miss them."

This brings a lump to my throat and tears to my eyes.

Keep in your thought and prayers Cpl. Chad Watkins and LCpl. Scott Bunker. I do not know the rank of these other two but Carl Schneider is in the burn unit in San Antonio and Colin West is recovering from shots in his legs and neck.

Love Peace.

Peggy & Jerry

And then we get a note from Mike.

"Hey Mom and Dad, How is everyone doing? I thought of something you can send me. Some of those microwave meals. I'll be leaving. I'll try to call you before I go but will be gone for two or three weeks. I'll talk to you again sometime in July. Love you all."

CHAPTER 14

Rage

I go to certain web sites each day that I hope will keep me informed. I find an article that is written May 30, called *Honor Our Children's Sacrifices* by Kevin B. Zeese (antiwar.com.) It is an interview with Cindy Sheehan founder of Gold Star Families for Peace. I have not heard of her before but she is beginning to get a name for herself. Following are excerpts from the article.

Zeese: Tell us about your son.

Sheehan: Casey was born on May 29, 1979, and was killed on April 4, 2005. He was my first born. He was an amazing kid who was very easy going. He had a deep faith in God, and he was the one my family would look to for moral guidance. He never wavered...

The official story of his death was that Casey was killed in an ambush in Sadr City by hostile fire. I have some speculative evidence that he was actually killed by friendly fire. The military lied to us and told us conflicting stories....

Zeese: What is the purpose of the Gold Star Families for Peace?

Sheehan: We formed to be a unique voice to spread the word about the lies and betrayals that killed our children and to put a human face on the suffering in Iraq...

Zeese: What are some of the lies and betrayals that killed your children?

Sheehan: They were sent to invade and occupy a country that posed no threat to the United States. They were used recklessly and ignorantly by their commander-in-chief, who should exercise more caution when he misuses our young people. They were all lied to by their recruiters, who will tell young people anything to get them to enlist, and then deliver nothing. They were all killed performing duties that they were inadequately or not trained for at all. Evan Ashcraft was suffering from dysentery before he died. He lost 25 pounds because of dirty drinking water and bad food. Sometimes they are rationed one bottle (of water) a day. Many times they have been killed guarding private convoys, people who make many times more money than they do. Sgt. Sherwood Baker was killed searching for weapons of mass destruction that didn't exist...

Zeese: Democracy Rising will be sending a letter to President Bush on Memorial Day concerning the lack of body armor and armor for vehicles in Iraq. What are your thoughts on that?

Sheehan: All of our children were killed because of lack of proper equipment or doing jobs that they weren't trained for, and it is so hurtful to us that with all the money being wasted and stolen in the Pentagon, and in the Provisional Authority in Iraq, that our children, over in harm's way are still inadequately protected.

Zeese: Do you have a Memorial Day message from Gold Star Families for Peace?

Sheehan: We at GSFP are insulted when people like Bush, Rumsfeld and Cheney say that America has to "stay the course" in Iraq to "honor our children's sacrifices." Our position is that no one, Iraqi or American, should have died for the lies and to make evil people fabulously wealthy. Just because our children were unjustly murdered, why would we want more bloodshed? Not one more drop of blood should be shed for the lies and deceptions. Honor our children's and our family's sacrifices by bringing the troops home as soon as humanly possible. Honor our men and women in the armed forces by using them only when America is threatened, not to invade countries that pose no threat to the USA. Honor the vets who have served America by meeting their every need. Honor the families of needlessly slain children by realizing that America is a country at war. Look in your hearts, look at the truth about this immoral war, and work for peace. Our children died for peace; make it so.

Her voice booms in my head. Much of what she says rings true from our experiences with Mike. While being recruited he was made promises that were broken or ignored. Mike knew he wasn't adequately trained before deployment but is told "You'll catch up." And then there are his reports back to us about the private companies in Iraq making bundles of money doing what the Marines are doing. And Mike is aware that their equipment is not the best. I want to scream. I raise a young man who envisions himself a warrior willing to serve and protect and I feel he is being used in a sham, a game, a bet for oil, a business of war. I can't accept this. And I don't know where to turn or what to do. I can't go over there and get him although I want to. My frustration and desperation grows stronger. I think at times I will just pop. I can't find any ideals to fall back on. I don't know how to save my son. I don't know where he is or what he is being asked to do. I just know that he is losing a precious part of himself. He is losing his innocence and his soul and can at any time lose his very life. It makes me crazy.

Cindy Sheehan has already lost all she can lose. I still have my son but I can feel and understand her rage.

CHAPTER 15

No News Is Good News

June 27th we receive a message from Mike saying he will try to call us again before he leaves on the next mission. We don't get that call. We know he is out.

Bagdad. June 28 (Reuters, U.S. Marines launch major operation in west Iraq) U.S. Marines launched a major operation in western Iraq on Tuesday, dispatching 1,000 troops against suspected insurgents in the western Euphrates river valley.

"Operation Sword began early this morning to root out terrorists and foreign fighters living along the Euphrates River between the cities of Haditha and Hit," the Marine said in a statement...

The operation... is at least the fourth battalion-sized operation the Marines have launched in towns in the western desert during the past two months...

The Euphrates valley has emerged as a strategic area in the counter-insurgency war, which has worsened since a Shiite- and Kurdish-led government took power two months ago.

Now we know where Mike is. And we wait. Not idly. We wait at the computer. We keep watch of the TV news stations and hope more information will be made known about this mission. When will we find out if our Marines have made it back to Haditha Dam safely? Are there any casualties? Wait. Be patient. "No news is good news." The daily mantra, "No news is good news." Somehow that isn't comforting.

Our Key Volunteer Network newsletter arrives. There are two letters from General Huck, the Commanding General. He sends what is called a Family Readiness Update.

The Marines, Sailors, Soldiers and Airmen of the Division are into a rhythm now and are carrying the fight to the bad guys with greater results. We've conducted several big operations in addition to the countless daily patrols. Whether large or small operations, the deciding factor is highly trained men and women. In the blink of an eye, our Warriors are able to make decisions to use deadly force or not to use it. It takes a special breed of highly trained and motivated professionals to work in such a demanding environment. They are a special breed.

The fighting forces continue to keep the enemy off balance by relentless pursuit. They are after the enemy twenty-four hours a day. We are disrupting his operations with large-scale maneuvers, raids, and searches for weapons caches and safe houses...

Iraqi Security Forces are making great strides as we train, partner and operate with them. They are getting better daily and there are going to be more Iraqi units this summer and fall to put into the fight against the insurgents. This is good news as it puts an Iraqi face on the security environment.

We are working hard and every day presents new challenges, but we are making progress. Our people need to remain focused and not become complacent. The dangers are real and a loss of focus can translate into a ruined day. With the Nation's support, the Marines, Sailors, Soldiers and Airmen of the 2nd Marine Division will prevail. Of that I am sure.

Keep us in your prayers and continue to write...
Need to close now. All of you are terrific Morale Officers and key to our success. Later and stay safe.

I study this letter, reading it over and over. I wonder where Mike is in this scenario General Huck describes. Has Mike been part of the "big operations?" Has he had to decide "in the blink of an eye" whether to use deadly force or not? Does Mike see "progress?" Does he "remain focused?" I realize how vulnerable Mike is on each of these daily patrols. Nothing in this letter makes me feel good but I accept the attempt by the commander to make me feel good. I think he really wants us to believe things are going well and, well, not to worry. Just continue to pray. "The dangers are real."

A second letter follows the first. I don't know the time frame of the letters because they are not dated and are sent in the same newsletter.

Greetings from Western Iraq and the Operation Iraqi Freedom, home of the 2nd Marine Division. This is Major General Rick Huck, the Commanding General, with another Family Readiness Update.

The men and women of this Division continue to impress Coalition Forces, the Iraqi Security Forces, and the Iraqi people with their professionalism and devotion to duty. It's been rubbing off on the young Iraqi soldier who wants to be like his U.S. counterpart. That's a tremendous testimony to our fighting forces...

A big part of our daily battles involved information operations. The Iraqi people are victims of the most appalling and outright fiction imaginable. The insurgents use any and all means to spin their lies and try to elicit an anti-Coalition Forces response from the people. However, we are countering their lies with an alternate source of information, utilizing radio. By expanding our radio coverage in Al Anbar Province, we hope to expose the propaganda of the terrorists and give the ordinary Iraqi family the truth about the affairs of their country ...

The days are getting longer, and hotter, but our Marines, Sailors, Soldiers and Airmen are dealing with it, as you would expect. They are great Americans and carry on in the same warrior spirit of those servicepersons who have previously fought our Nation's battles. It is a privilege for me to serve with them in the Global War on Terrorism.

I don't know how to feel about these letters. They are sent with the best intention to help families cope with the situations their loved ones are in. I am pleased to get some facts. But the truth about training Iraqi forces to someday take over what our Marines are doing seems unclear. If we can train our men in a few months, what takes so long for training there? What is the problem?

The Key Volunteer Newsletter also directs us to a web site, "Injured Marines Program." It contains news and information and useful links related to particular injuries, such as PTSD/ Combat Stress, Amputee/ Prosthetics, Paralysis/Spinal Cord, Burns, Traumatic Brain Injury, Vision/Hearing Impaired. This makes me take notice. We already have some injuries. We will have more. And so we need to know this.

In the same newsletter we receive an update on Carl Schneider.

I wanted to give you an update that you can share with everyone. My son, LCpl. Carl Schneider, of Cincinnati, was injured in Operation Matador on 5/11/05. He was transported to Ft. Sam Houston in San Antonio, TX on May 13th (his 22 birthday). He was admitted to Brooks Army Medical Center with bilateral 3 degree burns on his hands and arms, 2nd degree burns on his face and smoke inhalation injuries...

My main point in writing this is to share with everyone the incredible support and inspiration we have been given down here...

70

The community itself donates so much to give back to these soldiers and Marines. Most significant of all is the survivors. Many have burns covering half their bodies, a lot are amputees and the majority has life changing injuries. But they truly express the American spirit. In the gym and rehab room, they work through pain and frustration, but they don't give up. Most are wonderfully polite and concerned about the well being of their military brothers. Without a doubt, these guys are an inspiration to all with their optimism and strength of both mind and body.

I also want to take time to let everyone know that we are keeping Lima Company in our thoughts and prayers and we pray for the families of the fallen Marines who gave the ultimate sacrifice.

Brigid Schneider

Another item in the newsletter mentions that the Marine staff is working hard creating a "Garden at our Reserve Center in honor of our fallen heroes."

Finally, we are to reserve July 31st for Family/Loved Ones Day. This will be a picnic. Everyone will bring something to share. The Key Volunteers will provide grilled hot dogs and hamburgers. Greg Cifuentes volunteers to do the grilling. He is the father of LCpl. Michael Cifuentes.

July 11, 2005: Eighty-two days to go.

Good Morning Family and Friends of PFC Michael Logue,

"No news is good news," is our mantra. We haven't heard from Mike for several weeks. And we are told "no news is good news." But I have to say the mantra does not comfort me. Before he left he sent threes rolls of film home and a video.. We will scan some pictures for the web site.

On Thursday Lindsay got a call from Mike. It was the middle of the night in Iraq. One of the sergeants had a satellite phone and he was passing it from Marine to Marine. Each Marine got about five minutes to talk. One of the Cincinnati moms said her son left a message. She said he was whispering. Said he was on a roof top and couldn't say where.

Lindsay said Mike was mumbling. He said they haven't had a shower since June 28th. He said things aren't good where they are, said something about two car bombs that day. One hit a re-con vehicle and the other a humvee. He didn't elaborate more than that. He said he was okay. Thought they would be out there for a few more weeks.

At our Cincinnati meeting yesterday one of the parents reported that their son said we would not be able to send any packages after August 8th. The presumption is that they may come home sooner than planned. It takes about three weeks to get a package. If this is true, they may be home in September. The word is that maybe they have "battle fatigue."

I do not count on this talk. We have had no official word. Rumors have a certain energy and hope.

One of the biggest obstacles to the Marines now is the heat. They aren't able to sleep because it is so hot. Temperatures rise to 130* in the daytime. They are dressed in their "cammies" and flak jackets, carrying their gear, sleeping in holes that they dig, or in abandoned buildings without any plumbing.

We believe they are in the city of Hit. It is northwest of Baghdad, a city of one-hundred and sixty-thousand. They are doing a "sweep" through the inner third of the city, looking for weapons, looking for insurgents.

I think, Mike would be on summer break now, preparing for his sophomore year of college, enjoying friends, working at a job, partying, looking forward to fall classes. But he isn't on summer break.

Civic and national holidays never held so much meaning before. Hope you had a happy 4th.

Love PEACE.

Peggy & Jerry

A friend who lives in Florida sends me a note.

Just wanted to say hi!

Sterling bank employees took up a collection for spray water bottles with fans. We were able to purchase 145 bottles and Mike should receive them within a week. Wish we could have purchased enough for his entire troop. The package will say from Sterling bank.

Love, Carolyn

July 12, 2005: Eighty-one days to go.

Dear Family and Friends,

I received a call today from the Bengals football team. Brandon was calling for Mike's address. He said that Mike had emailed the Bengals telling them how much he enjoyed them. He told them where he was and what 3/25th Lima Co. was doing.

Marvin Lewis (Bengals' coach) wants to write Mike a letter.

I asked Brandon when they received the email. He said June 24th. Then I told him that 3/25th has been gone since then and will probably be out for a few more weeks. I told him how excited Mike would be to hear from Marvin Lewis. I also expressed my gratefulness for their attention and concern.

My voice began to crack and I apologized. He couldn't see the tears but he could hear them. He wished us all good luck. It will be great for Mike to get Marvin's letter.

Love PEACE

July 19, 2005: Seventy-four days to go

Family and Friends,

Our son lives!!! We heard his voice!!!

Mike called Monday at 2:15 am. We had a ten second conversation. The phone went dead. We lay awake waiting for another call. It didn't come.

Then at 4:00pm Monday I answered to a voice that said," *"Hey."*

I knew it was Mike before I picked up the phone. He sounds great. He sees light at the end of the tunnel. He was at a Camp outside of Hit, a place of relaxation that each squad is rotated to for a few days for rest. He had been there a day. "It's like being in a hotel. It has air conditioning and a mattress to sleep on and real food." He is very tired of MRE's (Meals Ready to Eat). While he was showering they were hit by mortars.[2] He said he would be going back to Hit today and another squad would be coming in for "vacation at the camp."

One of the things his squad had been doing is building a structure in Hit that would be used as a Police station.

Mike's squad was held back four to five days. As the Marines approached the city, gunmen shot at them from a mosque. Mike's friend, Dan Foot received shrapnel but he is okay. Also the Navy Corpsman, Travis Youngblood received shrapnel. Not sure of his condition at this time.

Mike was told that their window of opportunity to fly back to the states is September 6th - 18th. He is very excited about coming home. He has lots of plans in his busy little head. He wants to buy a tent and go camping, climb Mt. Le Conte, go to the Boundary Waters and a friend from Colorado wants him to come out there.

I am sure these thoughts are stimulating, motivating and give Mike new energy. It seems more real to him now, life after Iraq.

---

2   "There were Navy See Bees showering next to me. See Bees do construction and improvements on our base. They left our open air plywood shower quickly. I laughed and said to them, 'Ha, the fuckers missed. They're a few klicks (kilometers) off. I'm taking my shower.' I knew I could shower before they walked 'em in (bring the impact closer to target.) At least I would die clean. Much better than when you're in an overflowing port-o-jon. I was in one at the Dam and the mortar impacted right in the center of the river. Just on the other side of a concrete wall. That's the frustration of living in a combat environment." (Mike's comments)

Home is real. The places he wants to return to are places of family fun in his memory.

He said he thought they would be getting back to the Dam in a few days. I believe they are hoping there will be no more intensive operations.

We have been advised not to send anymore packages. All that has been sent since June is sitting at the Dam absorbing the intense heat, melting everything inside. He will have much to open when he returns. He chuckled when I told him. It's like telling a kid Christmas is coming.

Thank you for your wonderful support. It still is amazing to me to see how deeply compassionate people are. Not just family and friends, total strangers as well.

Love PEACE

This is a response from a friend of a friend as my communications get passed on to friends of friends.

This message made me cry. Both in the longing and relief of a parent to hear her child's (no matter how old they are they are still our 'children') voice and the longing of the child to be back 'home.' War as an abstraction is so different from the realities of the flesh and blood experience of it. My heart goes out to you and all the moms on both sides of the conflict. It will be 'Christmas' when he comes home. Hugs.

CHAPTER 16

Roller Coaster

I never liked roller coasters. I have a tendency for motion sickness and the sudden movements of the roller coaster from up, up ,up to down, down, down just is too much for my body. I don't much care for the emotional roller coaster I am on now either. I recover from being down, down, down and start to head up and there I am down again. This roller coaster is hard on my soul.

All, I would like to share an email with you that I have just received from the widow of a Navy Corpsman. Doc Youngblood was attached to Lima Company. Weapons Platoon knew him best. He came to us from the Great Lakes Naval Base in Illinois. I do not have any more details. Please ask your Marine if he can share any stories about Doc Youngblood.

Without further ado, here it is.(Isolde)

"I would like people to write letters about my husband so my children will learn how special he was. Our daughter will be born in September and she needs to know that he was an amazing person. I will be burying Travis on August 1ˢᵗ at Arlington Cemetery. His wake will be on that Saturday the 30ᵗʰ of July. He was the love of my life and will be always and forever. That is what we promised each other.

Laura"

This news is shocking. We didn't know Travis was badly injured. He was the Navy Doc for Mike's platoon. I write to my list after talking to Mike.

Family and Friends,

I spoke with Mike. He told me their Doc, Travis Youngblood, died after having his foot amputated from receiving shrapnel. The docs who take care of the Marines are Navy docs. Travis is the Doc for weapons platoon, Mike's platoon. While grieving about this, Mike said that their canine also died. He was a German Shepherd used for sniffing; He also died from receiving shrapnel. After telling me about these two casualties Mike said, "Yeah, that sucks." I know it is not the first casualty he has seen but it never gets easy. This is weapons platoon's first casualty. I tell you this and remind you that war is not nice. It hurts a lot of innocent people, including the unborn girl of Travis Youngblood.

Love PEACE

I responded to Laura Youngblood's request for notes for her children.

Dear Laura and children,

How sad to hear of the loss of your husband and father. Our son Michael is in weapons platoon. He knew "Doc." He is very upset. It hit him and the other Marines hard. Mike loved and respected "Doc." Please know that many people are moved and touched each time we lose one of our brave young men. War is not nice. War hurts a lot of people. Your father put his life on the line to help others. What a brave man. Be proud of him. He had the courage to do what most men don't. He served knowing the dangers and the cost. Be proud of yourself as a family. You too have courage and compassion.

May you be blessed abundantly as others were blessed to know "Doc."

Love PEACE always.
Peggy & Jerry Logue

My friend Trice was on line with her son Kevin. She forwarded to me Kevin's conversation about "Doc."

Hey, it's me again. To answer your question, no, that is not the same Doc that was with us in Hit. I didn't really get to know him that well because he was with Lima Company the whole time. It was really hard on the rest of the platoon. At first we were told they were just going to have to amputate his foot. Then they said they had to put him into a coma. Then the next day they told us he didn't make it. It was weird coming back to his room and seeing all his stuff by his rack, and his mail there waiting for him. There was a nice memorial for him.

I saw the Oliver North special. It was neat to hear them talk about us. I know LCPL Camp too. He is supposed to be getting a medal for his actions during that attack. He saved three Marines' lives. It was hard for the other Marines to watch the scene where the "trac" was on fire. One kids' cousin died in that fire. I am glad that they said good things about us...

Kevin Michael Mullins

Navy man dies in Iraq, leaving a family here to grieve (by Veronica Gorley, Daily Press) July 29, 2005. *Smithfield -- Debra Youngblood used to watch the grieving mothers of soldiers*

79

and Marines on television and wonder how they coped with their children's deaths in Iraq.

Now she knows.

"There is no way to cope," said Youngblood, whose son, Petty Officer 3rd Class Travis Youngblood, a U.S. Navy corpsman, died July 21. He was 26...

In January, he went to Iraq as a hospital man with the 2nd Marine Expeditionary Force. On July 15, an explosive device hit his vehicle about 100 miles northwest of Bagdad.

"He was a hero not because he went to war," said his wife, Laura Youngblood "but because of who he was."

Laura said she felt hope when she learned that he was stable enough to be transferred to Germany for medical attention. But he hemorrhaged just before he could be transferred," she said. "He held on for six days," she said. "He fought."

Laura Youngblood, 26, said they dated a month before they married, on Dec.31, 1999. She left the service in April 2004. They had a son, Hunter, who is now 4, and she will soon give birth to a daughter.

In his last letter home, her husband asked that the baby be called Emma.

Debra Youngblood... said her son's goal was to study medicine, possibly to become a physician assistant or a doctor...

When she first heard that her son had died, she couldn't believe it.

"I was like, 'This isn't true. This is a mistake,' she said. "You want to scream. You want to wake up everybody on the neighborhood and tell them that this terrible thing has happened. You want to make everybody aware that this young man died in the service of his country."

For her, nighttime has become nightmare.

"The worst time is when you lay down to sleep because the memories come flowing back," she said...

It's really hard to accept that you're not going to talk to him again, hear his laughter, hear his humorous stories of what he's done and what he's seen," his mother said, her eyes filling with tears...

Captain Glenn F. Thibault, MD described Doc Youngblood in his book *Sword in the Lion's Den.*[3] *"What are we going to do?!" a Marine sergeant screamed at the chief corpsman over the din of the spinning helicopter rotors. "What are we going to do? We lost our corpsman!"*

"Calm down, Sergeant," Chief Burkhalter said quietly.

"What do you mean, 'calm down!' How can I calm down?" he screamed, seething with anger and grief...

The incident from 15 July was an improvised explosive device attached to the inside of a mosque wall. As the patrol walked by, a triggerman detonated the bomb. Their corpsman down, the remaining Marines sprung into action to take care of him and the injured Iraqi soldiers...

When Operation Sword ended 3 July with no significant casualties, the city of Hit now in friendly hands, it was clear that holding the city was going to take more effort than taking the city. Since that date two Marines have been killed in the city from mortar and one from the IED mentioned - HM3 Youngblood, injured 15 July, died of blast lung on 21 July, the day after his foot had to be amputated due to a severe shrapnel wound."

A note from the father of one of our Marines tells us of a phone call from his son Shad.

Nikki just got a quick call from Shad. This info is not confirmed... Shad said two of our guys in 2nd platoon were killed (I am assuming from other info that Andre Williams is one of them), and about 8 were wounded, including 3 Iraqi soldiers. He couldn't give any

---

3   Sword in The Lion's Den: Navy Doc with 3/25 Marines in Iraq, by Captain Glenn F. Thibault, ,MD p 225, Publish America, 2008, Baltimore.

names, but said both boys had children of their own. He said it was a pretty fierce battle, and they had to call in air support. I don't know anything else about any of our guys, but thought I'd pass that much info along. We'll just keep praying for all of them. Hope to see you Sunday. Steve Biffle

I send a note to my list.

Family and Friends,

A few days ago we heard about two Marines who were killed from Lima Co. We didn't have any details and it wasn't confirmed. Yesterday it was. Cpl Andre L. Williams, 23, and LCpl Christopher P Lyons, 24, were killed when their company came under attack from enemy fire and rocket propelled grenades near the city of Cykla in western Iraq. Williams had talked to his ex-wife on Monday and was excited to be coming home and getting back together. He has a five year old daughter and a seven year old son.

LCpl Lyons left for Iraq when his wife was pregnant. He only saw his three month old daughter by webcam. Both Marines were in 2nd platoon.

We got a call from Mike this morning. He is fine.[4] He said they were brought back to regroup after the losses of 2nd platoon. He also said that his platoon was told that they were on stand-by so not to unpack. His platoon continued the sweep in Cykla after 2nd platoon's casualties. He knew Williams and Lyons and said they would have a memorial for them in a few days.

It is very hot there. He said, "It feels like when you open the oven door, like you are just baking. Even at night when it cools down we can't sleep because the ground is so hot, like a hot plate. Only between about 4:00am and 6:00am do I cool down enough to get some rest."

He said the homecoming plans now sound like late September

---

4   "I was at a vehicle checkpoint. We packed up and left for Cykla. When we got there, I found my friend Matt Angle. He had been shot in the stomach. Fortunately, at the bottom of the Sapi Plate, so he remained with us in the battle. After the air strike on the house, we aggressively assaulted through the small city." (Mike's Comments)

or early October. We won't know until it happens. He has also heard rumors that they will be quarantined at Camp LeJeune for a few weeks. Until official orders, it's all rumor. Mike is tired and ready to come home. They all are.

I asked him what he would do the rest of the day. "Eat and sleep," was his response.

Carolyn, they got the water/fan bottles. Thank you for the thoughtfulness. Mike is thankful to everyone for all your packages and prayers.

Please pray for the fallen young men who only dreamed of coming home.

Love PEACE

The following communication was between a 3/25th Lima Co. Marine and his grandfather. It got passed around at the Family Day picnic.

Saturday, July 30, 2005
Grandpa,

Thanks for the encouragement. We as a squad had been in 5 other serious firefights but this one was by far the worst. The others lasted only a few minutes each (a few very intense minutes) but very short nonetheless. From the first shot which hit my buddy in the head to the final bombs that we called in the whole fight lasted three hours. I had never been so hyped up and scared at the same time. It's amazing how the human mind reacts sometimes. I remember after we pulled back so that air could fly in and drop their payload everyone pretty much collapsed and passed out, the adrenaline was surely flowing pretty heavy through every ones system.

They told us a few weeks ago that only 2 other units have been in more combat than us since the end of Vietnam and that we have done more fighting than any other unit since the start of this war here in Iraq. Neat statistics to possibly sit back and ponder while in the safety of the U.S. but I know we all hope our fighting days are behind us. Lima Company has built itself a strong reputation around here. The other night when I got to the air force base for the x-rays, word somehow got out that I was a Lima boy and throughout the night about 5 or 6 Marines kept coming in and checking on me to make sure I didn't need anything. Although I started to get a little pissed because they kept waking me up it did indeed make me feel good.

Rumor has it that we will begin to turn in all of our optics and special gear towards the middle of August for the unit coming in to replace us. Hopefully things will now start to calm down. Tell Grandma I send my love.

Semper Fi
(Matt Mathew Mason)

We are staying abreast of your happenings as best we can. We are, of course, very concerned and relieved to know your injuries will heal without debilitating effects. I have the pictures you sent which I enhanced and printed for everyone. It is shocking to realize your friend in the middle has lost his life. It sure brings home the reality of the war we are fighting.

I understand and respect your desire to remain with your team, especially when one of your buddies went down. Somehow, someway, this mess will right itself and you will always know you did your part to make this a better world. Hang in there you old veteran, I feel like I am living some part of this with you. Semper Fi.

(Grandpa)

CHAPTER 17

"It's Depressing Here..."

August 1, 2005: Sixty-one days to go.

Family and Friends,

Sunday was Family Day in Columbus for the Marine families and loved ones. The first person we saw as we parked our car was the mother of Andre Williams who was killed during the week. She was greeted with hugs and tears. We all recognized her pain and grief. Are we strangers? No, we are families of Marines who are serving as brothers. Andre's ex-wife was also receiving hugs. She and Andre had talked earlier that week and were excited about getting back together. He was killed on Thursday.

Also at the picnic were ten Marines who are back in the States recovering from wounds received in Operation Matador with scars, some visible, some not. A false eye, an arm shackled in wires, legs with bullet holes, faces healing from fire, hands in gloves while skin grafts replace lost flesh and spirits wanting to be with their brothers in Iraq. These young men were not singled out. They didn't wear

*big stars on their chests. They had to be found. No one put them on
a stage and applauded them. They would say they were only doing
their job. They find comfort in the shelter of their brother Marines.
It was nice to see them together. They look healthy and like the finest
young men America has. They don't know their futures. They have
long journeys with lots of therapy. Most will not be able to continue
with the Marines because of their injuries. Some talked about going
back to school to pick up where they left off. One missed graduation
by a few weeks.*

*It was a sad day but because of the faith of these young men it
was a glorious day.*

*Carolyn Cifuentes told me that her son Michael called last
Thursday, the day Andre Williams and LCpl Lyons were killed.
Lyons was a good friend of Michael's. He was upset to tears and told
her "I hate it here." That upset Carolyn because there was nothing
she could do but encourage her son. They talked a few days later and
he seemed better, but anxious to come home.[5]*

*Our Mike is okay. He emailed us early this morning and asked
what our winter plans were. We treasure each day as it gets closer
to the homecoming.*

Love PEACE

What I didn't express in that letter to my List is how lost
I felt. How lost for words, lost for feelings, lost for answers. I
just tried to be present to the Marines that were there and the
families of those who had fallen. It was a numbing feeling.
On one hand there was relief because my son was still okay.
On the other hand, he was still there, at risk, in harm's way.
I was waiting for the other shoe to drop. Then there was that
incredible attraction to the Marines who had come home.
To talk with them, to assure them, to hear their stories was
cathartic. To feel that if I stay close enough to them, I am

---

5   LCpl Michael Cifuentes was killed in action, August 3rd, 2005,
    Barwanah, Iraq, by and IED. He was awarded a Purple Heart, Combat
    Action Ribbon.

somehow close to my son. And to watch the other parents, how they cope, what they say. I felt an amazing courage from the mothers. We had the same dedication and commitment to our sons. We were willing to do anything to assure the safety and protection of our own. And yet, nothing we did or said would do that and somehow each mother knew. So, we spoke gently to each other. We embraced each other and laughed when we could. The laughter was usually a memory we shared about our sons.

The saddest moment of the day was when the chaplain had a prayer for the two who had fallen that week. The families were there and I know they were still in shock. My God, how does this happen?

Responses to my email:

Sis, I sit at my computer this morning with tears streaming down my face after catching up on all the readings you have sent about Mike and his admirable comrades. My world lately, holding a beautiful baby boy hour after hour, and preparing my house and yard for a choir picnic that was held Sunday. And Mike and men can't even sleep or rest because it is just too hot. Watching their friends and fellow Marines fall in the line of duty. Preparing to attend their memorials. Thinking and dreaming about coming home. And yeah, I had a tough couple of days, sweating in the garden, shining and scrubbing my house so it would be perfect for our guests. Nothing like a little time for reflection!

Please know and pass along to Mike that he continues to be "wrapped in our prayers" and will be until he lands on the free and safe soil of the good old USA. (Sister)

"Hey Mom and Dad,
How are you guys doing? I can't wait to get home. What's new? What do you plan to do when I get back after Gatlinburg? Are you still going our west? And how's the rest of the family? Love you. Thanks. Mike"

Hi Honey,

We do not have definite plans for the winter. We would like to go to warm and sunny Arizona and then to Colorado to see your brother, John. What are your plans?

We had a nice Family Day gathering yesterday in Columbus. Saw several guys from Matador. Also Andre Williams' mother and ex-wife and family were there.

That was so sad. You can't get home fast enough for us.

Also saw Sgt. Davis. Yeah, he is limping a bit. He smiled when we introduced ourselves. He said "Yeah, I like Logue. He calls me the "gear guru."

Visited with LCpl Camp. He is doing well. He has gloves on his hands while skin grafts are healing. Scott Bunker still has some wires in his arm to help his bone heal. He lost his right eye and had part of a lung removed. Colin West is supposed to be on crutches, but he isn't. Watkins still has a foot problem. Mike Stahler has lots of scars but he is healing. They are missing you guys. Feel bad not to be with you. Looking forward to your return and welcoming home. These are all very nice young men. It makes us proud to know that you are their brother Marine. Miss you and can't wait to see you.

Love (Mom and Dad)

August 2, 2005: Sixty days to go. (Tuesday after the Family Day Picnic)

Family and Friends,

I returned home from "working the polls" and was getting my phone messages. The 5th message was from Trice. She asked if I had heard the troubling news from Iraq. I called her cell and she said seven more Marines were killed yesterday.

Whoa. We thought it was going to get better. If you go to www.ideologue.com and click on news you can read about the casualties.

They say the men are holding up well.

Love PEACE.

Hi Honey,
Heard about the other Marines KIA yesterday. You must be getting pretty down about all of this. I am so sorry you have to experience this. War isn't fun. You are so brave and strong. Keep up your motivation and focus. Your time is almost over. In a few weeks you will be turning in your gear. We can't wait for that news. You Marines have shown complete integrity and bravery. I don't know how to tell you how proud we are of you and how desperately we want you home. You have seen enough. You have done enough. It is time to come home.
Missing you and praying for your constant protection and safety.
Love you. (Mom and Dad)

In this note to Mike I attempt to keep calm. But I feel frantic. It seems each day brings more horror while we look for calm. I need to assure Mike as I reach my breaking point. I feel like I am being swallowed by a big monster. How ordinary my life has been. This is big stuff. This world of chaos and violence and my son in the middle of it makes me want to scream in fear. My soul is ripping deeper and I don't have any way to stop the ripping.

August 3rd, 2005: Fifty-nine days to go.
(Wednesday after the Family Day Picnic)

Family and Friends,
I awoke this morning hoping to find information about the seven Marines KIA yesterday only to see that fourteen more were killed near Haditha this morning by a road side bomb. This is the area where Mike and the 3/25th Marines are. This news is heart wrenching. We checked www.icasualties.com to find out that the

seven KIA yesterday were not 3/25th Lima Co. but other Marines from the 2nd Expeditionary.

I had just sent Mike an email to encourage him after getting through the loss of the two from last week and the seven from yesterday. At that time I didn't know about the fourteen from today.

Mike talked to Lindsay a few days ago before the seven were killed and told her that he was depressed. "We are all depressed. It's depressing here," he said.

It has been a few days now since anyone has heard from Mike. We know they are being called out day after day. Mike told Lindsay that they were called out on a day they thought they were going to get some rest. They had to assist an Army trouble spot. They had to bring in air power and bombed a vacant school insurgents had taken over. It was full of weapons and explosives.

What is there to say?

Thank you for your prayers, support and caring.

For our children and their future, Love PEACE.

We found this article was online.

14 Marines Die in Huge Explosion in Western Iraq: Week's Toll Rises to 21 For Ohio-Based Regiment

By Ellen Knickmeyer Washington Post Foreign Service, Thursday, August 4, 2005.

Baghdad, Aug. 3 -- A Marine Reserve company that was known as "Lucky Lima" before suffering heavy casualties in May was hit Wednesday by the deadliest roadside bombing of the Iraq war, a massive explosion that killed 14 Marines and the unit's Iraqi interpreter, according to witnesses and military spokesman.

The Marines were part of a convoy that was attacked on a desert road outside the western town of Haditha, one witness said. Rolling in armored vehicle after vehicle, the patrol was nearing the entrance to the town when a brilliant flash erupted in the middle of the convoy...

The bomb blew apart the personnel carrier, known as an Amtrac, and ignited its load of fuel and explosives…

The U.S. military gave few details of the attack.

Nine of the dead Marines were members of Lima Company--part of the 3rd Battalion, 25th Marine Regiment, a reserve unit from Ohio that had been sent to the Syrian border to play a lead role in shutting off the main route for foreign gunmen and suicide bombers entering Iraq.

As it turned out, Lima Company and the rest of the 25th Regiment were beginning four months in which they would be bombed and ambushed in the grimy Euphrates River towns where U.S. commanders say foreign insurgents had moved freely. During the tour, 16 members of Lima Company have been killed, according to a military spokesman in Columbus, Ohio, 1st Sgt. James Halbig…

Gunmen killed at least five members of the regiment on a foot patrol Monday outside Haditha, the U.S. military said, and the body of a sixth Marine was found a mile or two from the firefight. The same day, a suicide bomber killed a Marine in the town of Hit, about 45 miles from Haditha, the military said…

In Columbus and nearby cities and towns, Marine officers in dress blues went from house to house Wednesday, notifying relatives of casualties…

"Let me ask you, is 3rd Battalion of the 25th Marines fighting the entire war?" demanded Ken Hiltz, a police officer in Ohio and former Marine who has friends in Lima Company. "This battalion is decimated. I'm just losing count."…

"We've never had such a resistance operation outside town that cost the Americans a lot without hurting many civilians," said Mohammed Hamed Hadeethi, a professor at the region's Anbar University. "That's what gives this operation a whole different color than other operations. We call it the white operation."

CHAPTER 18

MARCH ON WASHINGTON

August 4th, 2005: Fifty-eight days to go.

Family and Friends,
A friend and neighbor says she is going to call our senators to tell them that it is time Lima Company Marines come home. They have seen enough and done enough. You might do the same. And we parents and wives and children of these Marines will be grateful for your action. Trice, after getting the devastating news that Michael Cifuentes was killed, said she felt powerless. I suggested to her that we call our senators. She thinks that is a great idea and something she can do. I will call the senators today. How about you? You will probably get a staffer. Tell them you want the senator to get the message that it is time for the Lima Company Marines to come home. Thanks.
Love PEACE.

A friend who has been receiving my emails sends a letter

to Senator Voinovich. A feeling of hope begins. It is possible to take action and not just sit and watch this terror of war. It is possible to say enough is enough: *I have met you several times before via the late Senator Barry Levey and I have supported you as I believe you are a thoughtful man of integrity. Please advise us as to what is going on with the latest group of Ohio-based Marines KIA this week. Why are the insurgent attacks killing all of these Marines? What is Congress doing to follow up and give them whatever they need to protect themselves? During your recess, I hope you all are not taking a vacation from the current news from Iraq.*

Sincerely yours,

Michele (Shelly)Abrams, Leadership Ohio Alumni Chairman

I send a note to Trina, a friend who is an activist for the environment and is against this war.

Trina, I hate this war and the complicated reasons we give for fighting it. I couldn't begin to unravel the agenda of our administration. I don't get into the violence of it and the politics of it now because I can only fight the battle of bringing Mike home safely. He did not see this coming. Neither did I. He thought he would go to college and become an officer and learn to fly as a Marine. War isn't a reality to a seventeen year old. They have trained him to obey orders and hopefully to survive. And until he returns home, I can't discuss this crime against humanity. But, it makes me cry. Thanks for being there and for your passion for justice and the good earth.

The feelings of helplessness and fear lead me to find ways to have a voice. Mike was enamored while in high school by a charming recruiter who made glamorous promises.[6] Recruiters come to our high schools and inspire our sons and daughters and make promises to get them to sign up. Each recruiter has a quota. How little we knew about the business of the military. I didn't want other parents to be broad-sided as we were. I was informed about a law passed in Cincinnati that would prohibit

---

6   " Remember, we didn't have a recruiter for several months and I would drive to Xenia and lead the polees meetings." (Mike's Comments) (polees… new recruits)

distributing the names of students to the military without parental consent. This law says that parents have a right to deny accessibility. I send an email to our High School Principal.

Hi Sam,

I hope that Lebanon can jump on this bandwagon with Cincinnati Public Schools. I really don't think that students should meet with military recruiters on the high school campus without parental consent, especially if the student is under 18 years of age.

This is how Mike got involved with the Marines. Maybe when he was a sophomore but definitely when he was a junior and only seventeen. We didn't know about the relationship with the Marine Recruiter until Mike was sure that becoming a Marine is what he wanted. He thought he was going to go through the Delayed Entry Program, become an officer and learn to fly, while attending college. He was promised this. His first year out of high school has been very difficult for him and for us. He wasn't able to complete the first quarter at Ohio University. And, of course, you know he has been in Iraq since March.

I want parents to know and have a choice.

Being in the military isn't a career many parents would choose for their son or daughter today. Meeting these military "heroes" on the high school campus without parental knowledge is disrespectful and irresponsible.

Mike will be fine when this is over. Maybe he is a better person for the way this has happened. And maybe we will be better people. But I would not want to go through this again.

Thanks for listening, Sam. I hope you can get this to the school board and/or to the Superintendent. I am planning to do something about this once Mike returns from Iraq. Right now I have all my energy tied up in getting him home.

Sincerely, (Peggy Logue)

I do understand and we should talk sometime. I am disappointed the Marines did not keep their promise. I, as you know, am not in favor of this Bush Foreign Policy nor his or Rumsfeld's idea of the military. I do believe, however, given the right circumstances, the military can be very beneficial to everyone.

Thank you for keeping me posted about Mike. I do pray for and look forward to seeing him when he is home. I do worry about all of our former students who are in Iraq as well as all American soldiers.

Sincerely, (Sam)

By August 4th I am sending a letter to my senators and encouraging my list of family and friends to do the same. Shelly sends the following note asking her friends to write to their senators.

Please keep the Marines and all the troops who are serving in Iraq and all through the world in your prayers. The most recent Ohio Marines KIA were serving with my Lebanon's son, Mike Logue, Lima Company. They are scheduled to return home soon, however the date keeps moving to later in the year. I am writing to our Congressmen that they receive the support they need so they might survive to return safely. Please consider writing or calling as well. My heart breaks for these families.

Peace to all, (Shelly)

Shelly also suggests that mothers get together and march on Washington. *I am prepared to volunteer… perhaps we should try to get all moms throughout the world together. Maybe we should start right here, "a million moms" march on Washington.* That idea registers a note of excitement in my head. But I know I don't have the energy to make it happen. I said to her, "*I will do anything to bring Mike home.*" I told Shelly, "*We have to weigh our costs. Right now the cost is too high. Let's re-evaluate why we are there and what we really need to do in the world to make it better. Maybe it is better to be feeding the poor and starving.*"

Trice sent a note out to all of her friends suggesting they write to their congressmen. She sent me a copy of her letter.

Dear Senators,

I am sending this as a follow up to my previous request for your action to "support" our troops. My son is a Marine reservist serving with Lima Company 3/25th . As you are well aware of the losses that the 3/25th have suffered this week and have continued to suffer since May, I am asking for your support. It is time to bring them home. Their ability to be efficient Marines dwindles as they wear out. While my son is fighting for others to enjoy freedoms that we as Americans enjoy. As a mother, I feel I must take on more power to see that our brave troops come home safely. Please take on the task to facilitate Lima Company's homecoming now.

As I write this Lima Company is involved in Operation Quick Strike and continue their daily patrols. And I fear of leaving my home. I fear the horrible visit from Marines that so many I know have gotten this week. My son is fighting so we do not live in fear. Please take action.

Sincerely, (Patricia Lehmann)

Momentum builds as I read the many letters friends forward to me that they are sending to friends and others encouraging them to write to their Congressmen. And the idea that a "Mother's March on Washington" could actually happen.

Also rising to the surface and encouraging is the news that a Marine who served in Iraq is pursuing a run for U.S. House of Representatives from Ohio. Paul Hackett is becoming known here for his disapproval of the war and his bid for this seat.

I send a letter to Mike's Marine List.

August 5, 2005: Fifty-seven days to go.

Family and Friends,
This is the letter I sent to our senators.
"Dear Senator (DeWine) (Voinovich),
It is time to bring our Ohio Marines home. They have seen enough and done enough. They have got to be spent physically, mentally as well as emotionally and spiritually. The families of these

*men ask you to use your influence to be sure they come home safely
and with honor and welcome. They don't need to see more combat.*

*I am a citizen. I am a Marine mom. This is enough. Do
something about it!"*

*I have been receiving emails and talking to others this morning.
Feeling powerless is not a good place to be. Rosemary Palmer one
of the mothers of a fallen son said on national TV that it is time to
bring our young home. She said we are throwing them away. "We
are throwing bodies."*

*I will do all I can to bring Mike home safely. He is my son. But
I will work for other mothers too.*

*The polls show that Americans are dwindling in their support
of the President's handling of the war. Fifty-nine percent are not in
favor as a poll reported today.*

*As I write this Mike with 1000 Marines are involved in
Operation Quick Strike. They had to call in air power to bomb a
building where they were receiving fire.*

*I and other mothers are wrought with anxiety as we wait for
news.*

I am inspired to call for a Mothers March on Washington.

*My heart goes out to the people of the world who are starving.
Mothers feed their young. This world cries to be fed, physically and
spiritually.*

*Maybe America needs to stop and listen to where it can best serve
humanity. If we let terror direct our actions we become terrorists.
And what about the Golden Rule?*

Love PEACE. (Peggy)

Trice sends a response to me. Her anxiety and lack of focus
is characteristic of how most of us feel who have loved ones in
Iraq. We can only focus on their safety and their quick return.

*I hope you don't mind me forwarding your email to others in
a quest for support. A Mothers March to Washington sounds like a
great idea and I am willing to help in a way. Warning: sometimes
I am useless. One thing that I have been dwelling on lately is my*

inability to make decisions and function at 100 per cent. If I was in the work force right now I doubt that I would be a very good employee. My anxiety I feel would keep me from being able to focus. I will focus now on bringing my son home before it is too late. I may need a lot of direction. (Trice)

Keeping people informed about real people fighting a real war in Iraq and how that affects the family generates interest in others and leads them to take action. Responses from those on my list follow:

I cannot speak for the other Moms, but I would support that whole-heartedly. I don't want to offend any of you, and I apologize if I do. I don't want to argue politics, but I care about all of you and I know you care about me and I need to vent and I know you can take it. I have been sitting here fuming about Presidents Bush's comment after the latest tragedies "remember we are in a war" while he is down at his ranch for a month-long "working" vacation. He needs to get his ass back to the White House and figure all of this out because his current strategy is not working. He declared this war. He told us in 2003 that the war is over and now he is "reminding" us that we are in a war. As if we could for one second forget that. I am ready for our boys to come home. These reservists are not expendable, as it seems they are being treated. They do not bring in help for them, they go to help others. They have done enough in their fight for our country. (Lauren Isaacs)

Peggy,

I hope you don't mind. I forwarded your letter to senators along to the addresses I have for "Dems In Action." That would be about eighty some names. Several of those are members of Ohio Progressive Action group. I'll ask them to forward to their lists. I'm still sending emails and making calls to the offices in Ohio of the senators. Lame comments by the politicians in this morning's Enquirer.

I got another letter from a group called "Out of Iraq." There are several groups circulating a petition to be delivered to Bush in Crawford, Texas on Saturday. You remember, he's relaxing on his ranch, for the next five weeks or so, sending condolences to the families of KIA, and reasserting that he will NOT BE DETERRED!

What a lot of bullshit! The group with the petition is saying that they want him to promise to send the twins to Iraq, to support his "noble" cause. They expect to be arrested. I'll put in for their bond. (Shirley)

Peggy,
I want to describe to you the moments I find myself praying for you, your family, Mike and his colleagues.

It is dusk and I am separating organic wheat from the weeds that it was hand-harvested with. It is a private time, a meditative task, with only birds joining me as I look past the hay wagon to the field.

As I separate each shaft of wheat, your emails keep appearing in my mind, my heart gets tugged, and I say a prayer for Mike and his company, Lucky Lima. For some reason, I feel close to "all of you" (the other families as well) during this time. I have been doing it every evening this week. I send you comfort and love. (friend)

The more frantic I become the more I need to direct my energy to ending the war and bringing the troops home. One of my friends said to me, "*Your fight for the life of your son can translate into the fight of all mothers for all sons and now daughters. I cry as I think about this. The more personal the story, the more universal it becomes, the more people can be reached. You are standing with Jerry and your family in the breach, split in honoring your son's bravery and willingness to die, and knowing how wrong the war is. What an awful, yet powerful place to be. May you have the grace to channel rage against the machine into speaking out through all the peaceful ways and skills you have honed through the years.*"

I become aware of a group called Military Families Speak Out (MFSO). I send an email to get more information.

The response from MFSO affirms my need to know that there are others who are against this war and have loved ones fighting in it. The last sentence in their letter to me says, *"Now more than ever, our voices must be heard. It is more important than ever that we speak out and say Bring Them Home Now!"*

Then, to my utter surprise and relief and excitement I read, *"There is going to be a march in Washington DC on September 24th where military families, Iraq Vets, and other veteran will be gathering in a contingent calling for an end to the war."*

I cannot believe this. Suddenly, I feel surrounded by a whole new group of friends. And what a relief, I don't have to organize a march on Washington.

There is one already planned.

CHAPTER 19

"We are Throwing Bodies."

Two hours before Trice sent me the note about helping with a Mothers March on Washington she sent me an email with a link to a story about the seven snipers that had been attacked a few days before. After viewing this I understand why Trice felt full of anxiety.

I'm very disturbed right now after reading an article that I found during a Google search. I'm not going to pass the link to you because of the content, but I will pass along the title of the link I found from my Google search for information from Haditha. "Spinning death uruknet, info, Italy." This was only three hours old when I found it. The article contains anti-American sentiment on this week's events that 3/25th experienced and an attached video of what may be one of the sniper's body. This is not something that I would want out on the internet if it was my son that just lost his life. So, I am not suggesting you to go to this site, but just sharing my frustration as I try to figure out what our sons are going through.

I am collecting information for a scrap book so that maybe twenty years from now maybe I will finally understand "WHY." Yes, this is making me crazy. I hope I do not offend you by sending this. I will not make it a habit.(Trice)

Reading the story Trice sent makes me feel sick. It is a video of the treatment of one soldier, a sniper, who was captured and killed. Sacred music is blaring in the background while angry voices tell the world what will happen to them or others who try to change the way of life in Iraq. It is filled with violence and very scary. These people have strong beliefs that they are doing God's work. It is their religious conviction that emboldens their violence.

I send a note to Isolde: *I have hesitated calling as I am sure you get many calls. These last few days have been very exhausting. You know that we have had a small Cincinnati group that has been meeting once a month as well as our Columbus group. Greg and Carolyn Cifuentes and Christina Kreuter are part of that group. So the death of Michael Cifuentes and David Kreuter has been particularly hard on us. We are afraid to leave our homes in case our sons may call. We are glued to the TV and computers searching for news.*

So, while we are hoping the Marines are taking a break, re-grouping and resting after their losses, we hear they are involved in Operation Quick Strike.

Isolde, I had a "melt down" tonight, afraid for Mike's safety. Do you have any news to share about weapons platoon, or anything hopeful, other than "no news is good news?" I am sure you are deeply concerned too. Thanks.

Dear Peggy & Jerry,

Unfortunately, I have no news but am aware of their new operation. I have not heard from Guy for a long, long time. I am so sorry that the stress and anxieties and fears are taking their toll on you and I can understand that. If I hear anything, I will call you right away. Wish I knew more but I really do not.

Trusting. (Isolde)

I am feeling stronger that this is an unjust war and the fact that my son is in it is tearing my heart and soul. As the dangers continue to threaten our men, my anger and fear deepens. I don't want to put Mike in any danger because of what I might say publicly. I am not sure how to speak out and be sure that it won't hurt Mike. So, I think I must be quiet.

I saw a mother on the evening news say after her son was killed that "we are throwing bodies." Wow! How that hit me. I read an article about her online that was in the Washington Post.

Washington post.com, Ohio Families Fed Up With Loss of Marines, By Joe Danborn, The Associated Press, Thursday, August 4, 2005; 3:36 am.

COLUMBUS, Ohio -- Rosemary Palmer and her husband were making plans to attend memorial services for six Marine reservists killed earlier this week_ five of them from the same battalion as her son, Lance Cpl. Edward Schroeder_ when two uniformed servicemen came down her street.

It was her family's turn.

"We knew. They didn't even get a chance to knock," Palmer said...

The Marines' death, along with two others slain July 28, brought the battalion's toll to 21 in a week. Eleven of those were part of the same Columbus-based unit, Lima Company that lost four Marines in a single day in May...

Isolde Zierk, 59, coordinator of Lima Company's family support group, found an answering machine full of messages from worried families when she got to her Columbus home after work Wednesday evening. A neighbor stopped by to see if she'd heard anything about her own son, Sgt. Guy Zierk, 29, who serves in Lima Company. She hadn't.

"My stomach's in knots," she said, choking back tears...

Jeff Mers, commander of a VFW post that has raised money and sent care packages to Lima Company, said that even before this week's attacks, he and other veterans were dazed from attending funerals of those killed in Iraq.

"I think I've been to nine of these just in central Ohio in the past few months," he said outside Lima Company's headquarters...

Palmer said she and her husband, Paul Schroeder, last spoke with their son about a week ago. He said he was tired of flushing insurgents out of the same places, just to have them reappear with better weapons.

"He said the closer they got to the time to come home, the less it was worth it," she said.

Jerry and I struggle with our feelings of hopelessness, of loss, of anger. But still the most important thing is how to be assured our son will come home in one piece. There is no relaxing now. We work to keep up with the news and to be prepared.

All, For me to add anything would be vain. Please read. (Isolde)

A Tribute to Christopher Dyer

Christopher Jenkins Dyer was 19 when he died in Iraq. He lived a rich life in those 19 years. He became a Marine, but not because he was poor or without options. He was a Marine out of duty and a desire to be among the best.

Chris graduated in 2004 with honors from Princeton High School. He played viola in the school orchestra and was on the varsity diving team. He took the most advanced science and math courses offered in high school. He had been accepted to the Ohio State University Honors Program and planned to enroll there in January to major in Finance. He graduated Parris Island recruit training 2 September, 2004. He was deployed as a member of 3rd platoon, Lima Company, 3rd battalion, 25th Marines.

Chris was an exceptionally intelligent and athletic child with enormous potential ahead of him. The Marines gave him the focus and resolve to achieve his potential. He was ready with a smile and a helping hand and was very caring of others. He thought of himself as a "squared away Marine." He was very proud to have achieved that title.

His loss is not only to his many friends and family, but also to his country.

He is survived by – and will be missed by – his father, mother, and twin sisters.

To his family, his friends, his country, and to himself, he was "Always faithful."

What we see in the families of the fallen is an enormous sense of pride. They seem to feel that their role is to continue to encourage those of us whose sons are still there. They have experienced the ultimate sacrifice and are so full of grace.

CHAPTER 20

"In Light of Our Most Recent Tragedies"

We receive word that the I&I (Inspector and Instructor) staff at the Reserve Center in Columbus is providing an opportunity for families to come together to ask questions and meet with professionals on a one on one basis " in light of our most recent tragedies." This is similar to what we did after Operation Matador. "Counselors, Chaplains, and the I&I staff are available to you all." Jerry and I want to go. We want information. We want comfort. We want assurance that our son is safe and won't be killed.

Isolde sends out an email...

All, We received the email below from a father whose son died with our Marines. No need to say more. As a Lima Company family, I know we have developed a support system amongst ourselves that is very helpful. I cannot but hurt for those attached to Lima who have no family contacts with their beloved Marine's brothers-in-

arms. Thus anyone wanting to send a card to the Bloem's, I am certain they would just love it. Here is the email. (Isolde)

"Our son Nick was from 4th Recon and attached to the 3/25th Lima Company, 3rd Platoon. He made numerous friends within 3/25th and we were able to meet some of them when the battalion went to Las Vegas in February.

One Marine with whom Nick was especially close was Lance Cpl. Eric Bernholtz. If possible, could you contact his family for us and tell them that we would love to speak with them if they are up to it.[7]

Our prayers are with all the families of the 3/25th, especially Lima Company. This Unit will go down in history as one of the toughest Marine Corps units of all time. These will be counted among the bravest of the brave.

If any other families wish to talk with us that would be great. Nick's deployment was especially difficult for us as we didn't really have any connection with the 3/25th since we're from Montana. Nevertheless, we will always feel a kinship with the 3/25th for the rest of our lives.

God bless and keep you all in the center of His hands.

Semper fi!

Al Bloem"

How faithful the parents are and how gracefully they go on while grieving the death of their sons. How generously they offer their help and support to those of us still frantic with worry. They amaze me. I feel like I will die on the spot if the Marines in Dress Blues appear at my door.

We begin to get messages that some of the families have heard from their Marine and we hope we will soon hear from Mike.

---

7   Lance CPL Nicholas Bloem and Lance CPL Eric Bernholtz were KIA August 3rd, 2005, Barwanah, Iraq, by an IED. They were both awarded the Purple Heart, Navy and Marine Corps Achievement Medal with Combat "V" for valor, Combat Action Ribbon

August 6, 2005: Fifty-six days to go.

Dear Family and Friends,

We have been housebound for several days waiting for a phone call. Trice called a few moments ago. She received a call from another Mom who just heard from her son and said they were passing the satellite phone around. He had only a minute to talk. As we were speaking, Trice's phone rang with an "unknown user." We hung up. A few seconds later she called back to say that it was Kevin and she was so relieved to hear from him.

We waited.

A while later Lindsay called. She had heard from Mike. He said they would be back at the Dam in a few days. It's night there now. He just asked how everyone was.

Anguish over for now. (Peggy & Jerry)

Dear Peggy,

Thank you for sharing your lives with me. I send you all my love and prayers and daily ask for the madness to end. Maybe with enough of us praying these thoughts all wars will end. In the meantime I know it will take work. I will continue that too. My heart is with you and your family. (friend)

Glad that Lindsay heard from Mike. It amazes me how these young boys are laying down their lives for us and yet when they call home they want to know how we are doing. Amazing. God bless each and every one of them. Keep them safe. Love, (Sister)

Hi Peggy and Jerry,

Your constant anguish will not keep Mike safe. (friend)

Sis,

There aren't many times when I am speechless. But now is one of them. My heart is heavy with grief and almost every waking minute I pause and ask the Lord's protection for Mike and all of Lima Company. I can only imagine the anxiety and anguish you

111

and Jerry are experiencing. Please know there is a continuous flow of our love, prayers, admiration, honor, and gratitude directed to you, Jerry and especially your brave and courageous son, Mike.

God Bless. Love and prayers. (Your Sis)

The news keeps coming about the funerals and visitations. It is sad and overwhelming.

From: Greg Cifuentes about his son LCPL Michael Cifuentes.

I have a tentative schedule of how things will go for the next week. If there is no delay, Michael should be coming home maybe Tuesday, but probably Wednesday, and will arrive at the Dayton Airport. He will be taken to Advance Funeral Home in Fairfield.

On Sunday, August 14, from 2-6, visitation for Michael will be held in the gym arena at Fairfield High School. The Marines will post an honor guard at the casket……. Carolyn and I are attending a funeral Saturday for one of Michael's friends killed a week earlier…..It is possible that Michael may be coming home a day or so later, if the identification process takes longer than expected….

We will celebrate Michael's life for the good that he brought to this world. With his buddies and fellow Marines, he was trying to bring a better life to a people who have suffered for too long. He was very upset when Corporal Bryan Richardson was killed in late March. There were more to follow. Most recently, Michael was grieving for the recent loss of two friends, LCPL. Chris Lyons and CPL Andre Williams. Michael died with his best friends in Lima Company on August 03, 2005. May it please God that all the sacrifices this country had made for Iraq and Afghanistan bring about the final victory…..

Our hearts will ache for Michael until in God's time we too take leave of this temporary abode.

Thank you, Lord, for blessing us with Michael for twenty-five years.

Carolyn and Gregory Cifuentes

Chapter 21

"My Son is Not Expendable."

After the meeting in Columbus with the I&I staff I wrote to my list.

August 7, 2005: Fifty-five days to go.

Family and Friends,

You have received many emails from me this week. If you want to be deleted from my list please tell me and I will remove your name.

The Marines are trying to help families deal with all the losses. Learning from the Vietnam War they want to be compassionate to the families. They are keeping chaplains and counselors available to us. When the Marines return this same service will be available... beginning with the quarantine at Camp LeJuene.

I will recap the meeting with the I&I staff.

Major "Somebody" (I don't know what he said his name is. The sound system is horrible) says he had a brief conversation via satellite phone with major "Somebody Else" in Iraq about what is going on. Major "Somebody Else" says the troops are "still in good spirit, they are focused and driven. They count on support from family and friends."

Our Marine families want to know when the troops are coming home and when to stop sending packages. The Major says they have six more weeks of combat so we should stop sending packages now but keep on sending letters.

Twenty-three of our unit of one-hundred and sixty have been KIA. The number of casualties is thirty-five. This is a lot for one unit. We learned today that our Marines are the spearhead for all of these operations. They are the front lines. They are the first to go in.

I want to say something so I raise my trembling hand. "Yes Ma'am," the Major says. I stood. My heart quivering and more nervous than I have ever been in my life, but with conviction deeper than I have ever had, I say that as a Marine Mother, I know it is time for the Ohio Marines to come home. "They have seen enough and done enough." Then I swallow and say, "With all the suffering this community has experienced with the loss of our men, where is the President, the Commander in Chief?" I sit down and hear the mumblings of the group. The Major replies, "I don't know if I can answer that question, Ma'am!" Then he repeats the stuff about "finishing the fight" etc.

I shout out, "MY SON IS NOT EXPENDABLE!"

Although I may sound strong I am scared and weak with anguish. How dare they take my son's life so carelessly? I had to sit or I would have passed out. I am speaking to a group of military and families who lost their sons and families whose sons are still there, many of them in full support of this war. The Marines and the families gathered here did not expect this.

But I have a huge investment in what is going on in the world right now. I will do anything to see my son come home, and not in a body bag. I stand my ground.

We are then in groups with a chaplain. A very nice Navy chaplain from the south turns to me and says, "You seem frustrated!"

"No, Sir, I am angry! My son is nineteen years old. He joined the Marines as a reservist. He is told he will go into the Delayed Entry Program. He is told he will go through college and learn to fly for the Marines. He is made promises that are never kept. Nine months after graduating from high school he is in a war that doesn't make sense."

Much conversation follows. The navy chaplain, who is a Vietnam Veteran, shakes his head in agreement as I rant. He knows there are no answers for me. He just hugs me.

A mother who has a twenty-five year old son in the Unit comes up to me and says, "I don't agree with this war my son is in. He is pretty right wing and I am moderate. He has called home several times and said 'Mom, I don't know why we are here.'"

This woman then told me she threw her water bottle at her TV when she heard the President's response about honoring the fallen "We will honor them by continuing what we are doing."

There is a march on Washington September 24th. Unless Mike comes home that day I will be there. Web sites to check out: Military Families Speak Out www.mfso.org . Also you may want to Google, Gold Star Families for Peace.

This week is full of funerals… for beautiful, young, idealistic Americans. They were part of our future. In their deaths, what do we gain?

Love PEACE.

Comments follow:

Good for you Peggy!!! I am so proud of you for standing up for Mike and the other young Marines in his Unit. It must have been very scary to stand up, with all the intimidation, and speak the truth to those in power. Military protocol would not allow any of them to speak out in strong agreement, but we know there are many of them who feel the way you do.

I'm glad to know about the March on September 24th. I'll spread the word, and do everything I can to support it.

I know those good young men over there are hoping for support in getting out of a terrible situation. Please when you talk to Mike, tell him we are on his side, and we know he has to follow the military line in his situation, but we WILL NOT be quiet!

The administration can no longer follow their pattern of "Deny, Deceive, and Distract."

Hang in there. Lighting a candle for Mike each day. (friend)

Wow!!! I respect the courage it must have taken to stand in front of all those aching and suffering parents and speak out Peggy. I can understand why you were shaking!!!! If Mike isn't home I will go to Washington with you. We all have a stake in what is going on... (Friend)

Hi Peggy and Jerry, You are in my heart and prayers every day. I cannot imagine the anguish that you all must be feeling. I tell many people about you and Mike, plus the fallen ones that you send info about, just to humanize this war. I felt so full of pride for you and anger about the whole situation when I read about your strong expression to "them." Good for you, sweetie. Love to you both. (friend)

Dearest Peggy,

The least I can do is to read your emails as they keep the war at the front of my mind, even though I might prefer to put my head in the sand. As it is I do not receive a newspaper nor watch the TV news.

Like your son, you are very brave. Living in the tension between hating war and loving your son and those who would lay down their lives for him as he would for them has got to be the hardest thing you have ever done. And the waiting.

The woman (on the link you sent) who lost her son, but is bringing it to Bush at his ranch gives hope. To see this kind of organizing, this early in the game, as opposed to the years it took for Vietnam, not to mention that it wasn't the military families or vets, but the antiwar activists who first organized. Then to see this kind of organizing gives hope that I have very little of. Bush is so hard.

When I was in DC with my daughter and grandchildren

we went to see the Whitehouse. Across the street, directly in front of the front door, a woman was camped with a tent-like shelter, surrounded by signs and evidence that she was there for the duration protesting for peace. I was so happy that the children could see her, after seeing the war memorials, WWII and Vietnam. Where are the peace memorials?

Well Peggy and Jerry, I pray that Mike's tour is over soon enough and that our politicians begin to "get it." No matter how nobly our soldiers serve, the cause is not a noble one, and they must recognize that.

Love PEACE. (friend)

CHAPTER 22

Yelling at the World

I am aware that I am beginning to sound "political." I know some family members and others on my list may differ in their political views and may object as I rant I want them to feel free to express themselves to me and if they choose, to be removed from my list. It is hard however, when I receive responses from my nephews who ask that I take them off my list.

How about this…keep me posted about Mike, but remove my email from the political list. I've agreed with what Mike's doing from day one, but I'm not going to debate it with you because family comes before politics. Thanks.

Love, d. (Darren)

I feel bad about this. I feel strongly about the "wrongness" of the war and the administration. I know how strongly others feel about the rightness of the war. I don't want a battle ground here. I just want my son home. I am dying inside.

D (Darren), I assure you I am not looking to debate with

anyone. I don't have the interest, or the desire, or the energy. I know where most of the family stands…that is why I accept the request of anyone to be removed from my list. I appreciate your support of Mike. And I appreciate and love you.

Love (P)

D (Darren) is Mike's godfather and my nephew. He is there for Mike always. Each birthday Darren has taken Mike out to dinner and for a night of fun from the time he was very young. He has been on this journey with us from the beginning. He came to Mike's graduation from Boot Camp. He flew to Vegas to see Mike before the deployment. He set up Mike's web site. He has been a dear friend, supportive and caring.

I receive a note from another nephew, Darren's younger brother, Adam.

I believe very deeply that these brave young men are fighting for a worthy cause of bringing freedom to those who have only known tyranny. Therefore, I respectfully request that I be removed from the mailings that deal with politics, but would like to continue to receive emails that give an update on Mike's status.

Thanks, love always. (Adam)

Adam, I appreciate your honest reply. It is not the intention of Jerry or me to be political. Our focus is to get Mike home. Our anguish, for what Mike is experiencing and seeing at nineteen years old causes a grief you may not understand. Our sleepless nights and anxious days stretch on and on as we wait to hear his voice.

We ask that you continue to support Mike in thoughts and prayers.

Love always to you too. (P&J)

Completely understood. I know how saddened I get when I think of him being away, and he is only my cousin, not my son. I feel for the emotional roller coaster you must be on. Mike will always be at the forefront of my thoughts and prayers, always. And I will continue to pray that the Lord comfort you and Jerry as well.

I cannot wait for his homecoming. It will be the biggest party southwest Ohio has ever seen! (Adam)

I am still feeling bad about the email from Darren so the next day I email him again.

Darren,

I am afraid I hurt or offend you as I express my anguish through anger. It put me in a funk all day. I know we disagree politically. I know many in the family disagree and yet they have allow me to express my grief. I am so thankful for that. I don't mean to be making political statements. They slip out in my anger and frustration. It is clear that we all want Mike to come home.

I do not want to hurt our relationship. Hopefully, we will both grow in understanding and acceptance.

More than anything, I love you, as a nephew and as a friend. And more than that I have a deep love for my son, as I know you do for your son, Elliott. I would consider my own death to bring my son home.

Love to you, Donna and Elliott. (Peggy)

I don't like what is happening here. I know I am voicing my anger in my emails. My disapproval of the war, my fear for Mike, my sense of helplessness, my desperation are all on a collision course as I see up close the results of war, the young dying, the children of my friends in flag draped coffins.

All of this slips out of my mind and heart and onto the keyboard as I reach out for help. I am yelling at the world.

CHAPTER 23

"For the Marine on the Right and the Marine on the Left"

In a documentary A&E Channel did on Operation Matador called *Combat Diary*, Major Lawson says, "Reserve Units are not always prepared for combat or death... We just had to kick them in the ass and keep pushing them."

Is this the way he keeps the Marines from falling apart or giving into their sadness after experiencing the many losses in the short time? Does he guide their anger into more combat and revenge?

One of the Marines feeling frustrated asks, "What more do they want? Do they want the whole unit?"

Jerry and I feel like we are living in a surreal world. Time has no meaning and will have no memory. There is no beginning or end. There are no seasons. No day. No night. No weekends. Time is just a line going from one tragedy to the other. Numbness is what we feel. We only experience fear and helplessness as these events surround us and continue to catch us off guard. It feels like we are in a glass jar with the lid screwed on and we are scrambling to get out. To get to safety. To breathe. To feel peace. And all we can feel are our nails sliding down the jar. And all we can hear is the tingling of our helplessness.

I am fortunate to catch Mike on instant messenger this morning. He says he is doing okay and has some excellent camera footage for us. One encouraging thing he says is he believes they will start doing only small missions now, but that he intends to "keep fighting until we leave." (Nephew)

Dear Peggy and Jerry,

I have thought of you all so much since I heard that Mike is in Iraq…I remember him several times a day in prayer. His presence in Iraq makes that horrible war even worse. I remember when I first met Mike. He was participating in one of the folk dances. I was so impressed with how comfortable he was doing that as a teenager and felt he must be a very special young man.

I just want you to know that I am one of the many praying for him." (friend)

Peggy,

This is a mom's moment. I have thought of you down there with Cindy (Sheehan), but often the first and most obvious thing is not the most personally effective way. I thought earlier today of saying, here is $100, if you want to go. However, I have often been in a situation where that initial passion could not be realized and then I needed to go deeper inside to find out what the passion means and then what other thing I should do about it.

But somehow Peggy, you are made for this moment. Bob (a friend) feels that this administration must somehow be impeached. The damage it is doing to the whole world is beyond measure. Now how do we do it? The moms seem the closest way I can think of. He (Bob) was seeing the streets clogged with moms, moms being hauled off to jail, moms everywhere. (friend)

We receive a note from Isolde.

All, While we are hurting deeply here stateside, please take a moment and consider how our Marines feel about the loss of their brothers-in- arms. Trust me, it's hundred-fold worse for them. They have the pictures of the tragedies engraved in their minds. Nothing we can possibly ever comprehend.

Let's not allow ourselves to get caught up in "small stuff" that seems big to us. We are not the ones in Iraq trying to stay alive 24x7. Our Marines and Corpsmen would really be proud of us in keeping the perspective.

This is just food for thought. No ill meaning. Nothing other than caring deeply for our Marines and Corpsmen, trying to put myself into their boots."

And then there are the ones we've lost. Think about that.

Just had to say this. Please don't criticize me for it. (Isolde Zierk)

August 9, 2005: Fifty- two days to go.

Family and Friends,

I had my first night of sleep in a few nights after being a "basket case" yesterday. I feel there is no way I can do this for six more weeks. Tears flowed all day. Then hearing his voice was like "being born again." We awoke at 6:00am. Jerry was on the computer and received an instant message from Mike. I rushed to the computer and we did instant messaging for ten minutes. He went off line and the phone rang. It was Mike.

He sounds fine. Says he couldn't say much about things that happened. He had already crossed over the IED and had turned onto another road heading toward the town when the "trac" (AAV) exploded killing fourteen Marines. He knew several of the guys. He says the last time he and Michael Cifuentes talked Michael was planning his honeymoon. Mike asked me how Mrs. Cifuentes is doing. I told him she is doing fine and that the community has come together to support and help them. And I told him that there comes a certain "grace" to fill the void in those who have had such losses. His concern for Mrs. Cifuentes reminds me of his caring and gentle spirit.

Then he tells us that they took over a bridge while receiving rifle fire, but in the past there was more hostile conflict at that same bridge… so they feel like they had made progress.

And he talked about a market area where they "set up" in five or six homes. During the day they would be on watch for several hours and then off for several hours. Same at night but he couldn't sleep because it is so hot.

A huge sandstorm came through Baghdad yesterday. He said "those are good because it brings a wind and it's not so hot because the sand blocks the sun."

He thinks they will be at the Dam for awhile but "ya' never know." They would do some "reset training and do small operations like vehicle check points, or patrols in the palms groves."

He asks how the news is in Ohio. I tell him it is sad and that everyone is concerned for them. But everyone is proud of them and wants them to safely come home.

Then he says, "I love you. I miss you."

His time was up and before he hangs up I tell him we are being interviewed for our local newspaper. He says, "You ARE?" I say yes, people want to know what it is like for parents and families with Marines in 3/25th. I ask him if there is anything I can say for him. He pauses for a moment and says, "Tell them we all have jobs. And we are doing our job for the Marine on the left, and the Marine on the right."

Present moment living!

Love PEACE (Peggy)

In the midst of all this, you must be proud of your boy! Keep the good news coming, my friend.

With much love. (friend)

Peggy

The healing power of Mike's voice must have been great. I am delighted to hear this blessing for you. I shared a bit of your email with my friends. It is important for all of us to hear this. They are praying. (friend)

CHAPTER 24

Semper Fi

August 9, 2005: Fifty- three days to go.

We receive an email letter from Captain Kasparian:

Dear Family and Friends,

We have the deepest sympathies for the families of our fallen 21 Marines and the other Marines who have given their lives for Iraq and for each other. We recognize that several of them came from other units, like 4th Amphibious Assault Battalion who has taken every risk with us. After the last week's incidents, when asked if they wanted to leave, every Marine from Company L said "We came here to do a job and we will finish it." A Marine dropped off six detainees who had just attacked his men. I asked him how it was going out there. He simply shook his head and said, "Busy." He quickly smiled and shook his head and headed out the door.

The last week has proven the most difficult for 3rd Battalion, 25th Marines and the families. We have participated in more combat actions than almost any other unit in Operation Iraqi Freedom.

129

We continue to take casualties and also kill, capture, or detain insurgents who have found no haven along the Euphrates. 3/25 has protected Baghdad and Ramadi from attacks and kept the hiways clear. Letters have come from Marine veterans from WWII to Desert Storm, thanking us for carrying on a proud tradition.

We will always keep honor and avoid hurting the Iraqi people. When Gunnery Sergeant Charles Hurley IV'S Platoon from Company L became engaged by heavy machine guns, he ordered his Marines not to fire back because the insurgents hid among innocent Iraqis.

We have had heroes like Lance Corporal Todd Corbin and Corporal Jeffery Schuller Jr. from Weapons Company who saved the lives of 11 Marines during an ambush when the enemy used a hospital to attack from. The Marines who gave their lives in the last week had courageously cleared a town in Operation Matador, going house to house, so they would not inflict injuries to the many civilians who lived there. We have had instance after instance of Marines going above and beyond the call of duty. Sergeant John Howarth, a scout sniper, ran out into a hail of enemy small arms fire in New Ubaydi to pull an Iraqi to safety.

Many times Marines have looked after their own. With a supporting M1A1 tank main gun firing, Captain Billy Brown from Company L walked in front of the fire power to a fallen Marine. With rocket propelled grenades firing point blank at him, he scooped the warrior up and moved him away from the enemy. 3/25 has continued to clear the roads and the insurgents. We have been the focus of main effort for the Regimental Combat Team 2 and 2nd Marine Division during major operations, recently during the clearing of the city of Hit.

Our job has always focused on keeping the rest of Iraq safe. The enemy will never use Haditha or Hit as a haven to launch attacks toward any southern city or town while we are on watch. 3/25 has always known we have to accomplish our missions so other Marines and Army brothers in southern Iraq do not get attacked from the enemy.

My friend Staff Sergeant Joseph P. Goodrich recently was killed in the city of Hit. We went to Reserve Infantry Officers Course together in the summer before we deployed. The entire time during this rigorous training, he had a grin on his face. I will miss that famous smile of his. He always remained positive and everyone felt better when he walked up to you.

"Semper Fi" has taken on a deeper meaning for many Marines here. 3/25 will remain "always faithful" to the Marines and families from past wars and actions who have given their all for the Corps.

From 3rd Battalion, 25th Marines to all those who we have lost and those who continue to press on in their memory, Semper Fi.

Captain John A Kasparian

Jerry and I have little reaction to this letter from Captain Kasparian. We are in a state of shock. Feeling overwhelmed from all the losses. And we are filled with fear for Mike and the other young men in 3/25th.

We aren't comforted by making the Marines heroes in death. In our eyes, Mike doesn't need to risk his life to be a hero and to be memorialized on a wall. I feel he is being asked to do more and be more than his young life can imagine. And that is what makes him a hero. And that is what makes us weep and makes us proud and keeps us faithful.

Semper Fi.

CHAPTER 25

War and Patriotism

As I try to deal with what is happening in Iraq and to our young men, I reach out for a way to vent my anger and frustration. I want someone to help me get my son home. I am buoyed by some of my women friends who are against the war and want to be involved. To a few friends I send the following email.

Hi Girls,

It seems like an opportunity to say something public about the "lack of feeling" President. A letter to the editor about the apparent lack of integrity of the Commander-in-Chief who hasn't attempted to make a presence at a memorial or reach out in any personal way to a community that has endured so much for his "noble war." We all know he would be here if there was an election... and then we would be sickened by his presence. "Feeling-less President Comes for Votes ... While Families Grieve."

Early morning passion... (Peggy)

I have been saying, "I would but you know I can't..."because of the belief that Blue Star Families dare not speak out against the President or the war lest they be accused of not only not being patriotic but not supporting the troops…their loved one. How dare this be happening? But it is. There is caution about what is said and what is made public. We who oppose the war keep much of what we feel to ourselves or to a limited number of friends. My personal fear is that Mike will think that I am not proud of him. I struggle to keep my mouth shut the longer this war goes and the scarier it becomes. I will someday speak out but only when Mike is safely at home. This is what I think. This is what I tell people.

Jerry and I receive a call from a reporter from our local Lebanon newspaper asking for an interview. She says people want to know how parents of Marines of 3/25th are holding up. We agree to the interview. I see an opportunity to get Mike's name out in the community. The citizens of Lebanon, Ohio should know him and what he is doing. And I believe they would have concern for him and pray for him. The reporter comes that afternoon and has many questions. We answer and then elaborate more when we find out that she is also against the war. But we ask her to please keep the political sentiments out of the paper because we are not sure how it would affect Mike. She promises she will.

The Western Star (August 10, 2005 by Sharon Smigielski)

For the families back home, the waiting is the hardest part. Before Tuesday morning, it was even more so for Lebanon's Jerry and Peggy Logue, whose son Mike is a reservist with the 3rd Battalion, 25th Marines Regiment.

Last week, the battalion suffered 14 casualties after an armored vehicle hit a roadside mine in Iraq's volatile Al Anbar province. Nine of the dead were from the Columbus - based Lima Company, of which Mike is a member; five of those were from counties in Southwest Ohio.

Tuesday, Jerry and Peggy Logue finally heard from their 19-year-old son, a 2004 Lebanon High School graduate. It was their first phone contact in nearly three weeks.

"Oh God, yes," said a clearly relieved Peggy when asked if she had heard from Mike.

Wrought with worry and constant tears, Peggy admitted to being a basket case the day before.

Hearing his voice was being born again, she wrote in an email to family and friends detailing the 20- minute conversation with PFC Mike Logue, who with the rest of Lima Company has returned to base camp at Iraq's Haditha Dam.

In recent months, Lima Company bore the brunt of U.S. casualties as it patrols desert roads along the Euphrates River, fighting insurgents. During the month of July, the company was in the field for all but three days. "Our Columbus Marines are the spearhead for operations in Anbar," said Jerry.

Besides last week's casualties, another eight of Lima Company died in May's Operation Matador. So far, 23 Marines of the approximately 160-member Lima Company have been killed in action. Approximately 35 have incurred injuries, said the Logues...

For the families back home, their anguish runs deep. "The deeper we've gotten into it, the scarier it's gotten," said Peggy, as she and her husband ride a never-ending roller coaster of emotions." This last month has been the longest down-slide. It seemed more intense, more violent, more casualties, more threat," said Peggy, a constant visitor to the Internet as she searches for the latest updates from the war front. "My son's not safe anymore. You run to the phone when it rings. You jump when the doorbell rings because you don't want to see those men in blue at your door," said Peggy, noting that the couple rarely leaves their home at the same time for fear of missing a phone call from their son, the youngest of three.

Family support.

In support of their Marines and each other, the families of Lima Company have banded together to form both a Cincinnati and Columbus based groups. Two Sundays ago, many of the families gathered for a picnic in Columbus, where the Logues passed the time with the parents of Michael Cifuentes. The following week, the Cifuentes would be among the five Southwest Ohio families notified of the deaths of their sons and husbands.

"Our little close-knit group was hit hard," said Peggy. "These are young men. They are our future," said Peggy, noting what she sees to be the futility of American involvement in Iraq. "In these deaths, we've lost part of our future. And what have we gained?" she asked.

Even so, their son and his comrades are staying to the task, the couple said.

Because of the paranoia about supporting our troop's means supporting the war, I am nervous about the statement, *"noting what she sees to be the futility of American involvement in Iraq."* I call the reporter and say, "I thought we agreed that you wouldn't say anything about the politics of the war or how we felt." She apologizes saying, "I didn't think it was too strong a statement."

I am afraid that someone reading this will know I am not in favor of the war. Will they then accuse me of not supporting my son? How painful. How dead wrong.

I send an email to Mike.

Hey Babe,

We made the front page of the Western Star. A picture of Dad and me holding your picture. It is a good story. I think you will like it. There were two other pictures of you.

Have you heard when you are shipping out yet? Please tell your parents ASAP. We have a system of notifying others. Hope you don't have any more big jobs to do.

We will be going to funerals this weekend and into next week.

Hope you are resting and winding down. It feels like more than a year since you have been able to really relax.

We are recovering from the roller coaster ride of worry... but won't relax until you are home.

Love you ... Miss you. (Mom & Dad)

We have one foot on the ground and the other on what feels like a very slippery slope. There is hope they are winding down. Hope that there won't be any more big jobs. But we have learned never to relax. We cannot outguess or figure the military. And they often can't outguess the enemy. The intensity of the war and the casualties 3/25th suffers and the funerals we now face bring the media to our doorstep. As the media reaches out to us, how do we walk the line of expressing how we really feel about the war and how to protect our son? Frustration arises because of the anger about this war and the questioning of our patriotism. We keep focused on the safety of our son but we are no match for the pros. We find ourselves getting deeper and deeper into the complexity of war, patriotism and love and respect for our son and the Marine Corps.

CHAPTER 26

Arrangements

The following are email messages from Isolde about funerals for our Marines.

> *Dear Isolde and the rest of our wonderful Lima Co. Family,*
>
> *Please know that we are so incredibly aware of your prayers and support as we grieve the loss of our precious **Justin**. We do not grieve as those who have no hope for we know that we will spend eternity with him and our wonderful Lord Jesus Christ.*
>
> *Wanted to pass along the information about the final earthly arrangements for saying our good-byes to Justin.*
>
> *Visitation will be Friday, August 12, 2005, from 2:00 - 4:00 and 6:00 - 8:00...*
>
> *Funeral service 2:00p.m. Saturday, August 13, 2005, Grace Brethren Church...*
>
> *Thank you again for your thoughts and prayers.*
>
> *With much love.*

Carole and Chuck Hoffman
May His Peace be with you!

All,
*"We bring **Michael** home early afternoon today.*
Visitation will be at the Fairfield High School gymnasium from 3:00-7:00p.m. on Sunday August 14.
Mass for Christian burial will be on Monday, August 15, 10:00am at St Julie Billiart Catholic Church
Burial will be at Gate of Heaven Cemetery..."

And...

Chris arrives in Cincinnati Monday, August 15.
Visitation is at Tri County Baptist Church Tuesday from 3:00-9:00 p.m. ... I realize this is long visitation hours. Previous Marine funerals have required this length.
Please note that family members of Lima Company should identify themselves to any Marine as needed.
Services are Wednesday, August 17 at 10:00am at Tri County Baptist Church...
Services are expected to last about 1hour 15 minutes...
Final services at Arlington will be Monday following at 1:00 p.m.
(From John Dyer, father of Chris)

All,
*Visitation hours for **Cpl. Kreuter** have been scheduled for Thursday, August 18 from 3:00-8:00p.m. at Spring Grove Funeral Home in Cincinnati.*
Services will be held on Saturday, August 20 at Tri County Baptist Church at 11am.
Anyone wishing to contact Cpl. Kreuter's wife may email her. Thanks. Isolde

CHAPTER 27

Life and Death

The emails that come describing the arrangements for these beautiful young men leave Jerry and me speechless. I feel like I don't know what to think or say or do. I just have a deep sense of inadequacy. We plan to go to each of the visitations and funerals. What to say? How do we support these parents and families? This is a deep hole. Where is the light?

Then, light, an email from Mike.

"Hey, I'm not sure but I think I'll be leaving around September 26th- 28th. So that's all I know about that. I will not be home until October 6th - 12th. I got promoted. I'm LCpl now. Will you let me know my pay rate and how much it increases and how much I have and where? Also, I was thinking about putting money into an internet bank. They have fewer services but more interest.

I have a month and a week left here...

I can't wait to go home. I've just been working out when I can now and running. I like getting letters. How are John and Sis and Snoopy?

Tomorrow I have mess duty so I'll be up at 500 and working chow hall stuff until 1900. I'll talk to you later. Love you".

Hi LCpl Logue!!!

What a pleasant surprise. Okay, I'll round up some folks to write letters now. We have been told not to send anymore packages.

Also they suggest we don't make big plans for you when you return. You will need a lot of down time.

We were interviewed by Fox news affiliates in Dayton. It played twice on the news last night. They were here for over an hour but used about 1-2 minutes on the show. Your Boot Camp Graduation picture filled the TV screen.

Hope you are resting. Let us know as soon as you can about your homecoming. John wants to come home for a few weeks when you return.

We went to Brett Wightman's viewing yesterday. His parents said to let you know they are praying for you and all the Marines to come home safely.

We are going to Timothy Bell's viewing this afternoon. Then tomorrow Michael Cifuentes' viewing.

Love you so much. Anxious for you to come home. We will have breakfast on the deck with your sister and brother.

We will check your pay rate and your other financial questions. Love you. So proud of you. (Mom)

Hey Babe,

Dad said if I get interviewed again I should start charging for it. I was interviewed by Channel 5 News and was on the 6:00p.m. and 11:00p.m. news. Also channel 64. It was on at 10:00p.m. We didn't get to see it because we weren't home in time. Kevin's Mom was standing with me.

Have to wash our Lima Company shirts tonight to wear tomorrow to Michael Cifuentes funeral. I told his Mom today at the viewing that you asked about her. Thanks for being so thoughtful. This has been very hard on the families.

Loving you and wanting you home safe. (Mom)

I send a note to a friend, late at night August 14, 2005.

Long hard days… viewing and burying these young men. So hard for the Mothers. Watching one Mother today. Two men tried to get her on her feet from the car when they brought her sons casket to the gym. She collapsed into their arms and they called for a wheelchair to get her inside. She did walk into the gym. I shared this with my sister who attended a viewing at another location. She said this mother did the same thing. Overwhelming grief.

Another funeral tomorrow….

Senator DeWine was in line for one of the viewings. Two other Moms and I approached him and told him we had written letters and called his office asking his help to bring our Ohio Marines home. One Mother told him that his office hung up on her when she asked them to repeat the message she was to give the senator. He was apologetic and said he cared deeply that was why he was here. He gave us personal numbers to contact him. Again I asked if there was any way he could advance their safe return. I told him our Marines have seen enough and done enough.

Late bed time and up early for another funeral. PEACE (Peggy)

I become aware of several web sites to check out. One of them that I find very interesting is www.Truthout.org. I view a video of Cindy Sheehan while outside the President's ranch in Crawford, Texas. The title is "One Mother's Stand." I decide to send her an email.

Cindy and All,

We are burying five of our local young men this week. All killed in Iraq last week when a roadside bomb exploded their "trac."

I have been reading and following your movement since then and wish I could be in Crawford with you.

I admire your courage and stamina and hope you continue to pursue answers…accountability.

Blessings and Love PEACE (Peggy)

Shelly, who has become active and written letters to senators and who inspired the idea of a Mother's March on Washington sent me the following email.

I drove to Fairfield yesterday in time to stand at the intersection of Gilmore and route 4 with two other women (A Marine Mom and a teacher) and the Fairfield fire department as the Cifuentes entourage passed by. I could see Michael's casket in the hearse and then the face of his Mom in the following limo. She could not believe the reception she was viewing. However, I must say, that by the time I reached the location, I was so upset by WLW"S Bill Cunningham and his diatribe about Cindy Sheehan. He called her a clown repeatedly, saying she was disgracing her son's efforts and in turn read the letter from her now ex-husband and his family saying they in no way supported her efforts. I tried to get through to the station three times during the broadcast. However the lines were busy. I could go on… I'll give you more details when I see you. The Mom with whom I stood was conflicted as she knows her son must return to duty in January following this R&R where he has been hounded by his recruiter six days a week and treated very poorly. She thinks her son's group may have been the group your Mike's unit relieved.

Keeping information in the press is the "power of the pen." Keep going. I sense a "tipping point" may be close at hand. (Shelly)

There is an OP-Ed in the New York Times by Frank Rich that a friend forwarded to me. It fuels my disdain of the war and my growing anger with this administration. The reality that my son is being used in what seems to be sham angers me more after attending the funerals of these young men who believed they were offering their lives for a noble cause. The families who just buried their sons believe this. We do not want to offend them by what we say. But inside lays the hurt and the disgust.

Someone Tell the President the war is Over, By Frank Rich, Op-Ed Columnist, the New York Times, Published: August 14, 2005

Like the Japanese soldier marooned on an island for years after V-J Day, President Bush may be the last person in the country to learn that for Americans, if not Iraqis, the war in Iraq is over. "We will stay the course," he insistently tells us from his Texas ranch. What do you mean we white man?

A president can't stay the course when his own citizens (let alone his own allies) won't stay with him.

The article blasts the President and the administration for the "false premises" that then sent brave young men off to fight. All the while it was politicians making military decisions and rebuking the Army chief of staff. As for the future, there didn't seem to be a plan. No exit strategy.

The article concludes with, "*Now comes the hard task of identifying the leaders who can pick up the pieces of the fiasco that has made us more vulnerable...."*

Reading articles like this at this time is adding hot coals to an already hot fire. How to handle this frustration and anger fearing for Mike's safety and the other troops who are so young and so dear, so innocent and so vulnerable. How mad this all is. How does this stop? I feel a sense of urgency. My mind is like a buzzing bee. I send a letter to my list.

August 15, 2005: Forty-six days to go.

Dear Family and Friends,

This has been a difficult time for the families of the fallen Marines and for those of us who still have Marines over there.

The grief for the mother of Timothy Bell, yesterday overcame her as she tried to get out of the car escorted by a Marine and her husband. She collapsed. After a while, they brought a wheel-chair and wheeled her in to witness her coffined son Tim receive military honors. She regained her courage and was able to walk out behind her son. We could see her pain and her pride. Tim will be buried at Arlington National Cemetery.

We were wearing our Lima Company T-shirts as we have at all the lima Company events since the Marines were deployed and we were sitting in the last row of the gym at Tim's funeral. A man tapped us on the shoulder and asked if we had a son in Iraq with 3/25th. We told him yes and he asked if he could sit with us. He introduced himself as the father of Christopher Lyons another fallen Marine whose body hadn't arrived home yet.

Later while standing in line for the viewing of Michael Cifuentes this same day, I saw the hearse car of Tim Bell's funeral we had just attended. It was the family of this Purple Heart Marine. The mother who could not walk to begin her son's funeral walked with purpose, dignity and sorrow to greet Carolyn Cifuentes, mother of Michael Cifuentes. Today we attend his funeral.

There was a candle light service last evening. One woman approached us and said, "It may seem like most of the world doesn't act like we care or even pay attention, but I want you to know there are many of us who do and we pray for you all even though we don't know your names."

It is sad that it takes such a huge loss to bring attention to these who die each day. Over 1800 have died since March 2003 when we were told the war was over.

Mike is a real person. He has dreams and desires to do something with his life. He has shown that already by his service and commitment as a Marine, a path too difficult for most of us to consider requiring that kind of courage and strength and generosity.

Jerry and I know that Mike is not safe until he returns home. Lima 3/25th is still doing missions. They have six more weeks. Your prayers surrounding Mike are still critical to us. Love PEACE (Peggy & Jerry)

And a quick voice message from Mike when we returned from the funeral.

"Hey Mom,
Just hanging out. Worked all day yesterday from 400 - 2000.
Then went to the gym. Feeling better and more rested the longer we
stay here. Going out for a couple of hours. Talk to you later. Love
u."

Okay Hon,
We got your phone message. I think it was the first call we
have missed since you've been gone. We were at Michael Cifuentes'
funeral. The funeral was sad. The Marines did a good job. We are
getting to know and like Major Greiner. He just came to Columbus
from California. He seems like a very fine guy. We keep hounding
him to bring you boys home. Of course there isn't anything he can do.
But we still hound him.
He said that when you come home you can opt to stay active
until January. They will put you to work in Columbus and you
would get military pay.
Have to catch the evening news. People came up to me at
Kenwood Mall today because they saw me on T.V. Lots of people are
praying for you and they know your name.
I am a warrior for you Michael, because I love you. (Mom)

CHAPTER 28

A Balanced Life

Pain and sadness, grief and depression, anticipation and fear fill my heart. War is madness. Whoever dreamed up war? Am I so naïve to think we would/could live peacefully? I don't see how anyone gains in war. Who really wins? Many are hurt and killed and injured. On all sides. And for what?

I don't have answers and think I must sound like a child asking stupid questions. Maybe I don't have a true sense of reality. Whose reality? Is this really reality? Deep inside I bleed and I can't vocalize the grief. I can't find words. Must I accept war as part of humanity? I resist and say "NO" there must be a better way. For now I must deal with my own personal madness, my son in this war and my anger, my frustration, my anguish until he comes home.

I find more articles on the internet about others who oppose this war and who want to see the troops come home. A movement called "Bring Them Home Now" comes to my attention. They say they are "*a campaign of military families, veterans, active duty personnel, reservists and others opposed to this ongoing war in Iraq and galvanized to action by George W. Bush's inane and reckless challenge to armed Iraqis resisting occupation to 'Bring 'Em on.'*" The mission is "*to mobilize families, veterans, and GI's themselves to demand: an end to the occupation of Iraq and other misguided military adventures; and the immediate return of all US troops to their home duty stations.*" *(www.bringthemhomenow.org 8/16/2005)*

The Statement of Purpose goes on to say that there is no just cause for this war. They state that, "*not one more troop killed in action. Not one more troop wounded in action. Not one more troop psychologically damaged by the act of terrifying, humiliating, injuring or killing innocent people. Not one more troop spending one more day inhaling depleted uranium. Not one more troop separated from spouse and children. This is the one way to truly support these troops, and the families who are just as much part of the military as they are.*"

This feeds my need to do something. I feel support and encouragement. There are people out there who understand and want to help. Obviously our senators aren't doing much. Back to the grass roots. But how? What can I do? I am still feeling the need to be discrete.

On www.military.com August 17, 2005 there is an article about Rosemary Palmer and Paul Schroeder, parents of Lance Cpl Edward Schroeder II who was killed in action on August 3rd, 2005 two weeks prior when a road side bomb hit his "trac" (AAV) and killed fourteen Marines. Rosemary says they feel we need to "fight this war right or get out." She is advocating sending more troops because there aren't enough on the ground to do the job right. She and Paul are against the war and have been from the start. Paul says that his son and other Marines are "being misused as a stabilizing force in Iraq. Our comments are not just those of grieving parents. They are based on anger…

not grief. Anger is an honest emotion when someone's family has been violated."

They urged Americans to speak out against the war. "We want to point out that 30 people have died since our son. Are people listening?" Palmer asks.

After reading this article I know I have to call this mother.

That afternoon I get a note from Mike.

"Hey Mom, Well last night I packed my sea bags and a chest to mail home soon. Next week our sea bags start to make the trip home. So for the next month I'll just have a pack for my clothes and my camera. I'll leave mid-September. The date was pushed up a little bit. I hope it moves up again. Our relief starts arriving about the first week of September.

Well I'll talk to you later. May have to wake you up for a call. Love u."

Mike, I was awake and thinking about you when you emailed your message. How exciting to hear about starting to send things home. I have been worried and longing to get you home. You call us anytime day or night. Don't hesitate. Talking to you is more important than sleep.

You must feel really good about packing up. We can't wait.

Going to Chris Dyer's funeral today. We wear our Lima company shirts and tell the family we wear them for you because you would be here if you could. They pray for your safe return. We saw Carl Schneider at the viewing yesterday. He is doing okay. Has a lot of therapy to do yet. His face is healing and he has his voice back.

Please be careful and safe this last month. If I have to I'll come over there and get you! Tell Kevin that his Mom and I have been hanging out and we want you guys home. NOW!

Can't wait to get your sea bag. Is there any way you can climb in it?

Love you. Miss you. Want you home.

Friends and other mothers of Marines continue to write to our senators and politicians with the request that our Marines come home. Trice writes a letter to Laura Bush. She expresses the feelings of many mothers. It is an attempt to reach out mother to mother. We think Laura might understand and show the compassion that her husband does not.

My son is currently stationed in Iraq at Haditha Dam with the 3rd Battalion 25th Marines Lima Company. I am asking you to speak to your husband about his policies concerning the war in Iraq....

I have spent this past week at memorial services for my son's brothers- in- arms. Many people at these services have said how proud I must be of my son for the sacrifices he is making. Yes, I am proud of my son, but pride is not the first emotion that I feel about his being in Iraq. I am in constant fear. Fear that the mortar attacks that they experience daily will this time be deadly. Fear that a sniper or suicide bomber will take him out on his next patrol. Fear that his fellow Marines will have to pick his body parts up after a deadly explosion. Fear that he will be traveling at any moment in an amtrac across Al Anbar Province. Would you let your daughters travel in these vehicles?

Your husband often states that we need to continue the course in Iraq to honor those that have made the ultimate sacrifice. How can he not honor those that are making the ongoing sacrifice? How can he continue to support a war that we are not properly equipped for? He needs to look these mothers, wives and children in the face and tell them why their soldier or Marine is no longer with us. Explain to them what the noble cause is that has taken their loved one away from them. Imagine living the rest of your life without your daughters. These young people are no more expendable than anybody else's loved one.

Please convey the deep sense of grief that we feel here in Ohio to the President.

Sincerely,
Patrice Lehmann

I am asked to speak at a local democratic meeting but feeling a need to remain out of the public eye I forward some thoughts for the meeting.

Tell them that there is growing disenchantment about Bush's war and people think it is incredulous that he hasn't done a thing to personally show concern for the families in Ohio who have lost so many loved ones at one time. These are not just democrats... these are people who voted for him and think he is a superb president but think he needs to take a step back and look at what is going on in Iraq.

Tell them we don't want one more death in Iraq for our families nor for the Iraqis because of our presence there. Tell them to do something, anything to help bring this to an end. Write letters. Speak out. Pray. Light candles. Do something to change the energy of this administration's agenda.

Tell them there are many mothers who are mourning and they should not be forgotten after the last funeral. Tell them we are in this together. We all lose when we lose one young noble life. We cannot underestimate the life of the young we have given up in a war that has no good meaning. Shame on us if we allow this to continue.

We support and honor our young troops whether we are in favor of the war or not. We all grieve deeply. Thanks. (Peggy)

I probably shouldn't spend time on the internet reading the articles about the war and President Bush. But I do. It fuels disregard for the president. Maureen Dowd wrote an article called "Biking Toward Nowhere" (New York Times August 17, 2005).

On Saturday, the current President Bush was pressed about how he could be taking five weeks to ride bikes and nap and fish and clear brush even though his occupation of Iraq had become a fiasco. 'I think it's also important for me to go on with my life,' W. said, 'to keep a balanced life.'

CHAPTER 29

The Wedding Dress

The Oxford Press runs an article about Michael Cifuentes and his funeral. The title is, "Marine recalled for his smile, sacrifice." (Friday, August 19, 2005). The article begins, *His smile was contagious. "Some of his classmates said that when he walked into a room the place lit up," said the Rev. John Ferone as he described how the life of Lance Cpl. Michael Cifuentes was received by others.... "He was a lover, a reconciler... a person who was able to give everything away so that this world would be a better place."*

The ceremonial playing of Taps echoed in the air and a 21-gun salute was fired in Cifuentes' honor.

Peggy and Jerry Logue, whose 19-year-old son Marine Mike Logue is a member of the Lima Company, were among those who stepped in to console the Cifuentes family Monday afternoon.

"The pain is deep and the pain is real. The American people need to see this" said Peggy Logue between tears. "Our son would be here if he could be. We all want our son's home. One of our Moms just left

because…. you feel a little out of control sometimes. You panic with fear that you might have to do this. I admire the strength and the courage of these people. I just don't think I can bury my son."

An article written by a friend of Michael Cifuentes surfaced on the internet from Pal-Item.com. It was published August 21, 2005. Title, "When they come home: After death of friend, war became real"

The war raging in Iraq fails to hit home for many in my generation. For me, that feeling lasted until 2 ½ weeks ago. When a roadside bomb ripped through Lance Cpl. Michael Cifuentes' lightly armored amphibious assault vehicle on August 3rd south of Haditha, Iraq. It also tore through the hearts of everyone who knew him.

… I called one of my best friends from college, Tara Reynolds, and cried with her, too. Michael was her fiancé. He was 25. They were supposed to be married next July.

The Visitation:

At 24 years old, I can count on my fingers the number of funerals I've attended. Intellectually, I understand the dangers of war. Now, seeing Tara cry and go through the motions of a funeral makes me sick to my stomach. She's 23 – too young to be burying the man she loved.

I'm not from the World War II or Vietnam generations. I never thought a war would break the dreams of one of my best friends.

The Funeral:

In the midst of a priest shortage, seven of them presided over Mike's funeral Mass on Monday.

The article goes on to relate the response of the community that lines the highways where the hearse will pass by. Firemen and enforcement officers stand at attention and salute as do veterans.

Michael with a degree in psychology was a substitute teacher in a local school district. He became a Marine because he wanted to. Knowing that he died doing something he loved is something his loved ones will hold on to. But nothing makes it easy. Strangers line the streets. An estimated 4000 people are present along the roadways to salute Michael Cifuentes. The article continues;

For me, the most emotional moments weren't the times when a priest was talking about Michael's life. He was my friend, and I didn't need anybody to tell me about how caring he was, or how much he loved kids and wanted to teach, or how devoted he was to Tara.

It was when two Marines finally folded the flag that had been draped over Mike's casket for days. Slow, steady and meticulous, each of the folds made his death and Tara's grief more real. Until that point at the burial, I had been hoping and praying that somehow a mistake had been made.

The Marine reading the proclamation about Mike's posthumous Purple Heart medal did so with a shaking voice and hands. Other Marines wiped away tears.

I don't know what she'll do with the wedding dress in her closet. She won it from a radio station for having the cutest wedding proposal story, and it was custom made. Some would question how you could keep it, but how do you give it up?

I have cried along with many others since the news of Mike's death - not just for what he had, but for what he never had the chance to have - a marriage, children and time to grow old with our friend Tara.

I share this because it is so real. How distant we can be from war and death and how overwhelmed we are when it hits home. When it is in our very house. When it is in our very hearts.

CHAPTER 30

How Does It Feel?

We are so visible wearing our Lima Company shirts at each of the viewings and funerals, the press spot us and want to get an interview. "How does it feel" they ask with pens in hand and cameras rolling, "to be here and see this with your own son still there?" They are quick with questions and seem to be in a hurry. I answer quickly with my emotions on my sleeve. "It hurts," I respond. Then I say how I admire the families. A few more quick questions and answers and they are off to another story. I think about this later. My heart says, "You really don't want to know how I feel. You don't have time to listen. You probably can't print it. Because most of the time I want to scream in sheer madness."

One day, after attending several funerals and viewings, with questions asked from the press swirling in my head, I journal my response to, "How does it feel?"

How does it feel?

You have asked me several times, "How does it feel?" How does it feel to be here with these families? How does it feel to see the young being buried? How does it feel while your son is still there?

Let me tell you about the many nights I wake up at 3:00am as though I am on night watch in Iraq. My thoughts immediately go to my son Mike. He is in Al Anbar Province, an area in Iraq we were told was quiet and "they won't see much action." Let me tell you how I panic and want to scream out in utter fear for my son, longing to see him and to know what he is doing and to know that he is safe. How I have been told that it is a crap shoot… he may be in the next amtrac that gets hit by an IED or the next attack on patrol. How I don't feel that there is anywhere there that is safe. So every moment is the next crap shoot. How devastating it has been to bury these Marines who were killed in action. How threatened and vulnerable I feel as my son is still there and knowing that his fate could be sealed. Let me tell you how many times I have seen him in a flag draped coffin like the ones that cover his friends. How many times I have received the folded flag with arms that could hardly rise up as I weep a silent deep weeping that has no sound in my numbed presence but allows tears to bleed from my heart.

Do you want to hear my scream? Primordial? Hysterical? Unearthly? Or see me collapse into absolute emptiness feeling I will never get up again? I don't want to get up. I am dead. Do you want to hear how I sometimes feel myself walking but I am not breathing? There is no air and I feel like I am dying and death doesn't matter. How I have thought, "would my death bring my son home?" How each step I take, each breath seems more than I can handle. How desperately I want my son to live and have hope. He is so young, so idealistic, and so confident, so trusting. Let me share with you that sometimes when I awake and my thoughts fill with the possible fate of my dear child my body trembles and I feel like I will throw up everything inside and everything I have ever known. And I am a stranger to the world. And I am alone in this grief.

I can't think of a reason or a cause good enough for me to willingly give up the life of my son. Not even for "my freedom." If he has to die for my freedom, I haven't gained anything. I would rather live with him alive in any circumstances than live free and comfortable while taking his life.

This is how it feels.

CHAPTER 31

Turning on a Dime

It is August 18, 2005 and Jerry and I are going to a candlelight vigil on Fountain Square in downtown Cincinnati to show support for Cindy Sheehan and her son Casey who was killed in Iraq. In agreeing to do this we feel we are committing to taking a public stand against the war. We will be labeled now for being unpatriotic and for not supporting the troops. I send a note to my friends inviting them to participate and end the note saying… *Supporting the troops by bringing them home…*

This is an eye opening experience for me about myself, my beliefs and my ideals. It starts out well and is to be a peaceful walk through part of downtown Cincinnati. We carry signs and chant things like "End the War," "Support the Troops," "Bring Them Home." etc. We walk to the ball park meandering around and since there is a game this night there are lots of people gathering. We carry our signs. We chant. We continue our walk to Bicentennial Park and come face to face with a large group of young people who are celebrating some occasion with lots of food and drink. We walk and carry our signs and chant not interrupting their celebration or even getting close to them for them to hear us. But they see us. One young man chooses to follow us and do his own chanting. He chants out "cowards," and says, "You are just afraid to stay in for the fight." He keeps following us chanting his insults. Someone asks him why he isn't serving since he seems so enamored with the war and the heroes that he "supports." He says, "Because I choose to go to school here and work here." Like that is reason enough to send others off to do his killing and be killed. He continues to follow and harass us. Finally before he turns himself around to go back with his friends and the lively party he says, "You are all just a bunch of yellow bellies." This does it for me. Having just buried five courageous men the age of this young man and fearing for my son and for the Marines who are still there in harm's way and listening to this suave alcohol filled clean cut all American boy call us yellow bellies, I turn on a dime and from a mean spirited place within me I swear at him. "You f___ing a_____! If you are so brave get your a__ over there and let our sons come home! They, my dear young man have buried pieces of their friends. And you are here drinking and going to school and talking like you have a clue about any of this."

I am quickly grabbed by Jerry and turned around face forward and told to calm down. "It's okay," Jerry says, "let's just go." I walk on mumbling under my breath, glancing back at him, tears in my eyes. Jerry holds my arm and keeps me forward. After walking awhile and being swallowed by the chanting of the group, I remember why I am there. I realize what I have done. I walk but can't chant. I am hurt. I am embarrassed. I am sorry and tearful. It doesn't take long for me to see how quickly I gave in to violence. I who proclaim there is a better way, responded in anger. "War is not the answer," I say, and then, I see myself become war. This is very humbling.

CHAPTER 32

Sacrifice

The next day, August 19, I am at my computer. I see Mike's name come up. I immediately message him.

Hey Buddy

"*Hey!*"

How are you doing?

"*I have watch in an hour. So I'm up now.*"

What do you do for watch?

"*Watch the vehicles.*"

I heard some Major was there...Odell?

"*General.*"

Oh! A General. I knew it was big. Tomorrow is the last of the funerals. David Krueter. Did you know him?

"*No.*"

We chatted about his military pay and how he could stay active until January and work out of Columbus. And I tell him about the people in the community that want to see him when he returns, his high school principal, his dentist, his friends, the news media. I apologize if I am taking his time because I know he has friends he likes to chat with on-line. But he assures me he is okay. So I keep up my harried pace of questions and superficial statements. Just hanging on and trying to keep him close. I tell him about a wedding Crista is in and that his brother John in Colorado wants to plan some time home after the homecoming. He asks if his videos made it home and if we have watched them. I told him we want to view them with him because it is hard to know what we are seeing.

We talk about his future and how he may need some time to rest and he agrees. And then we will make plans for school. I tell him that Jerry and I are thinking of going to Arizona in the winter to catch some sun. But nothing is definite.

Our only goal is to get you home, safe. Everything else is on hold. You don't know how precious you are to us, Dad, Mom, Crista, John. We have all shed some… many tears. But we are excited now. Can't wait. We won't let you go very easily next time.

"*I know you won't.*"

I am not afraid of the Marines… or the government… or the president. I am your Mom.

"*Ha! Ha! Love you Mom.*"

I love you more each day.

"*I have to go now... My time is up.*"

Hugs and kisses.

"*I'll try to call soon.*"

Love you.

Speaking with Mike through instant messaging is incredibly life giving. It is almost real presence. He is just a key stroke away. He is there. He can't die now I just talked to him. I am so thankful for these moments.

Bob Herbert from The New York Times, August 18, 2005 printed an article titled, "Blood Runs Red, Not Blue."

You have to wonder whether reality ever comes knocking on

*George W. Bush's door. If it did, would the president with the
unsettling demeanor of a boy king even bother to answer? Mr. Bush
is the commander in chief who launched a savage war in Iraq and
now spends his days riding his bicycle in Texas.*

This is eerie. Scary. Surreal.

*The war is going badly and lives have been lost by the thousands,
but there is no real sense, either at the highest levels of government
or in the nation at large, that anything momentous is at stake. The
announcement on Sunday that five more American soldiers had
been blown to eternity by roadside bombs was treated by the press
as a yawner. It got very little attention...*

*For all the talk of supporting the troops, they are a low priority
for most Americans. If the nation really cared, the president would
not be frolicking at his ranch for the entire month of August. He'd be
back in Washington burning the midnight oil, trying to figure out
how to get the troops out of the terrible fix he put them in...*

*For the most part, the only people sacrificing for this war are the
troops and their families...*

*For the second time since the war began, the Pentagon is
struggling to replace body armor that is failing to protect American
troops from the most lethal attacks by insurgents...*

*The President has never been clear about why we're in Iraq.
There's no plan, no strategy. In one of the many tragic echoes of
Vietnam, U.S. troops have been fighting hellacious battles to
seize areas controlled by insurgents, only to retreat and allow the
insurgents to return...*

The question about the sacrifices Americans are making
hits home more after my incident with the young man in
Cincinnati. He obviously is making no sacrifice for this noble
war. It seems only a few are involved and sacrificing. But if this
is such an important war why aren't we all sacrificing? Why
aren't all children called to serve? The privileged and this young
man as well?

I ponder this while my fear and anger grow and I want to
do something and want it to be the right thing. Not wanting

in the least way to hurt Mike or his Marines, or any of the military that are serving and the families who are sacrificing.

I read a few more articles that make my head shake and fuel my anger. Newsday.com carries a story about the U.S. military ordering an investigation into the death of a twenty-one year old cousin of Iraq's ambassador to the United Nations...*who alleged that U.S. Marines killed his unarmed relative in cold blood during a raid in western Iraq...Iraqis often make allegations of mistreatment by U.S. troops during raids, and Haditha, 140 miles northwest of Baghdad, is a center of insurgent activity in Anbar province. Some troops have been court-martialed or are facing charges for misconduct. (Navy to Probe Ambassador Cousin's Death by Robert H. Reid, August 21, 2005)*

Later, Mike tells me that he and others are called into questioning about this case. And that brings up other fears for me. Our Marines who don't know who the enemy is may end up in prison for shooting the wrong person. Even though there are rules of engagement, this is not a soldier's war. The enemy does not wear a uniform. How chaotic can that be? How would you know? How many chances do you take? War is crazy.

A few days later I find an article about "The Swift Boating of Cindy Sheehan." (New York Times August 21, 2005 by Frank Rich).

Though 14 Marine reservists had been killed days earlier by a roadside bomb in Haditha, his national radio address that morning made no mention of Iraq. Once again Mr. Bush was in his bubble...

When these setbacks happen in Iraq itself, the administration punts. But when they happen at home, there's a game plan. Once Ms. Sheehan could no longer be ignored, the Swift Boating began. Character assassination is the Karl Rove tactic of choice, eagerly mimicked by his media surrogates, whenever the White House is confronted by a critic who challenges it on matters of war.

The backdrops against which Ms Sheehan stands - both that

of Mr. Bush's what-me-worry vacation and that of Iraq itself – are perfectly synergistic with her message of unequal sacrifice and fruitless carnage...

The public knows that what matters this time is Casey Sheehan's story, not the mother who symbolizes it. Cindy Sheehan's bashers, you'll notice never tell her son's story. They are afraid to go there because this young man's life and death encapsulate not just the noble intentions of those who went to fight this war but also the hubris, incompetence and recklessness of those who gave the marching orders.

This same day I send a letter to Mrs. Bush. Thinking maybe she cares. Asking her to communicate to her husband how deeply we feel the loss and wondering where he is.

How degrading to our community that he thinks we could give up the lives of so many of our young men for his "noble" war and he doesn't have the courage to face us and mourn with us... Those who believe in this war and those who don't suffer the same grief and sorrow at the loss of beautiful, young and noble life.

Do you care? Tell the president.

How naïve of me.

CHAPTER 33

Another Day to be Alive

We receive our August Newsletter from the Key Volunteer Network. It contains a re-cap on our July 31st Family Picnic. That week we lost two Marines, Andre Williams and Christopher Lyons which followed the death of the Navy Corpsman Travis Youngblood. The Monday following the picnic five snipers are killed and one is missing. His body is found Tuesday. And on Wednesday, August 3, another fourteen Marines are killed as the "trac" they travel in is blown up by an IED. Greg Cifuentes, the father of one of the fourteen KIA , grills our hamburgers at the picnic on Sunday and gets word on Wednesday that his son Michael has been killed.

There is a note in the newsletter that the deadline for sending care packages has passed. And letter mail is to stop after September 1st. This is exciting. It makes me feel that nothing more can happen. They are on their way home. Oh! Thank God. Thank God. They are really coming home. The next meeting of the Marine Families is to be August 27th. There will be no special activities. The focus will be on learning what we can do to make homecoming successful for our Marines and Corpsmen. There will be representatives to address homecoming issues. We understand that they will be quarantined for about a week in Camp LeJeune before returning to Columbus. This is to allow for de-briefing, counseling, transitioning them for "civilian" life at home in America.

A poem, written by Sarah Dyer, the 17-year-old sister of Lcpl Dyer (KIA) is included in the newsletter.

Dear, dear Brother,
You have gone home
To your Father, your Savior
Your Kingdom is come.
Dear, dear Brother,
You fought bravely as a knight
You are a Devil Dog in the fiercest bite.
Dear, dear Brother,
We miss you so,
Your father, mother, sisters,
All your friends and Joe.
Dear, dear Brother,
We will see you again,
After triumphs, and troubles, and all of our pain.
Dear, dear Brother,
Stay tough on high.
We will remember you.
SEMPER FI.

The newsletter ended with the reflection of one Marine.

We didn't come here to plant flowers or sew pillows. But it is hard. So many. I have a hard time with it at times. It makes my back not feel as bad. It makes the heat not as unbearable. It makes the weight of my gear not that heavy. It makes me push. It makes me continue on when I feel as though I have no more energy to clear the next house. To move the next objective. These have been Marines I have both lectured and taught. Drank beer with and befriended. Now they are gone. Things are never the same after an operation where we have taken casualties. The pain of the memorial service grows each time. We remember where and who all we have been and those who will not return home to us. I have little fear of what may come from the next mission or the next op. I know that what will happen there on the field of battle will happen. I can only do my best and what I can with what God has given me. I joined the Marine Corps not to serve the country but to serve along side of those like myself. We are not here for ma or apple pie. The support we receive from home makes our lives easier but it is not a necessity. Our fight will still continue. Our op tempo will remain the same. The enemy is still out there. I love all of those back home. I'm glad that those back home do not need to be here. Nor do what I have done. Nor see what I have seen. We are all brothers here. We are all family. It doesn't matter what we say about each other or what we think. We are all one and we feel the pain of the others. I have no control of what happens. I just can control what is being done. This is what I think. This is what I feel. This is what I believe. All the things at home are petty. They are small. They mean nothing. While I am here. I have fought bigger battles here than I ever will at home and I am sure that I will fight even bigger battles before I leave this place. All I would want those back home to know is that we love our families and we love our 'ol ladies, wives and kids. Never second guess that. We knew the price that may have been needed to pay when we came here. Everyday we are prepared to pay that price over and over again. But nevertheless, for our brothers-in-arms, I no longer care what others may think of what I believe. I have seen what war is and it is the most ugly of all things. I pray for my return home. To finish college and become an officer. In hopes that I may never have to return but preparing for it. For this is what God made me. A soldier. A warrior. A leader. A Marine. It's simple really and that is what I have learned here. Life is simple. People make it harder than it really is by getting wrapped up in things that are petty and in the actions of others. Just take care of those that you love and everything else is easy. Well it's late. I have to hit the rack. I'm beat and I'm tired. My body is sore but in four minutes it's another day. A day closer to returning home. Another day to be alive. Unlike so many of my friends and brothers. (Author unknown)

CHAPTER 34

I Can't Begin to Title This

Voicing my feelings allows me to pass along some of the grief and the anxiety I feel. I can be as anesthetized as many Americans to the pain of the world. I am kept safe and all my basic needs are met. I have more than I need. I am comfortable. I am well fed. I have water and shelter and a job if I want one. I celebrate holidays by blowing off fireworks and think nothing of the fear those sights and sounds create in those who have known war. Nor the waste in energy and the pollution they may cause. After all, pleasure is most important. My American life is cozy. I don't want to be bothered by a world that is suffering and war that is always and has always been somewhere else.

I see a different view now and feel a different story. Now I feel immersed in this war and I realize grief and anxiety as daily baptism. So I pass it on to others so that they may know how close this reality is. How real it is. How painful it is. How universal it is. Maybe through the expression of my pain, others will feel the grief of war and help do something to bring it to an end. I reach out in my anguish and flame a deep, deep fire that eats away at our country until we find a better solution to war. And I know I will curl up and become an ember in that fire if my son loses not just his life or limb, but his soul. War does just that. It kills not just bodies. It kills the soul.

I write my personal reflection of the funerals and send it to my list.

Family and Friends,

I can't even begin to title this. The viewings, the funerals, the burials, the candle light vigils, the military honors are over for now. Jerry and I were able to attend the services for the five local Marines. We went in support of our Marine families. We went for Mike. What a tragic and huge loss. There are no words for the loss.

Each service had a full screen video celebration of the particular Marine's life from childhood to young death. The age range of these Marines was nineteen to twenty-six. Their lives had just begun. One was a new father with a seven week-old baby he never saw, or held, except in his dreams. "He was so proud to be a father," said his uncle while paying tribute.

We heard their stories. How proud they were to be Marines. How proud their families were of them. How treasured they each were. How they each wanted to make a difference.

Some of the songs chosen for the videos, "You're Still You," "A Breath Away," "The Dance."

We watched four mothers and one wife receive the folded flag. We heard a sister wail. We heard the 21 gun salute too many times. We saw the caisson carrying the flag draped coffins and the rider-less horse with boots turned backwards. We saw streams of people weeping, leatherneck motorcyclists who tried to attend every funeral of their fallen brother Marine.

We saw policemen, firemen, enforcement officers saluting and stopping traffic along the miles of those in procession on the road to the gravesite. People standing, watching, weeping, saluting as the whole procession drove by. We heard each minister try to bring words of comfort to those who had no comfort.

We saw Marines in their "Blues" being present, being strong, and being brave. Some were injured in Operation Matador and had returned with their wounded bodies and now came to bury their brothers who came home in pieces. We saw Marines weep. The Marine Major who just came to Ohio and is getting to know the state by attending these funerals told me he has an eleven week-old son." Oh," I said, "It's real now. You can relate." With moist and reddened eyes he gently nodded. The Chief Warrant Officer from Columbus, dressed in his formal Marine Blues who we had seen over and over again at the funerals, hugged me and said," I know we look and act strong, but we feel this deeply." He too had tears in his eyes.

And then there were the mothers. Although they already buried their Marine they continued to support the other Marine family by attending each funeral. But while watching the video tribute to another Marine, one mother saw a picture of her already buried son and could not contain her grief. We tried to hold her as tears poured while she struggled to catch her breath and subdue her shuddering body.

The rest of their life begins with tremendous pride, and tremendous grief: The mothers, the fathers, the wife, the children, the brothers and sisters. The families.

One father said to me" No one ever thought this would happen."

CHAPTER 35

Get Off the Fence

I find more articles online of people speaking out. Cindy
Sheehan has given the world permission, especially mothers
whose sons and daughters are serving in Iraq. Mrs. Sheehan
writes an article that the Information Clearing House picks
up. It is called, "Hypocrites and Liars" by Cindy Sheehan
8/20/05.

*I got an email the other day and it said, "Cindy if you didn't use
so much profanity... there's people on the fence that get offended."
And you know what I said? "You know what? You know what god
damn it? How in the world is anybody still sitting on that fence?"*

*If you fall on the side that is pro-George and pro-war, you get
your ass over to Iraq, and take the place of somebody who wants
to come home. And if you fall on the side that is against this war
and against George Bush, stand up and speak out...I have stood up
and said: "My son died for NOTHING, and George Bush and his
evil cabal and their reckless policies killed him. My son was sent to*

*fight in a war that had no basis in reality and was killed for it."
I have never said "pretty please" or "thank you." I have never said
anything wishy-washy like he uses "Patriotic Rhetoric." I say my
son died for LIES. George Bush LIED to us and he knew he was
LYING. The Downing Street Memos dated 23 July, 2002 prove he
knew that Saddam didn't have WMD's or any ties to Al Qaeda. I
believe that George lied and he knew he was lying... He lied and
made us afraid of ghosts that weren't there...*

*If it shortens the war by a minute or saves one life, it is worth
it. I think they seriously "underestimated" all mothers. I wonder if
any of them had authentic mother-child relationships and if they
are surprised that there are so many mothers in this country who
are bear-like when it comes to wanting the truth and who want to
make meaning of their child's needless and seemingly meaningless
deaths?*

*The Camp Casey movement will not die until we have a
genuine accounting of the truth and until our troops are brought
home. Get used to it George, we are not going away.*

This is what I want to say. This is how I am feeling. Like a
mama bear. This mother has lost everything. She has nothing
more to lose. She can speak out loud and clear and with no fear.
She can demand answers. How I want to be with her and feel
the energy and support she is receiving. And give her mine.

I read another article in the Pittsburgh Post-Gazette by
Missy Comley Beattie. The title is, "An Honorable Marine
Killed in a Dishonorable War."

*...For those of you who still trust the Bush administration –
and your percentage diminishes every day – let me tell you that my
nephew, Chase Johnson Comely did not die to preserve your freedoms.
He was not presented flowers by grateful Iraqis, welcoming him as
their liberator.*

*He died fighting a senseless war for oil and contracts, ensuring
the increased wealth of President Bush and his administration's
friends...*

So think of my family's grief – grief that will never end. Think of all of the families. Think of the wounded, the maimed, the psychologically scarred…

And then consider: The preservation of our freedom rests not on U.S. imperialism but on actively changing foreign policies that are conquest-oriented and that dehumanize our own young who become fodder for endless war as well as people in other countries who are so geographically distant that they become abstract…

And finally, think about flowers: The flowers for Chase Comley will be presented not by grateful Iraqis but by loved ones honoring him as he's lowered to his grave and buried in our hearts.

And then as I search for info about the war and what is happening in Iraq I come across an article in the Plain Dealer on Cleveland.com. *Mom Buries Fears Along With Son. (Monday, August 22, 2005 Connie Schultz, Plain Dealer Columnist)*

This is an article about Rosemary Palmer and Paul Schroeder whose 23-year-old son Augie, a 3/25th Marine was killed August 3rd along with fourteen other men when hit by a roadside bomb. Rosemary held a news conference the day after Augie's funeral. I see a brief clip on national news. It is a glimpse of another mother who has nothing more to lose. She is grief stricken but she is clear and says, *We have to fight this war properly or get out.* At an earlier time I saw her as she was interviewed from her home in Cleveland just after she got the news of Augie's death. At that time she said, *They are throwing bodies.* She and Paul are against the war but are not speaking out because of Augie. But now, *This is not my story. This is about Augie, and about all the men and women still fighting in Iraq. Now I feel like, you got a microphone? I've got something to say. … I was hoping the vigils would embolden others to speak out.*

Deep inside I know I must meet this woman. I need to call her but I am nervous. She has lost her son. How do I express grief mother to mother over the death of her child while mine is still alive? Am I selfish? Thoughtless? I don't know if she will even want to talk to me. I still have my son and yet I am so fearful for him. Will my cares seem insignificant to her? I don't know but I call her.

We visit on the phone for a long while. She knows I care and she knows I am scared. She shares with me that she too was continually on watch for her son. *I anguished and feared every minute of every day. It didn't let up until I got the visit from the two Marines who came with the news of Augie's death. Then my anguish was over, there was nothing else to be afraid of.* Her voice dropped. Now there is grief. And in that grief, Rosemary resolves action. She is determined to speak out.

I send her an email asking if she will be at the family meeting at the Drill Center on Saturday. I think that might be a chance to meet.

I would like very much to meet you. This Saturday isn't going to work. We have too many conflicts. Besides, my husband said he didn't know if he could bear being around so many people planning for welcoming their boys home. We will be at the official homecoming for the 3/25th, however.

Two things.

1) If you plan to be at the family gathering on Saturday, if you hear people questioning the "Bush plan" or speaking about Bush's lack of support for the boys, could you see if you could get their names and telephone numbers?

2) Maybe we could set up a meeting halfway between your home and Cleveland.

We have to come up with a clear message because we've learned that you have to be very direct with the press. They ask a lot of questions, and if you aren't "on message" 100 per cent of the time, they may use a quote that isn't really what you want to say.

It could be that that message won't be able to be disseminated until after the boys hit American soil. That's fine. It could be an even more powerful message if we said we held off with it for that very reason.

...our Key Volunteer said that the boys have a lot of "survivor guilt" (why not me?) and that tension is thick enough to cut with

a knife. Believe me, my prayers have gotten even longer because I want to be there for those guys still there.

Keep in touch. There are a lot more supporting voices out there than you might think.

Rosemary (Augie Schroeder's mom)

I am relieved to have the conversation with Rosemary. We form a bond immediately. We are mothers. We are against the war and we both feel a need to speak out. She has paid the ultimate price. A price I am not willing to pay. I feel I have support with her. Rosemary lost her son in a war that she is against. She has a right to speak out. She has nothing more to fear. She is a voice for me. I reach out to her and I feel her compassion and strength.

I send her a copy of some of the articles I have written to my email list, *How Does it Feel?* and *I Can't Begin to Title This.* She responds:

Thank you for sharing. Those feelings you reveal are just so familiar! Your stories are GREAT! Maybe one of the things we should all consider is a book telling the story of the 3/25th. If any of the other moms/dads/sibs/spouses write as well as you do, we would have plenty of material.

I tell Rosemary about my email list and how I have kept Mike in the minds and hearts of all of my friends and family. I tell her I believe those of us who have "skin in the game" have something to say, and that I will do anything I can to stop this craziness for Mike and for all that are serving.

I am beginning to find articles by military people who are speaking out. In an article by Tom Lasseter in the Knight Ridder Newspapers (August 25, 2005) I read statements from different military men.

"It doesn't do much good to push them out of these areas only to let them go back to areas we've already cleared," said Lt Col. Tim Mundy, who commands the 3rd Battalion 2nd marine Regiment...
"We're successful at taking some of his equipment and killing some insurgents, but the effectiveness is limited because we can't stay...

we go back to camp and then we get reports that they've come back in."

...In western Anbar, Marines have made a series of quick raids on towns including Karabilah, Haditha and Haqlaniya. But as soon as the Marines leave, typically after about a week sweeping through houses, the insurgents filter back in and set up base again. "If you go to an area and you don't stay in that area, the insurgents will return to that area and intimidate the local population," said Lt Col. Lionel Urquhart, who commands the 3rd Battalion of the 25th Marine Regiment.

Urquhart said he didn't have enough men to maintain a permanent presence in Haditha.

"You're going to have this constant need to go back and clean it up again...we have to go back in and make it clear to everybody that the insurgency does not control this country," said Urquhart of Akron, Ohio. "Is that a good way of doing business? I'm not going to say that."

When Marines re-entered Haqlaniya during a recent operation, virtually every downtown storefront had pro-jihad messages spray-painted on it: "Allah is our God, Jihad is our way"; "Long live the mujahedeen"; "It is your duty to fight for jihad in Iraq"; "Death to those who collaborate with Americans."

... "There's no way I can control this area with the men I have," Coffey, 37, of Burlington, Vt. said in a recent interview." The reports are that the insurgents are using these southern control points because they're open. We can't keep them closed because I don't have the manpower."

A few minutes later Coffey'e radio squawked. A rocket-propelled grenade had hit one of his Bradley Fighting Vehicles. Rushing to the scene, he found the driver and crew safe, but one of the soldiers in the vehicle looked at Coffey with large eyes and said, " I hate being up here by my f_____self." Without another Bradley or Humvee close by, it's easy for insurgents to pop up from behind, Coffey said.

I read carefully what the military is saying and it scares me. Our young men and women are in a battle without enough manpower and without adequate equipment. And our President is on vacation at his ranch for a month.

But there are others speaking out, getting people off who are "still sitting on the fence" and promising they will not go away until our soldiers and Marines are home.

CHAPTER 36

Instant Message

What was it like in other wars for the families left behind? Soldiers would be gone for months with no word back home. In this war we get a phone call once in awhile and we meet each other on the internet through instant messaging. I meet Mike on instant message August 23, 2005. He is at Al Asad, the air base held by Americans. He is there with other Marines being interviewed regarding the case of the Marines who are accused of killing the cousin of Iraq's ambassador to the United Nations. Al Asad is "plush," Mike says. "They have real food, a gym and a Sub-Way."

> *Are you staying there for the night?*
> "Yes."
> *Did you have a Sub-Way?*
> "No I didn't."
> *How are things going?*

"*Fine. Just ready to get out of here.*"

I bet you are. Any particular kind of work you want to do when you come home? We can start talking to people. I think there are many who would help.

"*I don't know what I exactly want to do, maybe something with the county, outside. But I don't know. Can't promise anything.*"

We can investigate and see who will help and what they can offer. You don't have to make a decision now. You really need a vacation.

"*I don't think I want to do lawn and landscaping right away. I don't know. I just need time off.*"

You really need to put your feet up, have a Miller, or marguerites and fajitas.

"*Yes.*"

We will treat you well.….. Crista and John want to spend time with you.

"*Okay.*"

Just think of relaxing for a few weeks… and breakfast on the deck.

"*Yeah!*"

Hang in there buddy. Like we are. We know this time will pass.

"*Yeah. We're getting close.*"

The countdown began at two-hundred and fifteen days. That was a long time ago. You now have about thirty-nine. That is to the end of September. So we can handle this. It does help to hear from you. It makes our day. Just to hear your voice.

"*Yeah.*"

So what will you do tonight?

"*I don't know what I want to do.*"

When is bed time?

"*Probably soon. But I may go to the gym first.*"

Do you have a room with other guys?

"*A big tent.*"

Is everyone finished being interrogated?

"Yes. They were pretty nice actually."
Do you want to do some online searching for yourself?
"I'm alright. We can talk."
Okay! I love it!
"I really don't look up anything except the Bengals and Ohio University web sites."
Have you heard from the Bengals?
"I got a package with a couple of t-shirts and towels and calendars."
Should we try to get a couple of tickets for a game?
"I wanted to."
Do you want to? Online? Or do you want us to follow up?
"Could you?"
Absolutely!
"I wanted to see if they would give tickets for me and some guys from my platoon because the Browns are giving like thirty some tickets to the Browns fans."
Anything we can do to help you have fun when you come home. We should be able to get something done on that. How many do you need?
"I don't know. Whatever they would be willing to do for our platoon. Time's up. Gotta' go."
Love you.

Now I have an assignment to get tickets to the Bengals game for Mike and his platoon. I have a few leads. My brother knows the coach, Marvin Lewis. Also, a TV station we have talked with might have some leads. Then there is Jody whose son David is a doctor serving in Iraq. She has many Cincinnati contacts. These are where I will start.

Weeks go by with nothing happening. My brother writes a letter to the Bengals and tells them about Mike and his unit. *This unit has been in Iraq since February 2005 and has lost twenty-three of their brothers, five of which we have just locally seen buried in the past couple of weeks. In addition, their casualties include thirty plus injured. This unit has been through hell since its arrival. Their seven months of duty has been almost non-stop activity. I invite you to visit my nephew's website http://www.mikelogue.com.*

It would be fantastic if the Bengals could reach out to these fine young men after their return home.

CHAPTER 37

I'm A Marine Now

It is August 26 and Mike and I meet again on the computer.

Hey Buddy. Waz'up?
"Hey!"
I just got a call from CNN. They want to interview me for a news program next week. They want to know how it feels to have a son in Iraq.
"For what we are doing? And my Marines? Don't get close to those people that blame Bush for killing their son or putting them in harm's way. We made that decision. And we do our jobs. We're not politicians. I'll try to call.
Love you."

Mike signs on again and we continue our instant messaging conversation. This is a sensitive time because I want to know how Mike feels and I want him to understand what I feel I need to do. I know this is important to him.

"Mom, if you do, say that now that we are here there is nothing to change about the initial reasons to come. Don't quote me either. Okay? But you know that in Al Anbar, it's still war out here. It changes day to day. It's a kinetic fight still. It's not like Baghdad and the rest of Iraq."

Mike, there are many people here who are against the war and want our troops home. I know you don't have enough men or the right equipment.

"I know. But if you do the interview I don't want a negative image of why we even are here and why my friends have died. That's all. Well, where I am they're tying our hands. Trying to win hearts and minds. It's not like that here. It's like that in other parts but not here. So, I don't know how you feel. Yes. You want us home."

I would have a lot to share with you but believe me, you are all considered noble and honorable. There is a serious question as to why you are there. Maybe even an illegal war. But that is all politics. You only need to do your job.

"That's right. Just if you do, mainly state all the great stuff about the unit and the hard work we have done and if you didn't know, we were chosen the best Marine reserve unit."

But the question is a serious one. And whether we can lose lives for a war that may have been started by lies.

"But even if it was. The only thing to do is not pull out or stay the course. Only one way it will be successful here is to start from cities like Baghdad, securing them and winning them completely turning them over to Iraqis. Not to go in and out of the cities like we have done. They need more people to do it like we did in Hit. We cleared it and now have two companies there and Iraqis. That shows more power and a realistic Iraqi army and it controls and secures and stabilizes the city. And that will spread out. But that requires more troops or Iraqis and the good officers to stay longer. Or, we leave and have a power struggle. Or we rape it of anything good

and bomb everything. And the last two aren't good choices. Unless Iraqis can control it themselves. But they are years behind that."

You must know that I am against this war. I have been from the start. But you may not realize why. It has nothing to do with you and honoring you and the Marines. It is because I honor you that I am becoming active in the anti-war movement.

"I know."

I love you and respect the work you want to do.

"But just don't let it be that these guys died for nothing."

They did not die for nothing. And anyone who tells you if you are against the war you are not honoring the dead are wrong. This war has a dead end.

"Did you see the lady from Texas? I saw a report."

Yes, and Kevin's mother and I were going to join her but we have the family meeting and so we can't. Mike, she is trying to get the administration to tell the truth about this war.

"I don't like the way she came across."

There are two sides. This isn't the time to talk about this. But I have hesitated to get involved until you come home.

"Saying Bush killed her son. Her son, like I did chose to sign up. We volunteered. For all the screwy politics that happen doesn't matter. We do as we are told. That is what we wanted to do."

Yes. She is a very sad and angry mom.

"I know."

But Mike, you didn't join to fight in Iraq. You joined to become a Marine, go through college and learn to fly. Become a commissioned officer. Yes. You are a hero because you gave it all up, because you are a Marine following orders. You don't decide wars. You fight them as you are told.

"I wasn't really a Marine though until I came here. Now I really am. We're compared here to men in Iwo Jima. We'll we both know I'm impulsive. Plans change. I don't want to get a commission and fly. Okay. I'll call now."

We sign off and Mike calls to finish our conversation. It goes like this...

"I joined to serve. To give back for the life that I have been given. For the life I have. For freedom. Like in all history even from the early settling we fought for freedom. Now at this time in history, this is where I have to be.

Strategy has to change. Can't just leave. We need to stay, secure and stabilize.

Our hands are tied here. It's stupid. Our escalation force has rules. If you do it wrong you can get NJP'd. Can't pull a trigger. If a car doesn't stop within fifty meters... and they come at you.... We have flash bags... like a pop can... not effective... flares are better. Then shoot at the ground... then grill.... then windshield. A woman was shot. Things happen.

We had two suicide vehicles with IEDs in Hit.

Never allowed to have a civilian or an Iraqi detainee open a bag or package on the road. You must do it or you are violating their rights and can get NJP'd (Non-Judicial Punishment).

Staying the course... hands are tied... strict rules.... Can't defend ourselves."

I only summarize the phone conversation because I am trying hard to listen and write as much as I can. I hear the Marine speaking. But I also hear my son Michael speaking. It is a painful conversation for me because he is so vulnerable. He is so young and I am so ashamed of and disheartened by this war. I can't confuse him. Not now. He is not there for argument or discussion. He is there trying with all his might to be a Marine and to survive. How do I say to him I honor you and your Marine brothers but I think this war is dishonorable? How does that sound to a soldier, a soldier still on the battlefield? I need to voice some of this to him because I feel myself getting more drawn into action against the war. I want him to know. But I want him to see the separation of honoring the Marine at war while not honoring the war itself. Is this all too complex? He is just there to do his job. Do what he is told. I will wait to see him and talk with him when he is safe. For now he has to trust and believe in his leaders. However, I question. This is my job.

Whatever I do, whatever I say, Mike shows nothing but respect for me. One more clue to his character. I hope he realizes how much I respect him.

The next day I email Mike.

Hey Mike,

It was good to talk to you yesterday. We will be going to the Family Day meeting in Columbus. We hope to hear about your homecoming. When? Etc. We know it will be a HERO'S WELCOME. We are all so proud of Lima 3/25th.

I talked to Augie Schroeder's mother last night. She was also called by CNN and encouraged me to do the interview. In the interview what she says will honor her son and all of 3/25th. She says to tell you that they are praying for the safe return of all of 3/25th.

Have you heard about the picture of the two Iwo Jima Marines holding up an Ohio flag? Yeah! You are compared to the Iwo Jima Marines.

I liked what you said about being a Marine now. You surely are a Marine and, Mike you are more than a Marine. Someday you will know that. No doubt! You have grown as you have experienced things most people never will.

You are special. How did we get such a wonderful guy? Love you,

Mom

CHAPTER 38

Mama Bear Meets Papa Bear

I correspond with Cameo George, from CNN, about the interview she wanted with me. She asks for a copy of the essay that I wrote, *How Does It Feel?*

Thank you so much for taking the time to write to me. I was very moved by your words and can't imagine what it must feel like to be in your shoes. Would you be willing to talk to me some more on the phone and possibly in person? I think you have a powerful point of view that needs to be heard by the public.

If you are willing, please send me your phone number so I can call you. You can also feel free to call me. . . . . .

I'd love to talk to you as soon as possible.

Sincerely, Cameo George (CNN Presents)

I got another email from Cameo after she had done some research.

Peggy, I was just doing more background research and I was searching the internet and some news sites for more stories on Lima

Company and I came across the website http://www.mikelogue. com.

Did you set that up for your son? It's fantastic! (Cameo)

Cameo, to answer about the web site, Mike's cousin, Darren, did the web site.

I just had a long conversation with Mike. It is midnight there. I told Mike about the possible interview. He had to sign off and then signed on again... more conversation... then he called me... more conversation.

I want to think through what he said to me. How he feels and what he thinks. I'll share this with his Dad and with Rosemary in Cleveland. Then get back to you.

I assure you... after Mike is home... and he understands what is going on... I will have more to say. Thanks (Peggy)

Peggy, I'm really happy to hear that you were able to speak to your son – that sounds like a welcome, unexpected surprise!

I want to offer up one last option before you make your decision. We don't have to use your last name or your son's name if it would help.

Either way though, even if you decide not to participate, our phone conversation was very helpful to me and I hope you know that I will understand and respect your decision.

Call me or email me when you get a chance. (Cameo)

Then I write to Rosemary hoping she can help me sort this out.

Rosemary, my thinking about the interview with CNN is to postpone until the boys are home. I feel like I have to be guarded not to appear to be unpatriotic or not supporting my son. I would not want him to hear anyone say that about me, certainly not while he is still there risking his life.

I also wonder if I would be more effective in what I say after the return.

What do you think? (Peggy)

Peggy, I think if you have ANY misgivings, you should wait.
You are a mom first and last.
Your friend, (Rosemary)
Rosemary sent me an article called, *An Open Letter to Cindy*
Sheehan From the Proud Father of a U.S. Marine, by Brantley
Smith, posted on August 17, 2005.

By your actions over the past two weeks it is clear that you
missed an important aspect of Civics 101: With rights come
responsibilities. You certainly have the right to voice your opinion
against the war in Iraq and the President's policies. You even have
the right to camp outside the President's home in Crawford and
demand he meet with you. Your status as a mother who has lost a
child in the war also gives your words and actions a credibility and
a larger audience than otherwise would be the case.

Now that your supporters have given you a broad forum from
which to be heard, making you a national figure, its time you
considered your responsibilities to all of us. I have a daughter set to
deploy to Fallujah in two weeks and I have a serious concern with
how your irresponsible and short sighted actions might impact her.
She is, after all, a volunteer, like your son, and she is going in harm's
way because she believes it is her responsibility to protect your rights
and freedoms.

Well meaning people like you always seem to forget the law
of unintended consequences and your vanity and arrogant self-
righteousness never bother to think through what it is you are trying
to do versus what you may actually accomplish. I am here to inform
you, Ma'am, that you will not change the policy of our government
by sitting outside Crawford making a spectacle of yourself in the
name of your rights to free speech; what you will do is provide more
propaganda for our enemies and cost the lives of even more brave
and selfless American warriors.

How long do you think it will be before you become a star on Al

Jazeera? For all I know, it may have already happened. One thing is certain, though, and that is that your actions and words will further embolden a ruthless and evil enemy and more American blood will be shed and some of it will be on your hands.

This article goes on and on about our responsibilities and that to end the war now would dishonor the sacrifice of "all of our fellow countrymen who have died in the cause of fighting terrorism." He also tells her she is "aiding and abetting an enemy."...*Ma'am, you have joined forces with an evil you neither understand nor apparently have tried to comprehend...instead of honoring your son's sacrifice you are inspired to comfort an evil enemy....*

Your son died in the service of freedom and my daughter will go in harm's way to protect and preserve it. Honor their sacrifice, Ma'am, by exercising it responsibly...

I will pray with you and I will grieve with you but I will not stand by silent while you needlessly and arrogantly endanger the life of my daughter and her comrades in arms. Please bless us with your silence and go home.

Brantley Smith
Proud father of a United States Marine
Tullahoma, TN

This letter is posted on <u>ohiomarinefamilies@yahoogroups.com</u>. I am taken back by the anger. It is this thinking that pervades our Nation. A tone set by our leaders. It is for this reason those of us who are against the war and have one serving "hold our tongue." This thinking keeps anti-war protestors quiet.

I read the article again and try to understand the feelings the father is demonstrating. I begin to feel compassion for this father. He is as desperate for his child as I am for mine. I realize this man is anticipating the deployment of his daughter and he is doing all he knows to keep her safe. He lashes out. There isn't so much difference between this father and me. He is papa bear.

Back to CNN.

Cameo, I wish this was easy !!! The hesitation I feel is for a reason that I must pay attention to. I have something to say and that makes it hard to turn down. But I think there will be a better time.

I don't want to take the risk to give my son or any of the troops the impression that I am not patriotic or that I don't support him or them. As long as he is in harm's way, I will wait for a more appropriate time to speak out.

There are many mothers who want to speak out.

I hope you will give us an opportunity to tell the story of 3/25th Lima Company Marines when they return.

Thank you for reaching out. Thank you for attempting to cover the deeper story. Thank you for helping to awaken the beautiful sleeping giant called America.

Peggy, I sensed your growing hesitation the second time we talked. So I can't say I am surprised. Although I am disappointed, I respect your decision. (I am also someone who tends to follow their gut.)

If at some other point down the line you decide you want a forum for your feelings, please let me know. I found you very compelling and I know others will too.

You and your family will be in my thoughts. I hope we will be able to speak again when your son returns home safely. Please stay in touch. (Cameo)

CHAPTER 39

Thou Shall Not Kill

I don't sleep through the night. I awake at three or four and lie there hoping to go back to sleep. I try to keep my mind quiet and not start thinking about Mike, where he might be. What he might be doing. Wondering if he is safe, or on patrol or on a mission. Wondering too how he feels. Is he scared?

Thoughts bombard my head and soon I get up thinking if I get to the computer, maybe he'll be there. I check my buddy list. Nope. He isn't there. Maybe he'll get on after his lunch. Wow! How out of touch that thought must be. I know most days they simply swallow MRE's (Meals Ready to Eat) quickly and keep focus on whatever they have to do. I go to all my web sites that have anything to do with the war and the Marines. Still he is not here.

I open a blank page and start to write. But keep AOL (America On-Line) open and will hear a sound if Mike should get on.

What should I write? Haven't I vented enough? Is there more to say? Is there more to feel that I haven't already felt and said about the war? About Mike being there? A friend told me not to let this consume my life. Well, I think it has and I really don't know how to stop that. While Mike is in such near and present danger, I don't know how to relax, to be normal. How do you do that? Before all of the losses followed by the funerals I thought I did fairly well.

But the deaths… and then the viewings, the burials… the grief, the pain. What do I do with all of that? The reality of war in all its ugliness takes me on a path of utter confusion and inadequacy. How did I get here?

Mike signed up to become a Marine never considering, I don't think, and I know we didn't, that he would be off fighting a war nine months out of high school. I didn't have any experience with the military and I trusted these uniformed men when they told me Mike's goals would be met.

War was not in Mike's plan. He was, for God's sake, seventeen years old. He had college on his mind. The recruiter told him he could live his dream and would receive many benefits in becoming a Marine.

Mike saw his dream crashing when he realized he couldn't complete the first quarter at Ohio University. He was ordered from one training to another. Finally he had to drop out of college. But he followed orders. He readied himself to do the job as a Marine.

I no longer can say we will send our children to war so we can be free. It is easy to say that and feel comfortable with that as long as it isn't my own child. No… I can't send my son to die so I can live free. How can I do that? Oh yes! I have said that before when I was sending someone else's child to carry a rifle. I feel now that we under value our young and give them away cheaply. And I feel I must work to stop this craziness. There are other ways to better mankind. War is not a good way. No one benefits.

Americans seem oblivious to the reality of this war. There are no draped coffins on the news. We are sheltered from the pain and the loss, and we are distracted by valuing news programs that talk of celebrity divorces and pleasurable romances.

It seems sick and petty.

But the good is there and it will rise. We need only wake up. I hope we wake up before we have created more enemies than we can stand off.

I think of the Ten Commandments that many want to place on our public buildings to show our commitment to a Christian way of life. How ridiculous we are. We want to see the words and yet we violate them brazenly. Three Commandments come to mind when I think of this war and our place in the world. "Thou shall not kill," "Thou shall not steal," and "Thou shall not covet thy neighbor's goods."

If we read them for their meaning, we might not want them placed where they can be seen and we can be held accountable.

These are my thoughts this night as I am awake and wait and hope that that sound telling me Mike is on the computer will soon ring.

CHAPTER 40

"Pissing in the Wind"

Through my continued search for media coverage about the voices that are speaking out against the war I review again information about the movement called, "Bring Them Home Now." This is a group of groups, Veterans for Peace, Military Families Speak Out, Gold Star Families for Peace. Iraqi Veterans Against the War, and others. They support the work of Cindy Sheehan and are going to lead a tour from Camp Casey in Crawford, Texas to Washington D.C. for the September anti-war march.

There are three tour groups covering much of the U.S. I see that one of the tour groups will be coming through Ohio.

At the same time I am aware that a bus from Cincinnati is going to the anti-war March in Washington. It is being organized by a person named Kristen from the Inter-community Justice and Peace Center in Cincinnati. I am anxious to become part of a group that is doing something to bring my son home.

I send a note to Kristen.

Kristen, I am a mother of a 3/25th Lima Company Marine stationed in Iraq. My son is part of the Unit that has twenty-three Marines KIA, and thirty-five plus WIA. Fourteen of his brothers have recently been buried. Another mother of a Marine and I want to travel with you to Washington for the march. I will call to make reservations.

My other interest with you is to see if there are any plans to join the "Bring Them Home Now Tour" of Camp Casey as it travels through Ohio on the way to D.C. I know they will be in Columbus September 7th to the 8th, and then Toledo September 8th and 9th and finally, Cleveland September 9th to the 11th.

It seems like a huge traveling support group would bring a clear message of the desire of many Americans to end this war.

Are you the person to talk to about this... or is there someone else? I'd appreciate a response.

Thank you, Peggy Logue (Proud Mother of Lance Corporal Michael J. Logue)

Peggy, thanks so much for writing. I have reserved spaces for you and am keeping your son, Lima Company, and all the families in my prayers. About Cindy, she will be coming here on November 5th as part of a teach-in we are organizing. I'm not sure if we'll be able to get on her truth tour before the big march, but I think we can look into it. There might be some possibility. I'd love to talk with you more. Feel free to call. Thanks!!! Peace. (Kristen)

I come across an article posted August 26, 2005 titled "Fighting unseen enemy creates psychological pressure on troops" by Tom Lasseter, Knight Ridder newspapers. Friday, August 26, 2005) *HIT, Iraq - The inability of U.S. forces to hold ground in Anbar province in western Iraq, and the cat and mouse chase that ensues, has put the Marines and soldiers there under intense physical and psychological pressure.*

The sun raises temperatures to 115 degrees most days, insurgents stage ambushes daily then melt into the civilian population and

American troops in Anbar find themselves in a house of mirrors in which they don't speak the language and can't tell friend from foe....

Officers worry about the enemy while trying to make sure their men don't crack under the pressure.

"I tell the guys not to lose their humanity over here, because it's easy to do," said Marine Captain James Haunty, 27, of Columbus, Ohio.

Asked for an example of the kind of pressure that could cause Marines to crack, Haunty talked about the results of a car bomb: "I've picked up pieces of a friend, a Marine. I don't ever want to see that s___ again."

The article describes an incident where a Marine Major receives a call from a patrol asking permission to kill an Iraqi. The man is out past curfew and appears to be talking on a cell phone. The Major orders the men not to shoot before getting a "f------- security check." They are constantly trying to discern the enemy from the innocent civilian. And have no way of telling who is who.

The article goes on about Marine Lt. Col. Jim Halderman who meets with local tribal sheiks in Fallujah.

The gathering was supposed to be an exercise in civic empowerment but quickly degenerated into the Iraqis demanding that they get identification cards designating them as sheiks, which would bar local security forces from arresting them on the streets.

"All of these guys are f_____ muj," Halderman said, using the Arabic term for "holy warriors," mujahedeen, which American troops frequently use to describe the insurgents.

"I've never been so nervous around a group of men," he said... he added that he was sure that a lot of the men in the crowd would have slit his throat if they'd had the opportunity.

Reading these articles I can't imagine what this must be like for our Marines and soldiers. How do they maintain respect for others and know they may be hood-winked. How do they know the difference between the bad guy and the good guy?

This is the daily drag of this war. So I wonder what Mike sees and thinks about this. How I wish I could talk to him.

The article continues:

Walking down an alley in Hit a few days earlier, stepping over pools of sewage, Lance Corporal Greg Allen had watched the Marines around him. They were picking through garbage, tugging on wires and kicking boxes, looking for bombs and mines and hoping that if they found one it wouldn't go off.

"They (insurgents) are doing a hell of a job fighting this war. They know they can't take us head on but they can do a lot of damage with bombs," said Allen, 19, of Syracuse, N.Y. "there's no one out here to fight."

I read about Sgt.1st Class Tom Coffey, 37, of Burlington, Vt. He had gone back to his base to pick up supplies when he got a call that a roadside bomb had hit one of his Bradley Fighting Vehicles.

A description of a vehicle possibly driven by the triggerman came over the radio. "The guy's already gone," Coffey said. "We're just p----ing in the wind now."

Later, he and his men walked along the Euphrates River, looking for a metal stake that an informant said marked a weapons cache. The sun burned, and palm trees and crops formed a lush green swath along the riverbank.

"There's been reports of a .50(caliber) sniper rifle out there. Maybe they called this in just to get us out here and take a shot. A .50-cal would go straight through our (body armor) plates," Coffey said, looking at the buildings across the river. "Why do I feel like I'm in a f-------Vietnam movie?"

And we wonder why so many of our men and women are returning with post traumatic stress disorder. More personally I wonder about Mike. There is the constant fear for his physical safety but there is more to be concerned about. And that finds a nest inside me and will wait for birth when he returns.

Now I can only deal with the immediate moments. Watching the news. Watching www.icasualities.com. Watching and waiting for the word that they are finished. Waiting to hear from Mike. Waiting for the comfort to know that he is at the base and not on a patrol and that he has survived another day.

Hi Hon,

We are so excited about you coming home. We got a note from the volunteer coordinator tonight telling us that they have moved up the official welcoming in Columbus to October 22nd. You will be home before that but this will be the big parade.

Question??? When you come home the first time, to Columbus, who in the family do you want to be there? They are not allowing the public in at that time. You will get to see others after that. Just family will be there when you first arrive. Then we will come home and have fajitas and marguerites!!!

I am not going to do the interview with CNN. I want to talk to you face to face first.

Another thing we learned. You will not be remobilized in two years, unless some global disaster comes up.

I asked Sgt. Halbig if you could consider continuing your college education. He said absolutely. You will begin drill again in March, 2006. But nothing is definite there. So... some good news!!!!

Love you. Mom

"Hey, when you talked to him did you tell him I was staying active duty? How's the family doing? Any plans for a trip to the Boundary Waters next year? The summer might be a good time after I see the scheduling for drills because I can't really get off of drill for something like that.

I am alright. I have a day off and tomorrow we're on duty so that means working parties (they are not fun) and mess duty for some unlucky people hopefully not me.

Ok Love you."

CHAPTER 41

Mixing Oil and Blood

August 28, there is nothing special happening this day, so why am I having a melt down? The adrenaline is pumped with thoughts of our boys coming home. And still I hold fear for them. It happens sometimes that one is killed just days before they are to come home.

Trice got an email from Kevin telling her that they are just doing three hour patrols and assures her not to worry. "Yeah right," she says.

The next day I send a message to Trice telling her about my bad day. I know she will understand.

Hi Friend, just want to tell you I had a hard day yesterday. Don't know why. I was weepy. Is it Post Traumatic Stress? Just longing to have Mike home, and still so worried.

I decided to send my journal notes, "How Does It Feel?" to my list. Guess I want family and friends to know that war is not fun and there is so much grief. And I want people to question what we are doing while these young are there dying.

I made reservations for us for the bus trip to D.C.

Up again at 4:30am and on the computer. Mike popped up. Says he was off yesterday. Off today. He assures me that they are fine. And he says, "perfectly safe." Maybe today will be a better day. But I think I need a vacation!!!

The journal entry that I sent to my list is the reflection I wrote answering the journalists who asked that question "How does it feel?" many times at the funerals. I get many responses.

Peggy and Jerry,

You are angels. You are heaven sent. You are there for us and you are there for everyone and you are there for the Marines. You are there for your son. We feel very thankful and blessed to know you. Thank you for that.

Sharon and Mike (father and step mother of a 3/25th Marine).

What a powerful writer you are. Probably powerful because it is the heart speaking. (friend)

I can only imagine how heartbreaking all this must be, and yet, a number of Marine moms seem to feel that staying the course is the only way to protect those who serve presently. I don't want to put Mike in more danger by allowing the insurgents to think that our will to remain is weakening; however, I do feel as if the tough questions need to be asked and answered. I struggle with possible solutions, and yet, I do think more diplomatic, people to people efforts will do more to quell both the insurgency and terrorists forever and bring the one world philosophy to reality. (friend)

I respond to this friend:

Dear Friend, I don't know how you feel about the war. But if it is an unjust and illegal war of occupation like I believe it is and there is plenty of proof for that, then staying the course will not protect our men. It will continue to kill them. The insurgents are there because we are there.

If we stay the course... in Mike's words, "We need to change strategy... to do that we need more men." So where will we get more men? Recruiters are having a hard time now. Can't meet their quotas. There is always the draft. Hold on to your boys!

Just a brief response to a very difficult situation. (Peggy)

And she responds:

Peggy, I watched the CNN special that you mentioned earlier. Certainly this war is based upon shaky grounds, and in retrospect, many now agree with those of us who were skeptical at the time of the Baghdad invasion; however, I think those who made the decision heard what they wanted to hear so as to justify their decisions!

Believe me, I have thought of my own boys throughout all of this, and my heart breaks to think of Mike stationed there. I just want to do whatever it takes to get the U.S. troops home safely. (friend)

Peggy, I am so sorry. I send you a very tight hug and lots of prayers. I hope you have your son in your arms very soon. Love (sister-in-law)

Peg, you know the suffering of mothers from the beginning. (friend)

Peggy, You have become a voice of the Marine family, of a mother of a Marine. Keep sharing your convictions, heart and soul. You need to send this to the media outlets. Let me know if you need their emails, fax numbers, contact people. With love, Jan (friend, co-worker)

My heart bleeds tears of grief for you. Frankly I think you should forward your letter of grief to your senators and the President of the United States. I intend to.

Love you. (former sister-in-law)

I receive a lengthy letter from my brother Tim who lost his five year-old son from complications of cancer treatments almost twenty years ago. I know he still carries that pain. But his letter is warm and compassionate and very real.

Dear Peg and Jerry,

I'm not sure if this will be of any help to you or not. Your email of "How Does It Feel" is reminiscent of our nine months with Timmy at Children's Hospital. The one major thing we learned from that experience is that we, as human beings, have no control of this life. That runs completely against everything we do as humans. We like to think we have control, but we really don't. We go through all the motions but it is futile. That can be extremely scary and unnerving but it is fact.

The scenes in your mind/dreams are similar to my scenes of seeing Timmy's obituary in the newspaper. Clear as day. How many times did I wonder, why is this happening? Why does a four -year- old have to endure this?

What got us through? Faith. People. People praying for us and Timmy. Realizing, as ugly as it was, God had some plan, and it went accordingly. We didn't like it. We really didn't like it.

So continue to pray for Mike, his safety and well being and that of his friends and comrades.

During our stint at Children's we always felt, really felt the prayers of people we did not even know. When we couldn't pray we knew others were praying for us. Take some comfort in knowing that Mike is being cared for in ways you may never know.

I hope this has been some help.

Love. (Tim)

Tim, how beautifully you wrote from your heart and we are thankful. I admire how you have lived through these years and I know your deep love for Timmy. Certainly I cannot think of a greater loss or a deeper pain than to lose a child. Tim, thank you for your heartfelt words and your compassion.

Love. (Peggy and Jerry)

The following response I received from a new friend I am beginning to connect with but have yet to meet in person.

Dear Peggy,

I do understand. I too have felt the nausea and panic that makes me rush to the bathroom with the runs and the waking up at night. The continuous awareness of this horror and the danger your son is in, more than mine, though as we said on the phone, who can calculate or compare the sufferings of each mother or father or family.

I am attaching a piece that David wrote two weeks ago and the correspondence from myself and Terry, my husband, back to him and then a short note from David responding to that. This is our journey. Please feel free to share this in private circles if it might be of help in any way. And I want you to know that I go to a shrine by myself and sometimes with my family where I light candles for your son Mike and those that died and all the Iraqis who died as well. And, that our sons may come home safe in body and mind.

I was really glad to talk with you tonight. It was comforting to share with someone who is in the midst of this as I am.

Hopefully we will get to meet in person soon. For now I reach out and hold you in my heart and mind and remember Mike and his buddies each day in my meditation. With compassion, Jody (mother of David, Army Doctor serving 2nd tour).

This is David's piece.

Iraq 2005
Recon teams humvee takes a hit and rolls.
Confusion, fear, dust, heat.
Strangling liquid cries.
"Why is it so dark in here doc?"
"What happened? Someone tell me what happened"
"My eyes! What's happened to my eyes?"
"What do we do with his arm? They can sew it back on right now right?"
Hot sweet slaughterhouse smell.
"Someone tell me what happened!"
Dancing and flowing through the precise moments
Of the work. The Calvary stations of my craft.

"Oh no you don't!"
"You are NOT dying here!"
Not in MY ER!"

217

At the LZ someone forgot to secure the long white sheet of exam
table paper hanging from the end of
    One of the stretchers and in the fierce prop wash
    From the Blackhawk it tears loose and rises and
    Hangs in the air in two startling calligraphic
    Curves against the shimmering amber sky.

    Back at the barracks I sit and lean against the wall
    And slowly peal and eat a perfectly ripe mango,
    Listening to the air conditioner hum, at rest.
    And it would be impossible to describe, at this
    Moment just what I feel.
    I think there is no word for it.

    Outside the camp darkness, I hear a quiet conversation,
    Gentle laughter.
    My boots and socks thrown in the corner
    Are soaked through with blood.

Jody's and Terry's response to their son follows.

    My dearest son, what can I say to this either, it is strange I have
injured myself twice today and am reflecting on the taste of blood as
well as I licked the small wound on my wrist and pressed it to stop
bleeding. We were getting the air conditioner from your locker and
the tailgate banged down on my wrist. And then, carrying bags
of groceries in I fell and a bottle of oil broke and exploded all over
the floor between the living room and the dining room and now
I'm bleeding from my right arm but trying to save the rug, calmly
calling for papa to help me with the mess.

    I thought of you all the time and wondered if you were in the
ER yet...

    What can I say? I say I am glad you wrote. Can you let tears
come?

    I stripped off my clothes soaked with oil and blood and threw them in the garbage with the oil soaked towels and cloths. Thinking, I'll clean them up later and can salvage the shoes.

I said to papa, what I should do is put on a pair of Dave's black army socks that I just put away downstairs last night and walk and walk over this floor to soak up the rest of the oil. I thought of true disasters, oil spills, war...

Then your email with this.

Yes, the Calvary station is there. You knew it would be like this, but I'm sure remembering or imaging is nothing like being in it now. How many of our forces died in this? I will light candles for all of them at the shrine and the injured too.

Shiva, Lord of the Dance of life and death. Tara, Kuan Yin, Mother of Compassion be with them and you.

And I and we are with you. Every step of the way.

With all my compassion and love. (Mama)

David,

I wept when I read your email.

Can one, in a weeping, weep for more than one reason?

I wept with grief for the bright life snuffed out, the eyes blinded, the fine young body maimed, the families bereft. I wept with rage for the cynical political caste that set in motion these events, with no apparent justification than their own greed and hubris. I wept with frustration for the blind, bloated, callow nation that put that cynical political caste into power. And I wept with pride for your own brave service to the victims of this tragic misadventure.

You are a servant of life. As such, it's your duty to stay clear and focused, never to be deceived by the machinations of those in whose interest it is to deceive the many, but rather to see everything with the eyes of critical compassion.

Is your email a statement that can be shared with others? If it is, should it be shared with a limited circle or with the public?

Stay safe as you can while serving life. We want you back with us.

Love. (Papa)

David's response back to his parents.

All will be well

And all will be well

And all will be well.

If you would like to share my ramblings widely or otherwise please do. Unfortunately I think most people won't have much of a taste for them. Hope you are well. Is mother much banged up? Is she OK? Please give my best to everyone.

Love. (David)

I sit with this piece for awhile. It is piercing to my soul. Anger, frustration, and compassion have nested in there. Too many emotions in one place. This horrible war. As if war itself isn't horrible enough. This horrible war has no good reason. So the anger. This horrible war has no answer and no end. So the frustration. This horrible war hurts so many. That toll isn't calculated because the hurt from this war will go forward to the next generations. It isn't just the obvious victims that are hurting now. I am beginning to realize it is a wound to the American spirit, our values, our virtue, our Nation's soul that is going to extol a price in the future.

I respond to Jody.

Powerful! I will share David's piece with my list. People have to communally witness the truth of war. Sharing our stories helps them see.

Whether there is agreement about the intent of the war or not. Pain is universal.

Hope to see you soon.

I meet with Jody and we begin a relationship of mutual care and respect. She is a counselor and later meets with us as family to help us reclaim normalcy.

I tell Jody about the request of CNN for an interview and she is able and willing to do it.

Chapter 42

Staying Active?

Early morning on the computer checking all the ritual web sites I get that ding that tells me Mike is signing on. He begins.

"Are you up?"
Yeah. Seem to wake up at 4:00am each day and start thinking about you.
"Oh!"
What are you doing?
"It's my day off. I just sent you an email".
I was just on your web site and checking out Lima 3/25th Marines.
"Yeah."
What did you do yesterday? Were you on watch? Did you go somewhere?
"No. I had the day off. Well we were actually on duty."
Doing what?

"Nothing."

I'm not following. What you did. Just off?

"Nothing. We didn't do anything."

Are you just not telling me? Or did you really not do anything?

"We really did nothing."

Okay… and you are off today too? This makes me happy.

"Yes."

I can't seem to stop worrying. Just want to get you home safe. It makes my day, just talking to you. Guess I was a little teary yesterday and I was afraid you were out somewhere.

"Well, I was here. All I did was work out at night."

Crista called and I started crying. She said, "Is your husband there?" I said "no." She said, "Get out of the house. Take Snoopy for a walk."

"Oh Mom!!!"

Then she called back today and asked me what I was doing. She said, "Do you want to go for a bike ride?" So today she is rescuing me and taking me on a bike ride.

"Don't worry so much. I'm coming home soon."

I'll be alright. I'm just having some post traumatic stress!!!

"Okay. But I'll be home soon and completely safe."

It seems like we haven't seen you for over a year.

"I know."

Have you heard about the hurricane that hit the Gulf Coast?

"Just read a headline."

Millions of people have evacuated New Orleans and Mississippi.

"Wow!"

Yeah. There are 25,000 people holed up in the Super Dome.

"Wow!"

Dad really wants to be in a warm sunny climate for winter. I'm not sure I want to be gone that long.

"You two will have fun. You can get him outside more. He can't use the cold weather as an excuse.

How's my truck?"
Great. Dad uses it to go to work.
"How's gas prices?"
About $2.70 a gallon but will go up today because of the hurricane.
"I'm kind of looking at motor cycles, but not too serious. Well my time limit. I have to go."
Okay. Love you.
"Love you, Mom. I'm alright."
Bye. You made my day.

As I have done each time we instant message, I printed a copy of it and re-read our conversation. I can feel my stress when pumping him about what he has been doing. I realize my imagination gets away from me. I am so fearful for him. I expect he is out there on these foot patrols or searching through garbage looking for bombs or in a convoy watching for explosives.

I went to my email and found his message to me and responded.

Mike, I didn't know you wanted to stay active so I didn't say anything to Sgt. Halbig. JUST DO NOT UP OUT FOR ANOTHER TOUR!!!! THAT IS AN ORDER FROM FIRST SGT. MOM!!!

You probably know better than we how to stay active, who to talk to. We haven't and won't say anything unless you want us to.

We are planning Boundary Waters next summer. Have to refine a plan when you and brother John are home. John can get our permit in January.

Great talking with you. I feel better today.

Love you. Miss you. (Mom)

"Hey, I want to figure out something. I'm thinking about staying on orders because it would only be like twenty-eight days of work in three months, because of weekends off and my accumulated

leave. And I want to find out about the G.I. Bill. At ninety or more days the pay raises to $400 a month. But at a year it goes to $600 a month. I was on Orders to make the deployment Nov. 30 to Jan 28th. Then taken off process. Then new Orders in which time I was at the drill center most days anyway. And on Orders on Feb 4th to Iraq until Jan 6, 2006. So, I'm screwed if it's cut and dry. I want to know if they can do anything for me or not because in my heart I deserve the full year benefit.

Love you."

This is very confusing. But what Mike is trying to say and figure out is whether it will be acknowledged that he did a full year and is eligible for the upgrade for benefits for college. No question, he did a full year but he was taken off the process for about a month when he attempted to attend college and was not supposed to go to Iraq. But he was back in process and adding up his time served it would be a full year. There are many rules for getting help after you return as a veteran. You would think their service would be rewarded with adequate help. Americans are out of the loop and would be as surprised as we are about how hard it is for veterans to get help.

I did not say anything to Sgt. Halbig about Mike wanting to stay active. This is a delaying action. I am not ready to speak out for that. It seems better to wait until he is home and has time to think it through. Then he can take appropriate steps. I certainly do not want to have any part in the possibility that he may be returned to Iraq.

CHAPTER 43

The Long Journey Home

My August journal ends with quotations from several articles that make their way onto my computer and into my head. These are posted the last few days in August. This is what Americans can read or ignore. I read in desperation. This month can't end soon enough.

The Vietnamization of Bush's Vacation by Frank Rich, (The New York Times, August 28, 2005)

Another week in Iraq, another light at the end of the tunnel. On Monday President Bush saluted the Iraqis for "completing work on a democratic constitution" even as the process was breaking down yet again. But was anyone listening to his latest premature celebration?

We have long since lost count of all the historic turning points and fast-evaporating victories hyped by this president. The toppling of Saddam's statue, "Mission Accomplished," the transfer of sovereignty and the purple fingers all blur into a hallucinatory loop of delusion…

In the wake of Ms. Sheehan's protest, the facts on the ground in America have changed almost everywhere. The President, for one, has been forced to make what for him is the ultimate sacrifice: jettisoning chunks of vacation to defend the war in any bunker he can find in Utah or Idaho…

It isn't just Mr. Bush who is in a tight corner now. Ms. Sheehan's protest was the catalyst for a new national argument about the war that managed to expose both the intellectual bankruptcy of its remaining supporters on the right and the utter bankruptcy of the Democrats who had rubber-stamped this misadventure in the first place.

Mr. Rich quotes the president saying that the best way to honor the dead would be to "finish the task they gave their lives for" and "as the Iraqis stand up, we will stand down." While Democrats offered no alternative two Republicans, Chuck Hagel and Henry Kissinger speak out.

For his part, Mr. Hagel backed up his assertion that we are bogged down in a new Vietnam with an irrefutable litany of failure: "more dead, more wounded, less electricity in Iraq, less oil being pumped in Iraq, more insurgency attacks, more insurgents coming across the border, more corruption in the government." Mr. Kissinger no doubt counts himself a firm supporter of Mr. Bush, but in the Washington Post this month, he drew a damning lesson from Vietnam: "Military success is difficult to sustain unless buttressed by domestic support." Anyone who can read the polls knows that support is gone and is not coming back. The president's approval rating dropped to 36 percent in one survey last week.

What's left is the option stated bluntly by Mr. Hagel: "We should start figuring out how we get out of there."

Think about this. Your son is over there. Already twenty-three of his brothers have been buried and there is this discussion going on now. I want to scream. And John McCain wants to send more troop over to secure the country. Where will they come from? The article closes with this statement: *In yet another echo of Vietnam, it's millions of voters beyond the capital who will force the timetable for our inexorable exit from Iraq."*

Several other articles site the fact that Democrats have done nothing but stand by and watch Bush continue this unprovoked war. As Helen Thomas states in her article *"Democrats Still Backing Senseless War," The Seattle Post-Intelligencer Tuesday, August 30, 2005.*

Are the Democratic leaders afraid to admit they were wrong? Does the credibility of the administration - and therefore, the country - mean anything to them? ... The fall back position apparently runs like this: "We're there and we have to stay there now. We can't cut and run."...Bush told the Veterans of Foreign War the United States will accept nothing less than "total victory over the terrorists and their hateful ideology"

His argument is that anti-war protestors who want the troops brought home quickly "are advocating a policy that would weaken the United States."

Bush himself acknowledged there were no ties between the deposed dictator Saddam Hussein and the 9/11 attacks. The 9/11 commission concluded that there was no evidence of "a collaborative operational relationship," between Saddam and Osama bin Laden's al-Qaida terrorist network.

Yet another article, *"Fighting in Iraq's Anbar Province"* by Tom Lasseter tells how "Insurgents have changed U.S. ideas about winning." (August 28, 2005)

Fallujah, Iraq. Insurgents in Anbar province, the center of guerrilla resistance in Iraq, are fighting the U.S. military to a standstill.

After repeated major offensives in Fallujah and Ramadi, and after the loss of hundreds of soldiers and Marines in Anbar during the last two years - including 75 since June 1 - many U.S. officers and enlisted men have stopped talking about winning a military victory in Iraq's Sunni Muslim heartland.

Instead, they are trying to hold on to a handful of population centers and hit smaller towns in a series of quick-strike operations designed to disrupt insurgent activities...

"I don't think of this in terms of winning," said Col. Stephen Davis, who commands a task force of about 5000 Marines in an area of 24,000 square miles in the western portion of Anbar...

Military officials offered three primary reasons that guerrilla fighters have held and gained ground: the enemies growing sophistication, insufficient numbers of U.S. troops, and lack of trained and reliable Iraqi security forces...

The insurgents have figured out by trial and error the different viewing ranges of the optics systems in American tanks, Bradley fighting vehicles and humvees.

"They've mapped it out. They go into the road and try to draw fire to see what our range is, and then they make a note of it and start putting IEDs that far out," said Army Maj. Jason Pelletier, 32, of the 28th Infantry Division, referring to improvised explosive devices, the military's term for homemade bombs.

I can't organize all of this in my head. It is very disturbing. Did we do our homework before the war? Maybe the press now will stir up others and they will also want our military to come home. But what about the KIA (killed in action)? Who is responsible? Who comforts the mothers?

Trice tells me of a project by one of the fathers to have a memorial and remembrance of our Marines at his church in conjunction with a remembrance of 9/11, tying the two together. She forwards the emails to me.

8/23: Trice I want to share something with you and as soon as I have confirmation, I will let everyone know. I spoke with Mike DeWine's secretary yesterday. If the Senator is available he is going to attend. Also I contacted Jean Schmidt's office. The same goes for her... I am also going to ask Senator DeWine to hand deliver a letter to the President. I am going to invite him to the homecoming. The reason is I felt several parents were upset over his apparent lack of sympathy when our Marines died in the explosion. I am going to suggest that he show up and thank our boys for their sacrifice. It may help to mend a few of the wounds. Don't know if it will happen, but all I can do is ask.

The thought of honoring our Marines in a ceremony involving 9/11 does not ring true to me or Trice. I do not want that apparent lie to be attached to my son's service in Iraq. There is so much hype around that event as a reason for this war. And then everyone later finds out the truth that Saddam had nothing to do with it. Perpetuating a lie and honoring our Marines. No! So, I decide that I will not be part of it. It sounds glamorous with huge pictures of our Marines plastered on the walls and stories of each. I want my son to be known and honored but not in conjunction with 9/11. It has its own terror and people to honor of their own. I do not want to be part of the politicizing of it. Hearing that some of us are not excited about it and even upset by it, Trice receives another email.

8/29: Trice, Hope the day finds you well. I just wanted to update you on the 9/11 service. I spoke with our pastor about the concerns of others. Although it is not a "9/11" service to honor the fallen of 9/11, there may be a mention or two of it. And I guess when you consider all that has taken place since that date, Iraq has ties to it. It is still a war on terrorism and 9/11 kicked it off. The one thing that rings true is that our Marines, Sailors, Army and Air Force personnel voluntarily joined the armed forces. And as much as I may agree or disagree with what has happened, the joining caused them to submit to the authority over them, which in this case is our government. They were asked to do a job and now they are doing it to the best of their abilities and some even beyond. And if we, as Americans or parents forget what they are doing and become disgruntled or develop an attitude of being against it, we have just undermined what they are doing and what they are standing up for. We would do them a disservice and I'm sure it could affect their outlook should they know that we were not behind them 100%.

I sincerely hope what I have said is not offensive in any way. Thank God we live in a country where we have the freedom to

229

express our views, say what we feel needs said, serve our God the way we want and be able to walk down our streets without fear of being blown up at any moment.

I personally speak to this gentleman at our Family Day in Columbus. I am sure when he speaks of some who may get "disgruntled" or "developing an attitude of being against it (the war)," I am included in that group. I am more than "disgruntled" and I am finding my voice. I muster up courage to face him and talk to him. I am aware of the strength of those who support the war and connect all the dots to 9/11 and have their churches and God on their side. I face him and tell him "NO, I will not be part of this. I do not want to honor my son in a way that connects him to a lie." We share a few thoughts and out of respect for each other because our boys are still there, we agree to let it go and let each find their own way. We think about the war differently, but our boys are both in harm's way. This is enough for us to allow each other the space we need.

I send a letter to Rosemary.

Rosemary, just checking in with you. How are you doing?

I had an interview with a Japanese reporter from New York yesterday. It is for a Japanese magazine registering a change of climate in the States about the war. Cancelled with CNN and asked my friend Jody to do it. But the reporter said she would like to hear from me when Mike is home.

We need to plan a strategy for Ohio Marine Moms to respond to the unpatriotic, non-supporting our sons accusations if we are against the war.

Also, I think we can lean on what some of the top military leaders are saying about not having enough troops to do a good and efficient job in Iraq. I want to have a good grasp on a credible stand when we speak.

Hope we can meet soon. (Peggy)

Peggy, I wonder if the Japanese reporter who spoke with you is the same one scheduled to talk to us on *Thursday? Guess if the media have us "leftie" military families in their sights, we get 'em all, right?*

The "We support our troops but send in more of them!" has been the mantra Paul and I have been chanting. Then, of course, they sent 1500 more and think that's enough. We're talking 100,000 more, at least. The problem is in Al Anbar Province where most of the Ohioans are.

I'm struggling with the Cindy problem because of all this. I'm concerned about how any links with her might sideline your and our more legitimate protests. We DO support our troops and want an end to the conflict that would be the best for the Iraqis and for the troops. Just walking away doesn't cut it.

The planned "drawdown" before elections next spring will only endanger the guys left behind.

When your son comes home, then we can hit the message from your end of the state. There are women in Columbus, too, who agree wholeheartedly, but their guys have to come home safely first, too.

I read a story last night that said that the mujahedeen are murdering anyone in Anbar Province who registers to vote. That would certainly make Ohio voter registration look simple by contrast. (Rosemary)

Rosemary, the Japanese interviewer is Takaaki Mizuno. He is the New York Bureau Chief for Asahi Shimbun.

I may not agree with everything Cindy Sheehan says, or how she says it, but she really has stirred the pot, which needs to be stirred. Through her other voices may be heard. So, for now she is the crack in the door.

Trice (another Marine mom) and I are planning to join the Camp Casey group as they travel through Ohio. Maybe we could meet when we get to Cleveland.

Did I tell you about the father of one of our Marines who is planning to honor the Marines on 9/11 at his church? He thinks it is great to do it on the anniversary of 9/11. You know the whole war on terror, axis of evil thing. I don't like the sound of it. They are using 11x14 pictures and bio's etc. It's hard not to honor my son publicly with his brothers but it feels like a sham to do it on that day and with that emphasis. I declined. He said there would be little mention of 9/11 but it would be patriotic babble. I told him I am not comfortable with it. Trice also declined. He sent her an email that upset her and she forwarded it to me. He told her he is asking Senator DeWine to hand deliver a letter inviting the President to the homecoming. I think I'll send a note to Isolde saying that Mr. Bush didn't have time to come to the funerals, why should he come here now?

I asked the Japanese reporter how the Japanese feel about Bush. They don't care for him.

Enough! (Peggy)

Rosemary extended an invitation for Trice and I to stay with her when we make the trip with the *Camp Casey Bring Them Home Now Tour* to Cleveland. I am glad to know that we will be meeting soon. Then she adds:

Thanks for the warning about the person wanting to invite Bush. I will also contact Isolde. Is the guy a father of a Lima Company Marine? Does he have the right to ask DeWine to issue the invitation? Should I write DeWine telling him we would invite massive pickets and protests if he has the temerity to ask that ___ to come to the homecoming party??? That's as strong as I can make my feelings known because I don't want the CIA to arrest me. However, just know that the above is as mild as I can be under the circumstances. Does this guy expect to use "the fallen" in his little display? Because if he does, tell him to leave our son out of it. (Rosemary)

It is now August 31. The last day of this very long and difficult month. I send a note to my list.

August 31, 2005: Thirty-one days to go.

Family and Friends,

We have had several conversations with Mike. He is looking forward to coming home. He misses Snoopy.

They will leave Iraq October 1st, give or take seven or so days. They will fly to Kuwait, be there for a few days, then to Camp LeJeune in North Carolina, for a week or so of debriefing.

They are doing vehicle check point patrols and patrols through the palm groves. He assures me he is "perfectly safe." Yeah! Tell a mother that!

As we have learned about the military… nothing is too definite until it actually happens. This could all change. But the word "homecoming" is sounding dear.

The long journey home is one for rejoicing.

Love Peace (Peggy & Jerry)

CHAPTER 44

"Wish I Could Help There"

A Can't-Do Government by Paul Krugman. (New York Times September 2, 2005)

Before 9/11 the Federal Emergency Management Agency listed three most likely catastrophic disasters facing America: a terrorist attack on New York, a major earthquake in San Francisco and a hurricane strike on New Orleans. "The New Orleans hurricane scenario," The Houston Chronicle wrote in December 2001, "may be the deadliest of all." It described a potential catastrophe very much like the one now happening.

So why were New Orleans and the nation so unprepared? After 9/11, hard questions were deferred in the name of national unity, then buried under a thick coat of whitewash. This time we need accountability.

First question: Why have aid and security taken so long to arrive? ...

Maybe administration officials believed that the National

Guard could keep order and deliver relief. But many members of the National Guard and much of its equipment- including high-water vehicles are in Iraq…

I don't think this is a simple tale of incompetence. The reason the military wasn't rushed in to help along the Gulf Coast is, I believe, the same reason nothing was done to stop looting after the fall of Baghdad. Flood control was neglected for the same reason our troops in Iraq didn't get adequate armor.

At a fundamental level, I'd argue, our current leaders just aren't serious about some essential functions of government. They like waging war, but they don't like providing security, rescuing those in need or spending on preventative measures. And they never, ever ask for shared sacrifice…

So America, once famous for its can-do attitude, now has a can't-do government that makes excuses instead of doing its job. And while it makes those excuses, Americans are dying.

Subject: Happy Labor Day, Friday, September 2nd, 2005
Dear Mr. Bush:

Any idea where all our helicopters are? It's Day 5 of Hurricane Katrina and thousands remain stranded in New Orleans and need to be airlifted. Where in earth could you have misplaced all our military choppers?…

Also, any idea where all our National Guard soldiers are? We could really use them right now for the type of thing they signed up to do like helping with national disasters. How come they weren't there to begin with? …

There will be those who try to politicize this tragedy and try to use it against you. Just have your people keep pointing that out. Respond to nothing. Even those pesky scientists who predicted this would happen because the water in the Gulf of Mexico is getting hotter and hotter making a storm like this inevitable. Ignore them and all their global warming Chicken Littles. …

No Mr. Bush, you just stay the course. It's not your fault that 30

per cent of New Orleans lives in poverty or that tens of thousands had no transportation to get out of town...
Michael Moore
A few words from our Marines about Katrina

"Hey, I'm back and I'm alright. Looks like the hurricane hit hard. I wish I could help there.
Well, I have about a month until I am home.
Love you. Talk to you later. Mike"

All, thought you'd like to read an email received from one of our Marines. (Isolde)

"Our trackers unit (the Marines who drive the AAVs that carry us around) is located in Gulfshores (or Gulfport, not sure which) Louisiana. A lot of the Marines, who we have all become very close with, have lost their homes and possibly families. Their town was 100% flooded. These Marines have been incredible with us. I could not imagine looking forward this long to going home just to realize with this short of time left that they don't have a home, or worse are missing people to come home to. Please keep these men in your prayers. When we lost 11 a month ago they lost 3 and the driver is supposedly in okay shape. They were there for us then, even though they had also suffered a great loss. Three Marines is a lot to them. Their unit is much smaller. I cannot stress enough how great these Marines have been to us. From bringing us water, to putting up with us, to listening to us during our mourning, to leveling houses with their MK19 and 50 cal machine guns before we had to enter them. I have no doubt that these men have saved my life many times. Next to my own platoon they are the closest Marines we have to us. Just please put them on prayer lists and keep them in your mind and heart as they go through these trying times ahead.

Thank you all. I love you all. (Bryan)

These men we send to war are caring generous people who always see a need and want to respond with help and support. How can we be anything but proud of them?

CHAPTER 45

Camp Casey Cincinnati

I receive an email from Military Families Speak Out (MFSO) of which I am now a member. It says the "Bring Them Home Now Tour" will be in Cincinnati September 7th. They request a press conference, a rally potluck or whatever would motivate people to contact congress and to go to the march in DC. The note comes from Beth Lerman (MFSO Dayton). She is asking for help to feed and house the participant speakers. This is the speaker list.

Vince George, MFSO.

Lietta Ruger of Bay Center, Washington, whose son-in-law and nephew serve in the 1st Armored Division of the U.S. Army and are currently in Germany. They have both served extended 15-month tours of duty in Iraq; they are both under stop-loss orders and due to redeploy to Iraq this fall.

Mona Parsons, MFSO, from Mt. Vernon, Ohio, Her son is currently in Iraq.

Bill Mitchell *of Atascadero, Ca, whose son Sgt. Michael Mitchell was killed in action in Sadr City, Iraq on April 4, 2004, along with Cindy Sheehan's son Spc. Casey Sheehan. Bill is a co-founder of Gold Star Families for Peace.*

Kallisa Stanley *of Kileen, Texas whose husband is in the Army and currently stationed at Ft. Hood. He served one year long tour of duty in Iraq and is scheduled to be redeployed to Iraq next year.*

Hart Viges *of Austin, Texas, who served in the 82nd Airborne Division and was deployed to Iraq from February, 2003 to January, 2004. After returning home, Hart applied for and was awarded Conscientious Objector status.*

Steve Fryburg *of Dayton, Ohio may be joining the tour in Ohio as a representative of Veterans for Peace and MFSO. His son was deployed to Iraq and has returned.*

I can't be more enamored and excited if I had been given a list of my most favorite people in the world and told they are all coming to my house. I write back to Beth offering my help and my home.

CHAPTER 46

Shaken Up a Little

September 7, 2005: Twenty-four days to go.

Family and Friends,
Yesterday the Cincinnati Reds honored the military and their families at a baseball game. We were at the Ball Park and were having a meal when we got a call from Trice. She received an email and read it to me. Trice was out of town but had computer and phone service. This is what the email said.
"All.
We found out today that my brother, PFC Seth Judy, and two other Marines were injured earlier today. All three are from weapons platoon. We know that they were hit with shrapnel and that they were flown to Al Asad. We also know that the injuries are not minor. They are potentially life-threatening injuries. Now we just wait. Please pray that they make it through."
Trice then said, "Seth's only (known) injury is to the left leg

but the chemical used in the bombs can cause suffocation days later. That is what happened to Doc Youngblood."

As you know, Mike is in weapons platoon.

Panic set in… again.

I called my friend and neighbor Shirley and asked her to get into our house and check to see if we had any phone messages. While she was doing that, we got another call telling us that Seth's mother had asked specifically if Mike Logue and Kevin Mullins were Okay. "Yes. They are fine."

A gust of air burst out of my lungs. I realize that as I let my guard down thinking they are not engaged in anything dangerous and are coming home… they are still in harm's way.

Mike called this morning. He told us about the incident. He was about seventy-five meters away. His roommate and buddy that took the shrapnel is okay and is in Germany for more surgery. The others injured are fine.

A suicide bomber tried to run his truck into their humvee. The Sgt. driving the humvee ran off the road to miss the hit, saving his life and the others. The suicide truck took five-hundred to six-hundred rounds but kept coming and then blew up as it rolled off the highway. Mike said there was such a huge blast that it blasted out the doors of the humvee and thus the injured men. There was so much dust no one could see right away what happened and they feared for their brothers. Such terror.

Mike said they will probably go out about two more times. Two more times too much for me. Then they will be flown or bussed to Al Asad where they will begin their trip home. This may happen in five or so days. Don't know how long they will be at Al Asad.

I asked him if he is anxious to come home. He said, "Yes! I can't wait." Then he said, "It's awesome to think that we will be leaving here in about a week…just not to have the stress… We don't realize the stress we have been under."

He talked about a politician from Ohio who came for a visit. He wanted to know how they all were. Mike says "they come in with huge amount of protection… black hawk helicopters etc. Then *the guy wants to know... 'Do you have your scopes? Well, yeah ... I paid $500 for a scope, and 'how's your boots?' Dude, it's a little late to ask."*

Peace. (Peggy and Jerry)

Trice forwards a note from Kevin to his family about this incident.

It's Kevin. Just thought I'd let you know I am alright. I don't know if you heard anything, but we are alright. No serious injuries occurred. It was a close call. We were all shaken up a little. Well, just thought I would let you know I am okay. Love you guys. (Kevin)

CHAPTER 47

"Thelma and Louise"

I am now part of the anti-war movement. I am to house ten of the "Bring Them Home Now Tour (BTHNT)" for their stay in Cincinnati and provide breakfast. I am excited. I have a hands-on work to do fulfilling my need to in some-way affect the ending of this war. I enlist other friends to help and set up a schedule of who is sleeping where and what food the host is bringing to the breakfast which will be at my house. Trice will take three of the speakers and bring fruit salad, juice and coffee. Shirley, my friend since Mike was a baby, will house two and bring egg casserole and cinnamon rolls. I will sleep three in my house and maybe two more will sleep in the RV(bus) that they travel in and will park in my driveway. I will provide eggs, pancakes and tea.

The tour bus arrives Wednesday September 7th and people start gathering at the Peace and Justice Center in Cincinnati to hear the presentations.

The meeting is inspiring. The speakers give their personal stories about how their lives have been affected by this war. They share their thoughts and feelings. Ending the war is their priority. The statement reads: *BRING THEM HOME NOW TOUR… From George Bush's door step to communities along the way, we demand that: Elected Representatives decide now to bring the troops home, we take care of them when they get here, we never again send our loved ones to war based on lies.*

The TOUR amplifies the voice of Gold Star families, who show the devastating human cost of this war; the voice of military families, for whom each and every day that this war continues brings the potential for the most devastating of consequences; and the voice of veterans, who can share the ground truth about war and the impact on those who were sent off to fight it.

Over the course of the TOUR, members of supporting organizations will reach out to military families, veterans and concerned citizens. The TOUR will spread the truth about the war in Iraq, mobilize people to Washington DC for September 24-26th and ask Congressional decision-makers the hard questions Cindy has asked President Bush and to learn what our elected representatives are dong to bring this war to an end.

I make this commitment to be involved now and consider some possible ramifications. The huge RV with anti-war/Bush signs painted all over it is to sit in my quiet very conservative neighborhood driveway. What will the neighbors think? That I am not patriotic? Don't support the troops? Dishonor my son? And then I remember that I must do this. I cannot hide from those who may accuse me of being unpatriotic and not supporting my son.

After the speeches in Cincinnati the speakers are directed to their evening locations. The RV arrives at my house. It fills my driveway. It is late at night so the neighbors won't see it until morning. Then they will see signs like "Crawford to Congress!" "Love the Warrior! Stop the War!" "For What Noble Cause?" And, "Birddawg Bush! You can't hide!"

In the morning we enjoy a wonderful breakfast on the back deck with the trees sheltering us. Several people come by to visit and ask questions of the Tour speakers. Then we pack up and begin the trip for the rest of the tour through Ohio.

The schedule for the stop in Columbus is handed out.

Military Families Speak Out, Gold Star Families for Peace, Veterans for Peace and Iraq Veterans Against the War:

To Speak in Columbus, Ohio,
Thursday, September 8, 2005

1:30   Tour arrives at the Ohio Statehouse

2:00   Rally and Press Conference on Statehouse Grounds, At Veterans Plaza, with tour members and Ohio military families (Trice and myself)

3:00   Delegations to Sen. DeWine and Sen. Voinovich's offices to deliver families' letters asking for the war to end and troops come home.

4:30   Senate Reaction/ Debriefing: Trinity Episcopal Church

6:30   Potluck Dinner with BTHN Tour participants, Columbus Mennonite Church

7:30   Program of Speakers, Presentations, Q&A

9:00   Outdoor Candlelight Vigil

Because our sons are currently in Iraq, and we are against the war, and are very passionate and are from Ohio Trice and I are asked to be speakers. We have already dubbed ourselves "Thelma and Louise." We are becoming dear friends both feeling a bit inadequate but very determined still to get our sons home safely. And here we are now on the road with an anti-war movement.

I will do anything to facilitate bringing our troops home so I agree to speak. Trice doesn't feel that she could keep composure and turns it over to me. I have already written some thoughts in my journals that I say I can read. I cannot imagine myself being able to just stand up and speak. I would do nothing but cry. So if they willingly accept that I read my words I am okay. "How Does It Feel" is one of the readings and the other is "I Can't Begin to Title This." They agree that it is appropriate to read my thoughts and so I do.

First we set up at the State Grounds in Columbus. Trice and I know that Mayor Coleman's son, J.D. Coleman is in the same Unit as our sons so we arrange to meet with him. He is proud to take us around town and introduces us to many people gathered throughout the city while they are doing a fund raiser for the Katrina victims. What we like most about meeting with him is that we know he is against the war. We cannot believe that we could be in such good company, a Mayor of a major city, capital of Ohio who is against the war and his son is in Iraq. He is very compassionate as he listens to Trice and me. We shed tears. He understands our fears. He lives them too.

We carry signs through town and meet a few people who think we are unpatriotic and they let us know that. But many people honk their horns in support.

Next we visit the offices of our state Senators. Wow! We are really getting into this. I am nervous because I feel so deeply and I know that my emotions sometimes get the best of me. I try not to cry.

We haul into Sen. DeWine's office. Of course the Senator doesn't have time to meet with us so he sends in his "Regional Director". For Senator DeWine it is Scott S. Corbitt. After he apologizes that Senator DeWine cannot meet with us in person he begins to repeat the company line. But wait a minute. This is not an easy silent group. The niceties aside, emotions begin to surface. We tell Scott about our sons and the experiences they are having with twenty-three of their men KIA and many injured. How sorry he is but the war must go on so that they "did not die in vain."

"How do we honor the dead by killing more?" we ask. Of course, decisions are made higher up. "But you are our representatives. We are asking you to tell our senator that we want our troops home and we want the war to end. That is what we want. You represent us. You must tell him how we feel. You work for us."

We quizzed him on reasons for the war, and conditions for the military like depleted uranium, not proper protective gear or equipment, etc. He stumbles on words trying to be present but he really isn't. He wants us to go away. He doesn't intend to give us a hearing, just pretense. As we walk by him on the way out the door I say to him, "You don't have to do this. You can look into your heart and listen to it. Truth be known you probably don't want another death either. Do what is right. Encourage the Senator to do the same. The people will follow and you will be honored." I don't know if he really heard me but he put his head down and shuffled papers.

Trice and I feel energized after this meeting. Several of the speakers have more experience at this since they have been on the road and have met with many senators and congressmen. They say they thought it went well. I am feeling empowered as a citizen. We just need to show up and keep showing up. It may annoy the staff. But they must at some point report to the Senators what they are facing. I can hear Scott telling Senator DeWine about the bunch who came in today!

Senator Voinovich's office is more of the same. We meet with the State Director, Beth Hansen. We feel stronger in our approach. This time we have with us a street person that we met as we walked through town with our signs, a veteran who is ill and homeless. We make them promise they will take care of him. We have them take his name and set up an appointment for medical help for him. I wonder if they ever really did anything for him.

On a lighter note, after leaving the Senators office we get stuck in an elevator. We call for help and finally the fire department is called in. We are able to get free before they bust the door down. Yes. The sirens are wailing and the firemen come in with hatchets and helmets. The whole works. What a scene.

Dinner is at a Mennonite Church. It is a huge selection of potluck from some very good cooks. I am asked to speak. I only know that I can read from my two journals, more than that I am not sure. I am too nervous and too emotional. I read and tears catch my throat and everyone is very understanding and waits as I regain composure and when I am finished, they all stand up and applaud. I am sure that it isn't that my words are so good but that I stand up for my son and am desperately pleading for his safe return. It is obvious to them that I will do whatever I can for his return home.

The next morning we have breakfast at the First Unitarian Universalist Church, another heart welcoming meal and some personal stories. I am beginning to sense that there are a lot of people that are against this war and will be willing to stand up and say so and they are very patriotic and they love my son and all of the Soldiers and Marines.

We depart for Cleveland at 10:00 am.

At home Jerry gets an instant message from Mike.

"Hey, what are you doing?"
Hey, Mike, Mom is in Columbus and Cleveland.
"What she doing? Is she protesting?"
Well, she's not really protesting. She met with Mayor Coleman in Columbus, J.D.'s father. She also met and spoke with the office staff for the two senators.
"Is she with Kevin's mom?"
Yes.
"I am down to one bag and a bag of food."
Sounds like you're on the go.
"Four days and I wake up at Al Asad. I have been checking out the Harley web site. Got to go. Just got mortared."

I receive a phone call from Mike while we are driving from Columbus to Cleveland. I assure him that I am in good company and am not undermining the work of the Marines of

3/25th. It helps to have Mayor Coleman on our side and to be with Trice. I don't think he understands what is going on with this. He can't be distracted. He is recovering from memorials and thinking about Harleys. He is anxious to come home.

In Cleveland we set up at 1:00pm. We have a meeting with Dora J. Pruce, District Director for Senator George Voinovich. We share much the same as we did in Columbus, with the same kind of reaction. They want to seem interested and concerned but really they just want us out of their offices. And this is a Friday afternoon. Again, we plead with her to please talk to the Senator on our behalf. We want him to listen and to do something. Not all of his constituents favor this war. He will be a leader. People will respond. He will be speaking truth. Yes! Yes! She says I will let the Senator know.

Maybe she will. Maybe he won't have time to listen. But we confine her for over one-half hour. We tie up her office. We are earnest. We are Americans. We do what we have a right to do. It feels good to voice our feelings and beliefs to those we elect and hire to represent us.

At 7:00 pm at the Congregation of St. Joseph attendants hear why we need to leave Iraq now. There are presentations, questions and discussion. It is the same agenda at 7:00 pm at Church of the Saviour. I speak at the Church of the Saviour. This is where I meet Rosemary Palmer and her husband Paul Schroeder, mother and father of Augie Schroeder killed in the amtrac explosion August 3, 2005. The room is packed. Several speakers give their presentations and then it is my turn. I had broken down in tears in Columbus and am hoping not to this evening. But, there are certain phrases that just latch in my throat and fill my heart with tears and make me pause... like, *how desperately I want my son to live and have hope. He is so young, so idealistic, so confident and so trusting.* I pause. I cannot hold in my tears. And the audience understands and they wait for me. The room is deadly silent. A sacred silence.

And my concluding sentence, *I can't think of a reason or a cause that is good enough for me to willingly give up the life of my son.*

The audience stands, they applaud. I am shaking. I am exhausted. Trice looks at me and says "Thanks Thelma."

CHAPTER 48

Calm Sweet Presence

This is the night Trice and I meet Rosemary Palmer and Paul Schroeder. They are there for my presentation at Church of the Saviour and then they lead us to their house where we spend the night.

We talk about the war and what our Marines are doing and how they might be feeling. We share our feelings of fear and our anxiety to get them home.

Paul tells us about Augie and shows us his truck which now has a picture of Augie in his "desert cammies" hanging from the mirror. We cry and we fall into moments of silence.

Then we watch an interview they did on one of the national news programs. I can feel their deep pain but also their commitment to all the other Marines and Soldiers. They will not let Augie's death be in vain. But it will not be by killing more Marines and Soldiers. It will be by stopping the madness of this war.

It is a sweet visit with them that evening. It is as though we have always been friends. But I am beginning to feel sick and know I need to get some sleep. Rosemary shows us to our rooms. I have a bedroom and Trice takes the office room with a computer and a hide-a-bed. Paul and Rosemary recently moved into this house that belonged to Rosemary's mother.

I stretch out on this regular size bed with unpacked boxes stacked around it and I begin to relax. I feel so deeply for Paul and Rosemary. They seem so strong and are so composed and yet the grief they carry is heavy.

The last three days have been full of activity, nervous energy and excitement. And now I need rest. I consciously try to relax my body and mind before I drift to sleep. Soon I become aware of an atmosphere of sweetness. I don't know what it is. I feel a lightness and then a smiling presence surrounds me. I just breathe and enjoy this feeling. Augie, whom I have never met, comes into my mind. The thought of him lingers and the smile deepens and I think to myself, "I wonder if Augie ever slept here." Soon I am in a much needed sleep.

The next morning while sitting around the table eating from a selection of bagels and wonderful cheese spreads, Paul asks Trice and I if we slept well. "Oh yes," I say. Paul then says, "You slept in Augie's bed." I gasp. I look at Paul and Rosemary, I take a breath. I have no intention of telling them about my experience of sweetness and the smiling presence that I felt the night before. I don't want them to think I am a kook. I'm not sure how to bring up something like this experience in such a sensitive time. I don't want to say anything to show dishonor. This feels like something spiritual and I don't want to offend them. I don't know how they will receive it. I hesitate. But before I can control my tongue any longer I look at Paul and words tumble out. "Oh Rosemary, Paul, I wasn't going to say anything about this but I had the calmest, sweetest sense of presence last night when I was in bed. I don't know where it came from. I wasn't thinking anything. But this smiling warmth came and it surrounded me and… I think it was Augie. It makes sense to me now that you say it is Augie's bed. I wondered if he had ever slept in that bed."

I look at Rosemary as tears carve a path down her face and she is swallowing back her pain. She can't keep the tears back and she nods her head. Yes. Yes. She is saying. And then Paul speaks up and says, "Augie always made people smile."

This is a precious moment. One I will never forget. I didn't know Paul or Rosemary until twelve hours before but I feel their son's presence. This brings comfort and it seals our friendship.

To this day I cannot adequately describe that experience. Yet it is as clear as day to me. Augie was in that room. His smiling presence filled the room and my heart.

As if this wasn't enough Trice then speaks up and says she too was not going to share her experience. While she sat at the computer checking her email she felt someone in the room. She actually turned to look. She felt as if the person was saying with a smile, "And, what are you doing here?"

How is this explained or understood? It is one of those "you would have to have been there moments." It says there is so much more to life. The calm sweet presence still lingers.

CHAPTER 49

Blog?

Meeting Paul and Rosemary and having the sweet experience of Augie's presence make the trip worth more than Trice and I can imagine. I am feeling more "under the weather" and think I better end my involvement with the BTHN Tour and head home. I am torn because I feel I am finally doing something rather than sitting at home on the computer or watching and waiting for news from Iraq. It feels good to be taking action. However, the stress and high energy is taking a toll.

We do a street corner vigil at West Market in Akron and decide after that to end our participation. It is a worthwhile experience and one we are glad to be part of.

After returning home, Trice gets at note from Kevin.

Hey everyone, it's me again. We cleaned up our rooms today, to get them ready for the next unit to move into. We are basically living out of our packs now. It won't be too much longer. Pretty soon

I will be out of harm's way for good. Love you all. (Kevin Michael Mullins)

Yeah Buddy, we are almost in the home stretch. I can't wait to see you. I got to talk to Mike Logue on the phone yesterday. Did he tell you about mine and Peggy's "Thelma and Louise" adventures? We also got hugs from JD's dad yesterday in Columbus. I am hoping he is going to be the next Governor of Ohio. He is on our side and waiting for his son to come home. I love you and can't wait until you're back in the USA. Love Mom.

Next day I instant message with Mike.

"Hey!"
Hey Bud!
"I've been up all night."
Are you on duty?
"Couldn't sleep all night… and have chow duty at 530."
You hate chow duty.
"Yeah! It sucks."
How come you couldn't sleep?
"At 300 they came by with this stupid siren… because the BNCO (battalion commander) wants us to do these drills where they ring the siren and we all get up into gear and go into the hallway ready to fight wherever they send us… it's stupid."

We had a really great trip and met lots of great caring people. But I developed a sinus infection and did not feel so good so we came home.

"Hope you are feeling better… Time limit is up."
Love you and talking to you makes me feel great.
"My computer was too slow and I couldn't email tonight."
What time do you get off?
"Love ya Mom. I'll be leaving soon."
Yes! Yes!!! We can't wait!!! Call again. Do you leave… Wednesday?
"Tomorrow 1900. Bye Love You."
Okay. Love you.

I am home now for a few days and reflecting on the experience in Columbus and Cleveland, and thinking about Mike coming home. It doesn't seem real. I am asked to write my reflection for the BTHN Tour newsletter and blog. It is titled "Ohio Caravan with Bring Them Home Now Tour" I begin:

I am a mother of a nineteen year-old 3/25th Lima Company Marine serving in Iraq. One third of his Unit has been KIA (killed in action) or wounded (WIA). In early August after losing twenty-three Marines in less than a week, fearing for my son's life and driven by conviction, I began my journey to change the direction our country has been going. I have been waiting for my son's safe return before speaking out publicly. There is such confusion in our country about patriotism and supporting the troops while being against the war.

I stood at a Marine Family meeting and told the Major and those present that it is time to bring the Ohio Marines home. I shouted out," My son is not expendable." I wrote to my senators asking for their help. I received no response. I refused to be powerless. I began thinking that Mothers had to win our country back and was planning to organize a Mother's March on Washington.

I found the web site, www.truthout.org. Here I found Camp Casey, Military Families Speak Out, Veterans For Peace, Iraqi Vets Against the War etc. I had never heard of any of these groups. I found that there is already a march planned for September 24th. Wow! Great! I don't have to take on the huge task of planning a march. Phew! I just have to go.

And this tells me there is a larger movement… that is in our souls and is beginning to surface.

I wanted to go to Camp Casey but couldn't because of a scheduled meetings with the Marines to prepare for the homecoming of our boys. I saw the Central Bring Them Home Now Tour plans to DC and realized I could caravan with them to Columbus, Toledo and Cleveland and maybe to Pittsburgh. I contacted a Cincinnati center to see if we could get them to stop in Cincinnati. So, my tour began in Cincinnati. I offered housing and breakfast. It was great to meet them. They are "my kind of people." They are not "off the wall," emotional fanatics. They are normal citizens willing to take risks as they speak out from their own experience and knowledge and with integrity against an incredible, illegal and disastrous war. They are compassionate people who suffer the loss of their beloved and they ask why. And they work hard to restore humanity, dignity and respect to our country. And they demand accountability and challenge our leadership to step up to the plate or get out of the way.

I was able to speak at the forums in Columbus and Cleveland. I spoke as a mother who watched five mothers bury their sons in the Cincinnati area in August. I shared the terror that I live with. The sleepless nights. The days and nights of anguish. "How desperately I want my son to live and have hope."

I was able to visit the offices of the senators who still had not responded to my letters. With others from the Tour we spoke of the many issues involved in war... depleted uranium, stop-loss, inadequate equipment, not enough men, operatives and the lies and deceit that led the American people into it.

We asked the aides, after we broke through the shell that tells you to "make it quick, I am busy and really don't want to listen to you," to ask the Senators what they want their legacy to be. We asked them to tell the Senators to look again at the war and why we are there, not with their jobs in mind or their political party, but to look with their human heart and their conscience. We told them if they see the truth and act from the truth... good will follow.

We participated in rallies and visited with many Americans who are sick of this war and the lies that keep us there and the dishonor it has brought to our country. We met enraged Americans.

There is much more to say about this BTHN Tour. It is an important moment. And the march September 24th will be historical.

I am convinced that our country is at a historical point... "And the people will lead."

I said to my son, "Mike, you have no idea how precious you are to me and dad, your brother and sister."

"I know."

"We will not let you get away so easily again."

"I know you won't."

"Mike, I am not afraid of the Marines. I am not afraid of the Government, and I am not afraid of the President. I am your MOM!"

Chuckling..." I love you, Mom."

I will work so Mike and other sons will not have their generosity, their courage, their integrity, their desire to serve, their desire to make a difference compromised. I want my son to always be proud that he is a Marine.

Peggy Logue (Ohio)

This article that I wrote is sent to the national MFSO and to other web sites and one person sent it to "the largest blog (8,000,000 hit per month) 'DailyKos'." He added, "You write very well- as if you have your own blog. If you don't you ought to." At this point, I don't even know what a blog is. This fascinates me. Then he sends me a list of web sites that he thought I should send it to. I really don't see myself doing that. Evidently he did send it off and I started getting responses from all over the world. Here are some of them:

What a voice this Momma Bear has found! The outpouring love brought tears to my eyes and I thank her for fighting for her boy, and for my twelve year old boy's future as well. (bobnbob)

As you noted, it is very difficult for a military family to come forward and speak against the war. It DOES have consequences. You can lose your job, you can lose friends, you can lose other military families, who you need...we are not going away. We will no longer be silenced. (hof1991)

Dear Mrs. Logue,

May I join what I hope will be a huge chorus of THANKS to you for your courageous words about bringing your Marine son and other sons home now. I read your beautiful and inspiring words on

Information Clearing House… I hope and pray your words will be heard and obeyed in the places of power. It will only be because of brave women like you in our country who will bring some sanity back to the political process. Keep speaking the truth to power, and know that there are millions of us "out here" who support you, because you have a credible voice and so many of us are rendered silent unfortunately by the press.

(Rev.) James E. Flynn (St. Mary's Church, Park City, Utah)

Peggy, I was much moved by your essay… I am very humbled before mothers and grandmothers who have children in the military, and in so many cases, lost them, or received them home, wounded and maimed. Humbled because my children and grandchildren are still safe. I have nine children and seventeen grandchildren. Nine of my "grands" are of military age, seven of them are boys and wouldn't Bush like to get his hands on them … When I look at my beautiful children and grandchildren, I ask myself, "was it for this we nurtured this family?" I do not intend to wait for the draft to come along and claim my grandchildren before I protest…I despair of ever achieving peace. I am going to be at the Peace Rally on September 24th in DC, as a Grandmother for Peace, and I will be joined by my eldest daughter, who marched in an anti-war demonstration thirty-odd years ago.

Peace (J.M. "Windy" Cutler, WV)

Another response asks me to become part of a group that is trying to "turn our Government around". She is a widow, retired, and "just plain fed up." They are gathering as an email group.

And this …

My Dear Lady, I am an Iraqi. I just like to say to you all decent Americans: What have we done to you to deserve to be humiliated in our own land, hungered, RAPED by your soldiers, imprisoned and above all killed in the thousands for no crime we committed against you. Our homes are bombarded daily, our valuable things stolen by your thugs! Tell me please one good reason that justifies what your Bush and the Zionists and his government are doing in my country? Bush lied to you and he still keeps on lying but you reelect him. What sort of people are you in God's name? Why do you condone his action? March against him and his criminal Neocons to retrieve the OLD good name of America. Yours (Prof. Dr.Q. Samarrai)

I receive the emails now from Military Families Speak Out (MFSO) and so the information about the convergence on Washington arrives. The Bring Them Home Now Tours would be crisscrossing the United States and arrive in DC by September 21st, in time for the United for Peace and Justice Mobilization September 24th-26th. The actual march would be September 24th beginning at 10:00 am on the Washington Monument Grounds. The March would step off at 12:30 pm. Many other events are scheduled throughout the weekend. Those who can stay until Monday will participate in additional protests as well as opportunities to visit with Members of Congress and Senators. The announcement ended with: w*e look forward to gathering together as military families in DC to let decision makers, our fellow Americans, and the world hear us as we say:*

End the war in Iraq!
Bring our troops home now!
Take care of them when they get here!
Never again send our loved ones - our service men and women - to a war based on lies!

CHAPTER 50

"I Can't Say"

"It's getting late."
Hey Mike. What are you doing?
"Just ate breakfast and now on the internet."
Are you on-line with anyone?
"No."
Wow! Breakfast. What did you eat?
"Some cereal and fake eggs."
Fake eggs. UGH! I'll treat you better when you come home. Did
you talk to Lindsay?
"Yeah."
What are you doing today?
"Nothing yet."
Are there plans?
"I'm going to go back to sleep soon."
Did you sleep last night?
"Yeah. I slept a couple of hours."

You must be tired. Have to get back into the rhythm of sleeping through the night.

"Yeah.... How's the Bengals tickets coming? I think I need to just buy some."

Are you doing a search on line?

"Just reading about the Bengals' win."

I'll check with Uncle Bob. He probably hasn't heard anything yet. I asked my new friend Jody. I'll check with her too.

"It's okay. I just want to get tickets but I hope they aren't sold out."

We'll check it out. Did you work out today?

"No."

Maybe you'll leave tomorrow? Today? Do they give you any notice?

"Mom, I can't say."

Okay. Sorry.

"It's okay... I'm tired."

Yeah. I know you are. I can sign off if you want to do something.

"It's okay. What are you doing this week?"

I don't have any big plans. Haven't felt good. Dad dragged me out to get a few groceries and ice cream. Snoopy got a hair cut Thursday. He looks like a skinned rat.

"Okay."

I spend a lot of time on line... mikelogue.com and several other web sites. I was just listening to an interview by two Marines who returned from Iraq.

"Yeah."

They have PTSD... nice young men. It's a web site Kevin's mom told me about. It's called www.welcomehomewarrior.org. How is the day time temp there now?

"Hot. It's still really hot."

It has been hot here too like eighty-five degrees. Not like your temps. You will be cold when you get here.

"I know."

You must be trying to read something.
"Yeah… hey I have to go, Mom. I'll talk to you later."
Get some sleep.
"I'm fine."
We love you. Bye.

Mike seemed a little distracted and jumpy in this conversation. He says he is tired. I am sure he is. How could he not be? It is always good to talk with him. But I never feel quite okay. I feel like he isn't telling me the whole truth. He is protecting me. And I question what he is really feeling, or doing. I always have a sense he "can't say."

CHAPTER 51

"...Kind of Forgot About Them..."

Dear Mrs. Logue,
 I thank you for all you are doing to get your son back home safely. I served in Vietnam from July 1968 to October 1970 - having extended my tour of duty three times. That too was an unjust and totally unnecessary war. I did not realize until I came home for good how much fear and anxiety I caused my mom until I was out of the Army. I am a Sansei, a third generation born American with Japanese ancestry. I only say this so you will hopefully understand that my mom did not want me to be in a war zone, but she could not speak out because we (Japanese Americans) are taught to be silent about what we perceive to be injustices.
 I hope you are successful in bringing your son home safely! He may be embarrassed by what you have done, but hopefully, in the future, he will know that you were right. This war is so wrong!
 Peace!
 (Lane Yoshiyama, East Los Angeles, California)

Hi Peggy,

GO FOR IT!! I applaud your stance and your actions. It is time for women to take their proper place on the road to peace. Tears come to my eyes as I feel the fear of mothers with sons in Iraq, and the anguish of those with sons who will not return. My son has spent six months in Afghanistan with the Canadian army... and I am all for ending these senseless wars that take our children away... throwing them into physical, mental and emotional danger from which most will never fully recover.

I send you lots of loving energy to continue, with the rest of America's aware women, to end this stupidity and bring the troops (and get rid of George Bush along the way if that is at all possible).

Love and hugs to you... Anne (Anne Lossing Coordinator, Projext Ix- canaan, El Remate, Peten, Guatemala).

Dear Military Families, I am a reporter with the Hartford Courant newspaper in Connecticut who is researching a series of stories about mental health among troops serving in Iraq. As you know, the military is now making an unprecedented effort to retain as many troops as possible for the war, with some serious and tragic human consequences. I am hoping to speak to families or close friends of Iraq troops currently or formerly or soon-to-be deployed, from anywhere in the country – who have concerns about the mental-health status of their soldiers... Thank you (Lisa Chedekel)

Dear Military Families, My name is Dietlind Lerner and I am a documentary film-maker based in Paris, France currently working on a fifty-two minute film tentatively called " NOT IN OUR NAME" for broadcast on Arte (Franco- German equivalent of PBS) in March 2006 on the 3rd anniversary of the US intervention in Iraq.

NOT IN OUR NAME is not a film about the Iraq war, instead it is a look at the anti-war movement in America during the last four years. Is there an anti-war movement and if so has it grown larger or lost momentum? If not, what is happening to Americans to make them either so apathetic - or scared. Who or what is behind the fact that anti-war crusaders might not be given a voice today? How easy or difficult is it to be against this war?

WOUNDED MARINE REFLECTS IN AKRON by Jim Carney (Beacon Journal staff writer, Monday September 19, 2005)

... "We lost a lot of Marines, and I lost a lot of good buddies ... I don't even know the number."

Turner, a lance corporal, is home in Akron after a month and a half in hospitals in Iraq, Germany and the United States, having undergone more than ten surgeries.

He was wounded in Hit, Iraq, on August 1 when a suicide bomber blew up a car and struck the humvee that Turner was in... The sandy-haired Marine turned twenty-one while in Iraq...

Turner's right eye is gone. He has little feeling in his right foot. His left arm is in a cast because his wrist was shattered. Still buried in his legs, back, arms and feet are pieces of shrapnel.

"I got way too many pieces to count," he said. "It would take all day to count it."

He walks with a cane and hopes he will get feeling back in his foot. He says he has lost forty pounds from muscle atrophy since his injury.

Turner was wounded after he and the three others volunteered to try and find Cpl. Jeffrey Boskovitch, a sniper from Cuyahoga County who was missing. Five other snipers had been found killed.

"Marines don't leave Marines behind," Turner said.

... He said he is self-conscious about the eye he lost. "I just want to get my fake eye," he said.

... He believes Iraq has been put on the back burner in the news since hurricane Katrina struck the Gulf Coast, and he wants Americans not to forget those still at war and those who are still

wounded and killed overseas… They don't talk about the guys that are over there fighting, the guys that are risking their lives day in and day out," he said, "It's like they kind of forgot about them."…

"I don't think I've ever been this glad to be home," he said. "When I go out, I don't have to worry about getting blown up or shot."

CHAPTER 52

"Now if This 'Helo' Won't Crash"

Kevin is at Al Asad AFB. This is the beginning. My son is on his way home. (Trice)

"Hey everyone, it is official, we are finally on safe ground. Well much safer ground. It was a good feeling stepping off that bird today. We all knew we had it made after that.

The food here is great. I think I ate too much for lunch though. It might take awhile to get used to this kind of food again. There is a lot of administration stuff to do before we come home. We all just wish we could go straight back, but we will get there soon enough. I will try to call as soon as I can. I love you guys and can't wait to see you. (Kevin Michael Mullins)"

All Families and Loved Ones,

Just received a call from our Inspector-Instructor, Major Greiner, asking me to please spread the word:

WHEN SPEAKING WITH THE PRESS, DO NOT

*GIVE ANY INFORMATION AS TO UNIT MOVEMENT,
LOCATION, OR DATES OF ANY KIND. THIS IS
CONSIDERED CLASSIFIED INFORMATION AND CAN
PUT NOT ONLY OUR MARINES AT RISK, BUT ALSO
OTHER MEMBERS OF THE ARMED FORCES.*

*Our Unit represents the heartland of America and has been in
the News more than we ever wanted them to be. Talking with the
press as to their whereabouts could launch an attack by the enemy at
their location. While they may be in a "safer place" they are not safe
until their planes land on US soil.*

*Again, any information as to the Unit's movement, location,
etc. is classified. Sharing it with the media is a 'NO- NO' (Major
Greiner's words).*

*Thank you very much for your understanding and cooperation
in this matter. Everyone is getting excited about the return, but
we must not provide information to the enemy. When stories hit
the news, it will also be on the World Wide Web, easily accessed by
everyone.*

Let's stay strong and patient. (Isolde Zierk)

SEPTEMBER 15, 2005: SIXTEEN DAYS TO GO.

Family and Friends,

"Now if this 'helo' won't crash!"

*Dressed in his "cammies," sea bag on his back, these are Mike's
thoughts as he jubilantly climbs aboard the helicopter that is to take
him to a "safer" place.*

"This is awesome," he says.

Such a relief. BREATHE! Now just BREATHE!

*It has been a long time since we have felt like taking a deep
breath. I can't imagine how the men feel to not be in a constant state
of preparedness to kill and to die.*

*Mike arrives at Al Asad today. He called us this morning. He
says they have been moving the men out all week. His platoon is the*

last to leave. They are mortared as they leave. Usually they may get a round or two mortars. This morning they got eight to nine.

I think of the Marines at Haditha Dam as "sitting ducks" and I always worried about their safety there. Mike says he didn't want to worry me more but confirmed my concern this morning when he told me that when they returned there after Operation Quick Strike in early August they found three IED's at the Dam. One went off. They were made to look like fire extinguishers. How did they get there? Each day hundreds of people are bused in from the city of Haditha to work at the Dam.

Mike's schedule at Al Asad is 6:30 revelry...PT...shower... eat...classes...lunch...classes...dinner...

time with the commander...PT...shower...bed.

They are in a huge tent that has eight air conditioners. They bus from one end of the base to the other.

The official homecoming has again been changed. It is now in November.

Nothing definite but I think they are combining it with the Veterans Day parade in Columbus.

Still no definite date as to when we can really, really breathe... when they arrive on American soil. Then they will spend some days at Camp LeJeune. Then...home.

The 3/1st Marines have replaced 3/25th Lima Company. They are already engaged in the operations they are called to according to their orders.

Now, other mothers, wives and families take up the worry and look for the meaning of this war and how it affects their lives.

Though our Marines are in a "safer place"...is anywhere there safe?

I have learned that we cannot count on anything. We just face each day as to its abundance and grace and are thankful for each breath...shallow or deep.

It isn't over yet... but thank you all for your constant words of wisdom, support and prayer.

And thank you "helo" for not crashing.

Love PEACE

Peggy & Jerry

CHAPTER 53

"They Lied" – "They Died"

Kristen, I don't have the energy to make the bus trip to DC for the march. I used up all my energy on the BTHN Tour. Or maybe it's the stress I've experienced and the anticipation of our boys coming home. I am disappointed but I know you have a waiting list and I hope someone will go in my place.

Thank you for doing this in honor of my son and others who have sacrificed so much so willingly and who deserve more from their government.

Remind everyone that our troops are noble and they are genuinely giving of themselves as they want to serve and help people and want a better world for all. Shame on a government that would abuse that noble desire by ordering our troops into a war that is illegal and wrong.

Please hold those responsible accountable and help restore honor to our military.

Thanks, (Peggy)

Peggy, I am sorry to hear that you are still feeling "under the weather" and that you have to cancel. You will be missed. I will keep your words in my mind. I think the email you have written is a powerful witness and reminder to those of us who are going. Could I read the email at the Send-Off Rally on Friday? Or, do you think you would feel well enough or would you speak at the rally?

Take care. (Kristen)

Jerry and I go to this rally but I feel exhausted and too nervous to speak. Kristen reads my email and introduces Jerry and me. We escort the many people to their busses and watch them go carrying our thoughts to DC to end the war and bring our troops home now.

Dear Peggy,

Rosemary Palmer gave me your email address and told me you were uncertain about wishing to speak to me but it was alright to email you and explain what we are doing.

I'm a correspondent with one of the main British television current affairs programmes, called Dispatches. We're making a one hour documentary about how the ongoing war in Iraq and the growing number of casualties is starting to affect public opinion in the US.

At this stage I am just trying to talk to anyone who is directly affected because they have a son serving there or they've had a son injured or killed in the war.

I just need to hear what people are thinking and saying – so that we know what we should cover in the programme.

So this is background research and it's all strictly off the record.

Once we've listened as widely as possible then we'll go back to people and see who is willing to take part in the programme and who would rather not.

We are hoping to film in a VA hospital, we are also talking to politicians and journalists about the coverage of the war and what images emerge and what images are suppressed. But key to the whole programme is the attitude of service families.

Because of the terrible death toll among 3/25ᵗʰ Reserve Marines we will be filming in the Ohio area and so we are trying to contact families connected with the regiment. Rosemary mentioned that you have a son in Lima Company.

I appreciate this is such a sensitive and emotional subject for any parent to talk about. If you are willing to talk to me on the phone - without any commitment to take part in the programme and on the strict understanding this is all off the record - I would really be grateful. If you let me know a time that's convenient I can call you - regardless of time differences.

Thank you very much. (Deborah Davies, Dispatches, Channel 4, London)

Before I respond to this request of the British I am wondering why there isn't coverage of the BTHN Tour and the March on DC. So I write to Cameo of CNN.

Cameo, question? Why is there no news coverage of the anti-war March in DC?

The news media seems to think that there is no news except the hurricane. So those of us who want other news go back to our computers and search through newspapers where there is very little news of the war to be found.

Americans have been streaming across the country, stopping in many states, meeting with senators, holding press conferences, conducting forums about bringing the troops home and there is no coverage of this. A big event is this weekend in Washington DC. Over 100,000 people are expected to march protesting the war.

Will CNN provide any coverage of this?

Thanks (Peggy)

STATEMENT OF US SENATOR RUSS FEINGOLD (Wednesday, September 28, 2005) as Prepared to be delivered from the Floor of the United States Senate.

Mr. President, I rise once again to comment on the deeply disturbing consequences of the President's misguided policies in Iraq. I have spoken before about my grave concern that the

Administration's Iraq policies are actually strengthening the hand of our enemies, fueling the insurgency's recruitment of foreign fighters and unifying elements of the insurgency that might otherwise turn on each other.

But today, Mr. President, I want to focus on a different and equally alarming issue – which is, that the Bush Administration's policies in Iraq are making America weaker. And none of us should stand by and allow this to continue...

The Administration's policies in Iraq are breaking the United States Army. As soldiers confront the prospect of a third tour in the extremely difficult theater of Iraq, it would be understandable if they began to wonder why all the sacrifice undertaken by our country in wartime seems to be falling on their shoulders. It would be understandable if they – and their brothers and sisters in the Marine Corps – began to feel some skepticism about whether or not essential resources – like adequately armored vehicles – will be there when they need them...

Make no mistake, our military readiness is already suffering. According to a recent RAND study, the Army has been stretched so thin that active-duty soldiers are now spending one of every two years abroad, leaving little of the Army left in any appropriate condition to respond to crises that may emerge elsewhere in the world...

We are not just wearing out the troops; we are also wearing out equipment much faster than it is being replaced or refurbished...

And, Mr. President, recent reports indicate that the divorce rate for men and women in the Army has jumped more than 80% since 2001. This is not a casual aside – it's a huge, glaring red flag. What we are asking of the Army is not sustainable, and the burden is taking its toll on our military families. This cannot go on...

As my colleagues know, I have introduced a resolution calling for the President to provide a public report clarifying the mission that the US military is being asked to accomplish in Iraq and laying out a plan and timeframe for accomplishing that mission and subsequently bringing our troops home...

How much longer can the elected representatives of the American people in this Congress allow the President to rack up over a billion dollars a week in new debts? This war is draining, by one estimate, $5.6 billion every month from our economy...

I cannot support an Iraq policy that makes our enemies stronger and our own country weaker, and that is why I will not support staying the course the President has set... There is no leadership in simply hoping for the best, we must insist on an Iraq policy that works.

Newspapers across the country carried a full page add paid for by the Win Without War Coalition. On the left side were pictures of Donald Rumsfeld with a quote, "We know where (the WMDs) are. 3/30/03.

Next to him a picture of George Bush with the quote, "We found weapons of mass destruction." (5/29/03) Also, "There's no question that Saddam Hussein had al Qaeda ties." (9/17/03).

Then the picture of Dick Cheney, "We will in fact be greeted as liberators... I think it will go relatively quickly... (in) weeks rather than months." (3/6/03) "We believe (Saddam) has, in fact, reconstituted nuclear weapons." (3/16/03).

Finally Condoleeza Rice, "We do know that (Saddam) is actively pursuing a nuclear weapon." (9/10/02)

Above these pictures and quotations are the words **"THEY LIED."**

On the right side of the page in a framed box are the names of all who have been killed. Again in bold, black large letters... **"THEY DIED."**

A question followed... "Mr. President, how many more?"

CHAPTER 54

"That's About All I Got"

Hey Peggy,

Good to hear from you. I'm sure you were happy to get Isolde's message this morning about the guys coming home. Too bad the message wasn't that they are ALL coming home!

We're doing okay here. We had Augie's best friend Brian over for dinner on Friday night. He told us a lot of fun stories about how they used to crash parties at OSU(Ohio State University), that sort of thing. He also told us he only saw Augie use force twice: once at a party when a host pulled a gun on someone who was picking at him (Augie put a headlock on the guy who was doing the picking and tossed him out to avoid something worse) and once at Augie's apartment when a drunk co-worker grabbed a girl, intending to hurt her. He barricaded the aggressor into his bedroom until the guy sobered up. So, each time, he was playing the protector role. Paul says he sees Augie as very similar to the angel in the 1996 movie "Michael." A true angel, but not angelic!

Amanda (Augie's sister) is having it rough in New Jersey. She is angry. She's mad at everyone and at God. She has lost faith. She goes to see a psychologist, but working through grief isn't something that happens overnight…

As for me, I'm exhausted.

Thanks for asking. (Rosemary)

Rosemary, it's the middle of the night. A gust of wind came through my window at 2:00am and I got up and saw that the floor was wet. So, I guessed it had rained. I checked through the house for other opened windows. Then, of course, I was wide awake. So here I am.

I am so glad you got to see Brian and hear the good stories. You know… I can't imagine working through this grief. Yes, I am happy that Mike is on his way home. But there is such a sadness that they all aren't coming home. There was a picture of Michael Cifuentes on TV tonight. Miami University was doing a memorial at a football game because Michael was in the band. Just seeing his picture… I say to myself…I couldn't do this.

I am thinking of you, Rosemary. I know I can't come close to know how you are feeling… I do care but feel inadequate at expressing my compassion…

And it fuels my anger… Yes, my next breath is anger.

I know you are doing the interview for the British. I talked with Deborah Davis yesterday, again. I told her I would love to be the family they document, but need to discuss it with Mike. He called from Kuwait last night. I mentioned it to him and he didn't sound much in favor. So, I may not do it. He is going to think about it. No one in my family feels like they want that kind of scrutiny. For me, it is a chance to get some of the reality of the war into the face of the general public… who merely give lip service to "supporting the troops" while flashing the yellow magnetic ribbons on their cars but don't even know where Iraq is or how many have already been killed.

As for Mike, I think there is so much to un-do. He can't think too far ahead and doesn't want much to deal with.

Take care. (Peggy)

I read a moving article quoting Paul Schroeder about the homecoming of 3/25th Marines. His son, Augie has already come home, in several boxes.

HOMECOMING BITTERSWEET FOR OHIO MARINES COMING TO CAMP LEJUENE by Cinnie Mabin Associated Press, September 29, 2005

For 3rd Battalion, 25th Marines families, Friday's homecoming to Camp LeJeune, N.C. will be a bittersweet ending to a tragic tour of duty in Iraq. The hard hit unit deployed in January suffered 150 injuries and 48 deaths…

"I had hoped to be greeting my son," said Paul Schroeder, whose son Lance Cpl. Edward Schroeder II was killed in August. "I see all this happening and I'm glad all these guys are coming home, but I wanted him to be there too, so it's difficult to take."

Until August 2, the day his son known as "Augie" died, he too had been planning a homecoming. It was going to be a big bonfire, complete with a lamb roast in the family's large backyard near the vegetable garden." Hopefully on one of those glorious October days and we were going to invite the immediate world," the father said with a heavy voice before pausing to collect himself. "I got the garden. I got the firewood. That's about all I got."

CHAPTER 55

"Oh My Gosh! Oh My Gosh!"

Friday September 30, 2005 12:26 am. ONE MORE DAY.

Family and Friends,

We just found out that the news channels are on their way to Camp LeJeune to film the homecoming of our Marines!!!!

Mike called from Kuwait last night. He didn't know when they would leave there. We were told they were trying to get them to LeJeune by Friday. I can hardly believe this. Watch the morning news. Oh my gosh! Don't think I can sleep now. Just sit up all night and watch the news.

Oh my gosh! Oh my gosh! OH MY GOSH!!!

(Peggy & Jerry)

Sis – I woke up to the news on TV this morning… in my semi-conscious sleepy state, I heard on Channel 5… "And Lucky Lima returns home to Camp LeJeune this evening at 5:00"… OH MY

GOSH, OH MY GOSH, I sat up in bed as if I had been shot out
of a cannon. Tears of joy! With a joyful heart and thanksgiving –
you're in my thoughts all day.
Love. Your Sis, Eileen

Family and Friends,
Little sleep last night. We heard 3/35th Marines left Germany
about 8:00am. They have one more stop before getting to Camp
LeJeune. And now our tears are of joy and excitement. Wish I could
jump in the car and be at LeJeune. They are going to be "quarantined
to the base for the entire length of stay at LeJeune. This is to give
the Marine Corps a chance to debrief and decompress our Marines
before they see their families. Families are encouraged to wait until
the return to Columbus for their reunions with their Marine. "There
is no guarantee that they will be allowed to even see their Marine
while in LeJeune, if they choose to go there." This is the official word
as given to First Sgt. Halbig by "our Major and his staff."
So we will wait.
Channel 12 is supposed to do live coverage from LeJeune from
4:30pm – 6:30pm on their big screens in downtown Cincinnati. If
you are downtown you might take a look.
Get out your flags and welcome home signs ready.
Peggy & Jerry

Hello again Family and Friends,
We are informed that WKRC is going to be at Camp LeJeune
and all family members are welcome to go to the TV station today to
see the satellite footage of the Marines getting off the planes…Just
tell them at the station that you are there to see the Marines and
they will show you where to go. (Peggy & Jerry)

And then an email from Deborah for the documentary for
the British news channel.
Dear Peggy,
I don't know if you've managed to speak to your son – and talk it

through with your family – but if you are willing we would hope to film a little bit with you before the homecoming, any preparations you are making and to talk to you a little bit about your feelings in advance of seeing your son…then to follow you – with whatever ground rules you want set – to the homecoming and meeting your son… then either return with you that evening or if you prefer – the following evening – to see you all reunited and complete the interview.

As we discussed on the phone – this is going to be a hugely emotional time for all the family and of course we will respect that. It will be down to you and your family to agree what we can film and what we can't – and you can only finally decide that in the moment.

I put this down in an email because I thought it would be easier to consider if it was all written down. I will call you either this evening or tomorrow. Best wishes (Deborah)

Deborah, this is difficult to discuss with Mike without being able to really visit with him. I talked to him about it on the phone last night when he called from Kuwait. He is tired and hungry and not feeling well. Guess they have been traveling and there is nothing opened for them to get food.

His response does not seem favorable. The timing may be bad. He said, "I don't want them in my face… and they mess up what you say, anyway." The embedded journalists were not their favorite people because it took so much to protect them.

Jerry and I are willing to do some interviewing with you before Mike gets here. But we are not sure we will be able to finish the interview as you wish. Please know we are parents first and last. We have to see what Mike's needs are.

I appreciate what you are doing. The world needs to see this and I wish we could do more for you. (Peggy)

Peggy, I do understand – and I don't want to add stress to the next few days…

I am really grateful for all your help to date and if you decide you don't want to be involved in any way – of course that's your decision – we don't have any right to force ourselves into people's lives especially at times of such turbulence – I'm always astonished and feel very privileged when anybody does allow us in – all we can do is try and do justice to their stories and offer a conduit to the wider world – whenever I give lectures to journalism students I always tell that at the end to constantly remember – it may be your story but it's someone else's life. (Deborah)

Saturday, October 1, 2005.

Family and Friends,

LCpl Michael Logue, or as we call him, Mr. Mike, is at Camp LeJeune. They arrived about 11:00pm last night. He called us at 1:00am. He sounds really excited and happy to be back.

They will have formation this morning then classes and clean their equipment. A friend of ours from Lebanon whose son is stationed at Camp LeJeune is visiting his son and called us this morning to say he will be taking Mike to dinner tonight.

We don't have a definite time for their arrival in Columbus but it will probably be this week.

There is also sadness... all didn't come home... can't imagine ...

We will have a day for you all to celebrate with us. We have to follow Mike's lead as to when he is ready.

We are so thankful for your generous and constant support and for allowing us to express our sometimes joy but oftentimes grief and sadness.

Love PEACE

Peggy & Jerry

CHAPTER 56

"Last Marine in Squad Mourns..."

Paul Schroeder sent a note to his group of friends.

"Dear Friends,
Augie's unit returned to the US yesterday, September 30.
Augie's box of gear -- mostly clothing--also came home yesterday.
Needless to say we thank God the unit is back, but it's a bittersweet
homecoming.

While the good days are now outnumbering the bad ones,
the sadness remains. And, in typical fashion, it is quite easy to go
from deep sadness to anger. This is especially so when we read the
assessments offered in the attached article. You will recall we sent
you a picture of Augie's unit with nine of the eleven Marines in the
photo killed. Of the two survivors, one was the dog handler. The
other LCpl Travis Williams.

His story is attached. Pay close attention to the comments of the
squad leaders quoted in the article. Here is a sample:

"*Even commanders acknowledge that with the limited number of U.S. and Iraqi troops in the region, the mission is focused on 'disrupting and interdicting' the insurgency – that is, keeping them on the run – and not controlling the cities.*

"It's maintenance work," said Col. Stephen W. Davis, commander of all Marine operations in western Anbar. "Because this out here is where the fight is, while the success is happening downtown while the constitution is being written and while the referendum is getting worked out… If I could bring every insurgent in the world out here and fight them all day long, we've done our job."

For Williams, the calculation is much more visceral and personal.

"Personally, I don't think the sweeps help too much," he said quietly on a recent day, sitting in a room at the dam, crowded with Marines resting from a late mission the night before.

"You find some stuff and most of the bad guys get away… For as much energy as we put in them, I don't think the output is worth it," he said.

This is exactly what Augie told me two weeks before he was killed.

This also bears out the point we have been making that those in command of American troops in Iraq -- the civilians in the Pentagon and the Administration -- HAVE NOT AND DO NOT -- support the troops as they want all of us to do. This has been going on now for twenty-nine months (since "Mission Accomplished" on May 1, 2003) and most likely will continue to go on. Our troops are sitting ducks.

There is something horribly wrong with this administration. I think it has to do with cold blood. (Paul Schroeder)

Paul,

I am thinking of you and Rosemary. Many times throughout the day I think of you. I forwarded your message to my email list. I read the whole article (Last Marine in Squad Mourns 11 Friends Killed in Bombing by Antonio Castaneda, AP).

During our time of joy as we greet our son… I am aware of you and Rosemary and your loss.

PEACE (Peggy)

Hey, are you there?
"*Yes, but talking to many people.*"
Okay. Did you buy some shoes?
"*Yeah. They didn't have exactly what I wanted so I had to pay more. They were $90.*"
You deserve them.
"*I spent $160 so I wouldn't have to buy something when I first get home.*"
I bet your feet don't know how happy they could be.
"*I wanted something new to wear.*"
I was in your room today trying to get some of your clothes ready for you.
"*I have to go now. Love you guys. Tell everyone 'hi.'*""

We receive a note from Isolde.

LIMA'S ARRIVAL IN COLUMBUS, *October 4, 2005*
Dear All:

The long awaited word has just been received! Lima Company Marines and Corpsmen will arrive at Port Columbus on FRIDAY, OCTOBER 7, 2005.

Please plan on arriving at the Reserve Center between 7:30am - 8:00am.

Everyone will have to enter through the back gate and show an ID. Please tell them the name of your Marine and he can check you off.

It is anticipated that the Marines and Corpsmen pull into the drill center between 10:30am and 11:00am.

Finally, the moment has arrived and we know when we can welcome our heroes home. I just wish so much that the entire Lima Company would have been able to return this very same day.

Semper Fi. (Isolde)

CHAPTER 57

"We Get Attached."

Family and Friends.....no more days to go.

It is so incredibly overwhelming for Jerry and me to have so many of our family and friends up at 5:00am and on the road to Columbus to await Mike's arrival. The rain...the cold...the noise...the crowds. I look at the pictures and there you all are... most wearing your Lima 3/25th t-shirts and holding signs and American flags.

I can see the newsmen and cameras hungry for the event, the motorcycles revving, the firemen and policemen practicing their salute, the bands, the flags.

The weather is freezing. It is raining. It is early morning. The sky is gray and covered in clouds. But we have no feeling except utter anticipation and sheer joy.

The Marines board busses at the airport and their whole journey to the drill center is paved with citizens waving flags and signs of pride and gratitude. Repeatedly we are told how far away, how close our Marines are.

As we wait for their arrival our banner is oozing ink as the rain hits it and tears the welcome home letters to the ground.

The helicopter that is following our Marines can finally be heard over head. There is a crescendo of sound from the families gathered as the Marines get nearer and our joy overflows.

I am asked to wear a micro-phone for a Cincinnati TV station. They tell me they will hear everything I say. But I have no awareness of what I am saying. What does relief, anticipation and joy sound like?

Finally we are told, "The Marines are on the property and will be seen momentarily." We begin to hear the cadence of their marching boots. And our hearts are beating with the same strong rhythm. And then through the legs and dripping coats of other people we can see the camouflaged legs and worn boots of our Marines. They round a corner and march in front of us. Screaming fills the Earth.

That picture plays over and over in my head and still brings me to tears. Finally seeing our Marines marching in their "cammies" into our sight. Marching…eyes forward…and then "snapping in" on command to face us. There is something so sacred about that moment. A freeze frame in my mind. The quick order "DISMISSED!"

"I do not know what the TV station hears because I rush toward Mike with a scream that comes from somewhere deep in the Earth. I do not see any of the hundreds of people in front of me. I only see Mike. I do not hear anything except my scream as my pain lets go. I cannot feel the rain or the cold I only feel myself clutch the thin body of my young son. And I hold him. And I hold him. And I weep. I sob and can't let go for a long time. I hear the voice of his dad crack as he hugs Mike and tears are everywhere.

Each of you then greeting Mike, hugging him and loving him, brought comfort and reality back to us.

And then listening as our Marine leaders speak eloquently of how bravely our Marines served and watched as they could not contain their tears in mentioning those who were not coming home.

We visit other families for a brief moment and then load up Mike's sea bags and begin that long awaited journey home.

Our drive home is full of conversation and touching as we pushed down the wet slushy highway. It carried all those tears wanting release.

The Welcome Home party on Saturday is awesome. As Mike watches the fire department raise the flag on the extended ladder to an amazing height right out our front door, he says, "This is awesome." Then family and friends fill our home with love and comfort and relief and celebrate with us the joy of our son coming home.

Mike is overwhelmed with love and support. His aunts and uncles and cousins gift him with a lap top computer. His voice cracking he can only utter, "this is too much!" And Uncle Bob assures him it is not… "and you don't need to say thank you," he says, "you have done that already! We say thank you!"

It is a spectacular homecoming. One brother says it is the most emotional event he has ever experienced. Another brother says next to watching his wife give birth it is the most powerful thing he has ever seen. And many family and friends greet Mike with tears in their eyes.

A nephew is overwhelmed just driving up our street and seeing the flags and knowing Mike is home safe. And the neighbor whom I had met once approaches our house with tears flowing down his cheeks. He shakes Mike's hand and turns and walks away tears still flowing.

There are no words for us as a family to say "Thank you" to all of you for supporting us during this seven month nightmare. We are relieved. We are happy. The reality of what next will surface soon enough.

Mike is happy to be home but interestingly he says "if it wasn't for you guys I might have stayed."

I gasped and said, "Really!" I swallow my shock. "Mike?" I swallow harder. " Why?"

Nonchalantly he says, "I guess we get attached."

Love PEACE
Peggy and Jerry

Lima 3/25ᵗʰ Marine flag and the American flag flying over Haditha Dam, Iraq. Area of Operations for 3/25ᵗʰ Marines.

"We are temporarily sleeping in a hallway. It's about 500 feet down from the top. It's a haul with all our gear and two sea bags…This is a nasty hallway. It smells like sulfur, very strong. It's poorly lit and the water leaks from pipes."

We see and hear explosions constantly.

A continuous mission was to secure weapons
and explosive caches.

Medevac carrying wounded away while trac continues to
burn at Al Quaim. This is the trac I got out of just 30 seconds
before it hit an IED.

What was left of the trac that hit an IED in Al Quaim, Iraq,
May 11, 2005. We lost four Marines.

Memorial service at Haditha for the Fallen after Al Quaim.

Mike having a first smoke after his position took machine gun fire and an RPG. The machine gun fire had strafed the wall behind him at chest level. The RPG hit the wall four feet overhead but was a dud.

After the fire fight, Kelly points to
the machine gun and RPG impacts.

Mike Logue and Austin Hyde
on a short security halt in Hit, Iraq.

Mike Logue and Austin Hyde inside trac traveling back to
Haditha Dam after a few weeks in the field.

Providing security on a roof top for a building in Hit.

Mike removes his gear and tries to relax while other Marines take a defensive position securing the building in Hit after a short patrol in the 120-140 degree heat.

Our lightly armored humvees with open backs and thin metal frames.

What is left of a humvee after a suicide bomber detonated 25 meters behind it. The bomber took 700 rounds and still continued his pursuit of the humvee.

We dig a hole in the sand to provide a fighting position. Sometimes we throw a poncho on top for cover from the burning sun.

Day-off training for man overboard exercises in the Euphrates River.

The remains of the trac that hit an IED on August 3rd, 2005 in Barwanah, Iraq. Fourteen Marines were killed.

Mayor Coleman met with Peggy and Trice in Columbus when they were on the Bring Them Home Now Tour. Coleman's son, J.D. also serves with Lima 3/25th Marines.

Mike, family and friends watching the fire department raise the American flag on a ladder truck at the welcome home party.

Memorial for 3/25th Marines dedicated at the 3/25th Marine headquarters in Columbus, Ohio.

Having a great time at the Marine Ball, November 2009.

Mike's tattoo memorializing the deployment of Lima 3/25th Marines, especially the trac explosion in May, 2005.

Marine buddies having a night out, Austin Hyde, Collin Brintlinger, Greg Hughes and Mike Logue.

CHAPTER 58

"Everyone is Stoked"

I planned to end my book here. I thought with Mike home my grief would end and all would be well. And all would be normal. But the truth is it takes years to get back to some sense of normalcy and wellness. Counseling helps. But the task of healing is not instant. So we are still working on that, each of us in our own way.

This book probably doesn't have an end. Just this month we received a poem (author unknown) about Lima 3/25th Marines. You will find it later in the book. It tells me someone else is still dealing with the grief of the experience.

There are some loose ends I didn't finish telling you about and some new items too, so the remaining chapters fill you in and bring you up-to-date as Lima 3/25th are about to celebrate the fourth year of their homecoming. And so, here it goes:

After several failed attempts to get tickets for a Bengals football game for the Marines I reach out to one more possible source, my niece Brigid Niesel. Brigid lives in Colorado and often flies home for the Bengals' games. She has many Cincinnati contacts. She received all of my emails during the deployment. After telling her what I needed for Mike and his platoon she emailed me for more information about Mike's unit. Here is the rest of the story.

Marines to see Bengals battle (John Kiesewetter, Cincinnati Enquirer December 21, 2005)

Marine Reserve Michael Logue and his buddies won't forget their Christmas gift from the Cincinnati Bengals.

The Bengals have given 112 free tickets to Saturday's sold-out game against Buffalo to Logue and 47 other members of the Columbus based Lima Company, which lost 16 marines in Iraq this year.

"It's really awesome they were able to do this for us," said Logue 20, a 2004 Lebanon High school graduate.

Said Maj. Stephen Lawson, 36, of Middletown, the unit commander: "This is a great Christmas gift. Everyone is stoked."

Logue's cousin, Terrace Park native Brigid Niesel, started the football rolling in October when she asked WKRC-TV reporter Paul Adler to help her get some Bengal tickets for Logue and some of his Marine buddies. While serving in Iraq Logue and fellow Marines received Bengals shirts and a note from head coach Marvin Lewis inviting them to a game.

Niesel, who lives in Denver, was amazed to learn that the team would provide more than 100 tickets to the soldiers and their family and friends...

"I couldn't be happier. If I had been given ten or fifteen, I'd been pleased," said Niesel, 36, a lifelong Bengals fan who is flying home to attend the game...

Tickets to the 48 Marines were mailed with notes from Bengals owner Mike Brown and Adler.

"Your commitment and willingness to serve makes our way of life possible," Brown said.

"I think we all see the value in giving to the Marines. I truly

believe that I'll never comprehend in my lifetime what my cousin experienced over there," Niesel said. "We can't do enough to pay them back for what they've done."

CHAPTER 59

Beyond the Silence

I speak again with Deborah Davis from the British news "programme" Dispatch's. We agree to be interviewed by them. Before the homecoming they come to our house and spend many hours shooting video and talking with us. They are very respectful and very sincere and compassionate. It really feels good to tell our story and be part of documenting this aspect of the war. Jerry and I are interviewed at home and then are surprised to see them at the homecoming in Columbus because we are told there will not be media there. Deborah asked me if it was alright for them to come to our homecoming party. We feel very comfortable with them and decide it is okay for them to come. They are professional and don't interfere with what is happening. They interview Mike and they show the warmth of our family and friends who gather for the homecoming.

They also go to Cleveland and interview Paul Schroeder

and Rosemary Palmer who share how it feels to see these boys come home but not their son.

The program is well done and very comprehensive. It is an hour long and titled *America's Secret Shame*. It is shown in Britain but we are told that unless a news agency picks it up in the States it won't be seen here. And it wasn't. We are given several copies with permission to make more copies and show it wherever we can. And we do.

Jonah is one of the team and he asks to see some of the videos that Mike brought home. Mike is playing them on the computer during the homecoming party. They are difficult to look at and I am not sure about the security of it all. I respond to an email from Jonah asking about Mike.

Jonah, how good to hear from you. Re-entry has been slow. For the most part Mike seems okay. He signed off with the Marines last Tuesday. So he is now de-activated until called up. He is more relaxed since then.

The first week we noticed he didn't want to be alone. He didn't sleep in his bed for about five days. We are troubled thinking about what he saw, what he may have had to do. How he felt being where he was hated and hating other people. We realize he had to do what he had to do for survival. It is hard to pick up the pieces of war.

We have had one visit with a counselor whose son is on his second tour in Iraq as a Surgeon. Mike has chosen not to be with us for these visits.

Jonah, you asked about viewing the videos Mike brought home. They are so graphic and set to music. They seem like video games. Maybe they do this to soften the reality of it. But they are disturbing to me. I don't think I would want to share these.

Thank you for your work. We were impressed with your team and how you were able to tell our story. My son John said, "They are real journalists." (Peggy)

My counselor friend Jody becomes someone to share thoughts with as time goes on because her son is doing a second tour and he hates it and she does too.

Jody, glad to hear from you. Mike worked a few days this week in Cincinnati doing re-bar. It is outside in 15 degree temperatures. From one extreme to another! From desert heat to arctic cold! He isn't satisfied with this work and is still looking. We talked about it and I tried to say to him, "Mike, you don't need to do any more tough stuff." The words didn't come out before the tears fell. I turned away so he wouldn't see but he did. "I am sorry. I thought all the tears were gone," I said. He hugged me and said, "I know Mom and I don't have to prove myself."

I asked him later how things were with him in relation to Iraq. He said, "Fine, but I am still jumpy." He shared a story about flashing Christmas lights and how it felt like it was an explosion.

It all makes me cry. (Peggy)

By October 26, 2005 we hold a vigil for the 2000th U.S. Soldier killed in Iraq. I get an email from Kristen from the Inter-community Peace and Justice Center.

Please join us in a solemn vigil to honor all who have lost their lives in Iraq and help highlight the human cost of the war in Iraq.

People from Greater Cincinnati will join people from more than 390 communities from 49 states across the USA to honor those who have died and to say that the country's pro-peace majority wants Congress to stop the deaths by stopping the dollars that are funding the war.

I receive a note from Paul Schroeder on December 17, 2005 after I tell him how tears still fall.

Tears are the heart. How long they last depends on the wound.

Amanda mentioned to me today that when she thinks about Augie, it's only about his death. She is just now realizing she needs to think about him alive, remembering all the good, happy and fun times. This too is hard because the tears come.

I've just now started to think about those times. Believe me I'm tired of thinking about the military. I think what Augie would be doing right now if he were here. He planned to work at the Marine Center until the holidays, and then go back to his old job printing checks. I don't know how he would have handled the return home.

He took so many things in stride and tried to find some humor in everything. Still, Iraq was a different experience. Mike will work it out, I'm sure in time, with a different focus, when his daily activities become routine again.

We've started ever so slowly going through Augie's stuff. We found the attached. These were done when he was in 8th or 9th grade. There is another book of cartoons he called "Heir to the Throne" which we can't find. Those were done later in high school. He took a drawing class at OSU and I always told him he should try to do cartoons. I also told him to go to film school.

Had he come home, I would have suggested so many things to do. I think, in his heart, all he wanted to do was own a bar like Cheers! You know where everybody knows your name.

We plan to get the Christmas tree out this weekend and do some shopping. It certainly isn't the same. I guess we're in the middle of what was and what will be. I hope so, because I don't want this to be the what will be.

FOF (Families of the Fallen, an organization Paul and Rosemary started) is now nearing 800 members. I've sent letters to all the leadership in both houses of Congress. I don't know if we are making a difference. Perhaps. At least now we're beyond the silence, beyond the debate, and into how best to do it.

Best wishes. (Paul)

CHAPTER 60

Empty Boots

Mike gets a job working for a company that audits property for the county for tax purposes. He is able to be outside and pretty much on his own. He has to turn in his work each day and go to morning meetings. He walks from house to house taking measurements and noting any structural changes. He feels a need to carry a kabar in his truck and a small pocket knife in his dress pants pocket. He had a similar job in Iraq going house to house breaking down doors, hoping death didn't greet him on the other side. The lack of security and trust he brought home. He carries that in his heart.

Jerry and I keep up with the war the best we can. But for awhile we don't want any news.

We become familiar with a movement called *Eyes Wide Open*. This is a visual experience that attempts to make war real to people by lining up an empty pair of boots for all the KIA Soldiers and Marines. Also on display are shoes of all sizes representing the human cost of the war to Iraqi families. I attend a local display of *Eyes Wide Open* for Ohio KIA and find it very moving.

In June of 2006 a national *Eyes Wide Open* display is held for several days on the State grounds in Columbus, Ohio. Jerry and I are asked to speak.

Empty Boots at statehouse to show human cost of war. (Jim Siegel, the Columbus Dispatch)

Nearly 2,500 pairs of boots in military formation representing fallen U.S. troops will stretch a full city block across the Statehouse west lawn along High Street- one of the most visible locales in all of Ohio.

For Peggy Logue of Lebanon, whose son Michael served with Marine Reserves' Lima Company, 3rd Battalion, 25th Regiment, the exhibit is a chance to see close up the cost of a war she thinks has been badly mishandled by the Bush administration.

"We have young people dying, and if we're over there fighting a war, we better know what we're doing it for," said Logue, who, along with her husband, Jerry, will speak at the exhibit early Wednesday afternoon.

Twenty-three members of Lima Company, many from Ohio, died in Iraq.

"I don't dishonor their service," Logue said. "I think their lives may have been wasted because our administration has not done its job."

The sight of the empty boots lined up as if the soldiers were standing in them overwhelms me and I need a few moments to collect myself before I speak. I am handed the microphone and try to speak but my voice trembles and tears come. Jerry takes the microphone and begins his presentation. It is hard to deliver my thoughts while looking at the empty boots knowing brave men stood in them and gave all. I did what I could.

After our presentation Jerry and I walk among the empty boots. It is a spiritual time, a quiet time. Many people are doing the same. Everyone feels the quiet and the reverence.

We see the boots of those we have recently buried. I find Augie's boots. Dear Augie, a calm sweet presence.

CHAPTER 61

Tears

November 13, 2006 tears keep flowing. It has been over a year since Lima Company returned home. How long is grief? When do the tears stop?

We celebrate a memorial to the fallen Lima Company Marines this Veterans Day. Just hearing the names called off again brings tears. The Marine platoon leader who is reading the names only gets to the second name before his voice cracks and he pauses and swallows and tries not to be obvious. This ceremony is another step to healing.

We meet other families of the fallen. I wonder how they do it. I so respect and honor them. My son is home. He seems to be okay physically. What are his memories? What are his fears? What makes him feel different? What experiences are buried in his darkness?

In a moment of grace which comes quickly and unexpectedly Jerry is able to share some thoughts with Mike. He tells Mike that we saw the movie "Flags of our Fathers". One of the statements by a Marine in the movie is that they experience shame sometimes for what they have had to do and what they have seen. Jerry tells Mike not to wonder if what he saw and what he did is anything to be ashamed of. "Your Mom and I know that what you might have seen and what you might have done you did to survive. Not just for yourself but for that Marine on the right and the Marine on the left. You have no reason to be ashamed. We are so proud of you." Then his voice wavers as he holds back tears and says, "I love you, Mike." Tears now in Mike's eyes well up and he says, "I love you, Dad."

Mike has been given tickets for a Bengals game that someone from the VA wanted to donate to an Iraqi vet. Mike takes his sister and two other Marines with him. By the time Crista, Mike and the Marines come home from the game they are feeling pretty good. Crista enjoys the chance to be with her brother and his Marine buddies. She tells us that Mike is with the right people. "These are the ones he needs to be with," she says several times stressing it so we will understand. Finally, with tears in her eyes she looks at me and says, "These are the ones Mike needs to be with. His other friends are fine but these ... these are the ones he needs." She sees how they can talk and be with each other in a way no one else can. They experienced death, cruel and harsh and up close on a daily basis. They saw together things they don't want us to see. They faced every day the dark tunnel of the unexpected. They braced themselves to face the terrible.

Some Marines and military returning from combat do a lot of drinking and in their drunkenness they share their thoughts and memories with each other. And some of the time they wrestle and fight with each other. They are buddies... for life.

Now ours are home. We cry for them. We love them. Not knowing how to get to their dark places we come to realize that they can only go there with each other.

And I realize that only families of combat Marines or

Soldiers can understand our grief and our tears. Tears that come at anytime in any circumstances and unannounced and from a very deep place. Tears that cannot be explained. Tears that you think are over. Tears that sometimes seem unnecessary, tears nonetheless. And for our families that lost their young men, tears don't end ... they just go dry.

It is hard for me to think of my son as a veteran. The word has never meant much to me before. I have been so disconnected from war and the military. I have learned so much. I am thankful and grateful and have deep respect for every veteran from all wars.

And yes, we go on. And today the war goes on and more families are crying here and there, moms, dads, wives, and children. Tears...more tears.

CHAPTER 62

"It's About Humanity"

It's 2007 and Mike is at Ohio University pursuing a degree in aviation which he loves. He is asked to share his opinion on the Iraq war for the University newspaper. Here is a summary.

Iraq war creates debate at home as well as in Washington (The Athens News, 4,09,2007 by Bryant Greening)

Nearly four years after President George W. Bush's decision to send American troops to Iraq divided the country, United States citizens seem to be coming together on one issue - the need to wind down our military presence in Iraq. The only question now, according to local Iraq veterans and political pundits, is how and when.

Troy Weber, an Ohio University junior and veteran of the war in Iraq, said leaving Iraq is hardly a black-and-white issue. While he did say the United States has a responsibility to the Iraqi people, he conceded that America may be overstaying its welcome...

Michael Logue, an OU freshman and veteran of the war in

Iraq, said he can understand both sides of the issue. However, he ultimately said that when American troops were sent to Iraq, the Unites States implicitly agreed to assist in rebuilding the country.

Peace and stability, Logue said, are the ultimate goals for Iraq. Without establishing a safe homeland and democratic government for Iraqi civilians, he said the United States' efforts will be in vain.

"A victory for us is that when we leave, innocent Iraqis won't be killed (like they were under former dictator Saddam Hussein)," Logue said. "Our efforts wouldn't be a wash."

...Logue said that because there are anti-American forces in Iraq, U.S. soldiers are in a position where they must maintain strict authority. If democracy and peace are ever to become a reality, the veteran said, all Iraqi civilians must learn to respect rule, law and authority.

"You can't just be nice and expect them to follow," Logue said.

Logue also said he is worried that if American troops withdraw too soon, the Iraq government will collapse, giving terrorist organizations the opportunity to take over. "In 10 years, we would have something like what's happening in Somalia," Logue said, referring to terrorist breeding camps.

He also worried that a premature American withdrawal would send a dangerous message to the rest of the world. "(Terrorist organizations) would feel like they just beat one of the top military forces," he said. "That confidence would give them more power."

...Logue, for one, said Americans need to stop arguing about the legitimacy of entering the war and concentrate on the future of Iraq.

"People don't always agree with Bush (and his decision to occupy Iraq) "Logue said. "But we need to see this be a success. There are certain things I agree with in life. And I don't want people to be denied their freedom. It's about humanity."

CHAPTER 63

No Place to Hide

It is Memorial Day 2008 and Jerry finds an article on line titled, *The Making and Un-making of a Marine*. It is written by Lawrence Winters.

I was awake early the morning of Memorial Day. I lay thinking about why I wanted to get up while my wife slept restfully. Seeing her repose made me wonder what it's like to truly be at rest. I can't remember the last time I actually felt a state of complete relaxation. Of course I sleep, some. I even attain different levels of calm but real peace, a feeling of safety or surrender in my core of my being; I lost in the Vietnam War.

It being Memorial day and all the talk about war veterans coming home with Post Traumatic Stress Disorder (PTSD), I remembered something I'd read years ago. I thought it might apply to PTSD. The author said when we are hurt physically or emotionally, the traumatization causes our muscles to tighten up in protection. The example was given of when you stick an amoeba with a pin, its cell wall tenses; but after a few minutes it will relax to normal. If you keep sticking the amoeba, it will take longer for the cell wall to relax. Eventually the cell wall will go into stasis never recovering its relaxed state. The author went on to say that humans that are emotionally, physically hurt or frightened repeatedly developed a stasis that he called "body armor." Body armor lets no emotion out or in. It occurs to me that this is what it's like to have PTSD.

When a soldier is on the battlefield, pin pricks come in every size and shape. To make my point more current the battlefields of today's wars in Iraq and Afghanistan are the entire country – there is no such place as behind the lines. There is nowhere for a soldier to rest safely, not even the green zone. To over use my analogy of the amoeba, today's soldiers have no place to hide from the pins and no time to recover once they've been stuck. The pin pricks in these wars come from daily exposure to direct explosions which have become the lethal background music of Iraq. The ever present drone of war's machinery in soldier's ears carries the menace of death, either their own or someone else's. The pervasive awareness of road side bombs makes all movements life threatening. The suicide bomber has made a potential death threat of all unidentified human beings.

How beautifully written and how scary the reality. I called it a roller coaster but I think pin pricks as tested with the amoeba is more accurate. I found it hard to let my guard down after so many pricks. And I was in the safe arms of America, not in a desert with IEDs and RPGs and all kinds of bullets flying passed my head. I don't know that I ever developed the "body armor" that the author speaks of. I feel like until Mike came home I was in a constant state of being pricked.

A wonderful book has come to our atttention, *War and the Soul...Healing our Nation's Veterans from Post-traumatic Stress Disorder (Edward Tick, PH.D. Quest Books, Wheaton Illinois, 2005)*

In his book Edward Tick talks about the need for soldiers to tell their story. Then their story needs to be validated and become part of the collective wisdom of the community. How often does this happen? Most vets don't share their stories. Many don't want us to know what they saw and did. They struggle themselves with what they had to do. They feel individual shame or confusion. Or:

Veterans most often withhold their stories, not only because of the pain evoked in telling them but also because they fear that, in our culture of denial, we won't properly receive them. Without telling their stories they, *become stuck in the role of scapegoat, carriers of the tribal shadow. If we are to redress this situation, we have a profound responsibility to be a supportive audience for those who went to war in our name.(page221)*

This book deals with many of the issues I, as a mother of a young Marine, fear. That Mike would lose himself and not know how to get back. Jerry and I gave Mike a copy of this book. We also gave his doctor a copy and the mother of his girl friend. We would like everyone to read it so that as a culture we may better be able to help those we send off to war to return to some sense of normalcy by honoring where they have been and what they have had to do. Our military is asked to "descend into the abyss of human and earthly nature," and there to learn, "that which he or she did not want to know - the brevity of life and love, our human capacity for destruction, our smallness and helplessness against existential forces."(page253)

I am learning with Mike what it means to be a warrior. Edward Tick, in his book says it well. (War and the Soul p252)

A veteran does not become a warrior merely for having gone to war...He becomes a warrior when he has been set right with life again. A warrior's first priority is to protect life rather than destroy it. He serves his nation in peace as well as in war making and dissuades his people from suffering the scourges of war unless absolutely necessary... A warrior disciplines the violence within himself. Internally and externally, he stares violence in the face and makes it back down. A warrior serves spiritual and moral principles, which he places higher than himself. The role of warrior has a high, noble, and honorable status.

Jerry and I feel that Mike has high and noble visions and we are honored to have him as our warrior son. He has led us to a place we never dreamed we would go. He has shown us courage and integrity.

A Memorial is dedicated to the Lima Company Marines in May 2008. Jerry and I are there with Paul Schroeder and Rosemary Palmer. Many 3/25th Marines are there including some still recovering from injuries. And there are many dignitaries to speak including Senator John Glenn. Speeches are made honoring the Marines and the work they accomplished in Iraq.

And the artist's who created the memorial speaks. She like many in Ohio was grieving when she heard the continual stories of the deaths of our fine Marines in August, 2005. She wanted to do something to help but didn't know what. A vision awoke her in the night and she saw the memorial she was to create. She began the work of creating it, eight life size portrait panels of the 22 Marines and the Navy Corpsman who died during their tour. This memorial is dedicated this day.

Mike comes to Columbus to attend but then chooses not to. He isn't the only Marine who doesn't come. Some do. Some don't. Some can't. They will see the memorial and pay their respects when there is no one else there. All the people and the speeches seem to be too much for some of them.

I see the wife of the Navy Corpsman, Travis Youngblood with her children, her young son Hunter, who was only four when he lost his daddy and her now three year old daughter, Emma, who never saw her father. She is telling them as she gently strokes the artist rendition of her Travis, to "say good-bye to daddy," all the while she is trying to say good-bye but can't pull herself away. When she finds no place to hide maybe she and her children will develop "body armor". But I hope that his story will be told over and over to her children so they will understand that their father did something for the community that few men do. He gave all.

CHAPTER 64

Everything Else is Easy

It is October 2008, the third year anniversary of the homecoming of Lima 3/25th Marines. Life has a marvelous way of bringing healing.

While in Arizona in the winter Jerry and I receive an email from Beth Lerman. She is the one who in 2005 sent out a note about the Bring Them Home Now Tour coming through Ohio and requested housing and food for them. Beth is the Coordinator of the Ohio Chapter of Military Families Speak Out. Her message this time is about needing help with setting up a house for an Iraqi refugee family coming to Dayton.

I am immediately drawn to that request. I return a message to her saying how much I want to help and ask if there would be more families coming so that Jerry and I could help when we return from Arizona. She says "Yes. There will be many."

We return home in April and we receive word of another

Iraqi family coming and a request for help. Jerry and I respond, "Yes, we want to help."

We hear it is a family of seven. We are still cleaning and getting the house ready as the family walks through the door, five beautiful children from age six to fourteen, four girls and one boy. The father carries everything they came with and everything they own in one duffle bag.

We take them through the house and the two little ones run back and forth to their bedroom. They have huge smiles on their faces. They seem overjoyed with their room. And there are no toys or bright colors or games or anything child-like. The only thing in their room is a used bed sparsely covered with a used bed covering. But delight fills these children.

I am showing Asraa, the mother, items in the bathroom; toothbrushes, soap, shampoo, towels. She is so grateful and repeats, "Thank you. Thank you." I look at her and say, "Welcome to America." And tears fill my eyes and my voice cracks and I have to look away. There is no way to hide my tears. I don't know why they are there. There is no warning. They just show up. I excuse myself and shyly walk away feeling embarrassed. The social worker sees me and I say to her, "I am sorry for this. I don't understand my tears. I am so happy to be here and help these people. My son was in Iraq. Many of his friends were killed or injured. Maybe this is why I cry. I don't know."

The social worker takes my arm and smiles and says, "If you want to talk with me I am available." I thank her and try to hide my face. She has enough to do with this new family for now. I don't know why I want to help these people. I don't know why I cry. Maybe because these are the people Mike was trying to help. Is it for these people that some of his friends died. Is it for this family that some of my friends' children gave up their lives. I don't know. This is so unexpected.

Jerry and I become very close to this family. We are seeing

them through many onstacles and hardships as they settle into American life: medical, school, jobs, driving, shopping etc. We help them in any way they need and any way we can.

After several months, we grow closer to them and we invite them to our house for a sleepover. We make room for all seven. It is a delightful time of picnic, swings, movies and ice cream. We look forward to many more experiences with them.

Reflecting on this experience we are amazed at how full of blessing we feel. This family has taken our wounded hearts and filled them with love. They help us heal the scar left by the war our son was caught in and their family lived through. One they had to escape. We feel a deep connection. One we cannot explain. We instantly bonded with this family and we love them dearly. We see beauty in their faces and warmth in their smiles and we are incredibly amazed and so pleased to know them.

Mike, our warrior wants to serve and help others and has led us to this page of our personal history. Working with Iraqi refugees has brought life back to our souls. We could not choose a better way to heal, a better way to serve.

Sometimes the Iraqi parents, out of respect, will say to Jerry and me when we have brought them something or helped them with something, "No! No ! This is too much for you. Let us. We can do it. This is too hard for you."

They say we are doing too much or something we are lifting is too heavy or the hour is getting late and we should go home, they will finish etc.

After saying this many times in different circumstances I finally respond to them emphatically, "No. No. This is not hard. This is not too much. Having my nineteen year old son in a faraway country with a rifle in his hand. Shooting at people. Being shot at. Seeing his friends die. And seeing my friends bury their young men. This is hard. This is too much. Everything else. Everything else is easy."

CHAPTER 65

A Tribute to our Marines

(author unknowm)

Note: (August 15, 2009)
I am sharing this because it is such a loving tribute to our Marines. It is the story of Lima Company in the year 2005.
Faithfully,
Isolde Zierk

It started out so easy
But May would soon arrive
And we would lose our first Marines
Ubaydi'd come alive

Then on across the river
To the north and west we rode
In tracs that smoked and shuttered
And one would soon explode

First platoon was hit again
Unlucky had they been
For in three days in early May
They'd just lost eight good men

Before the month was over
New Market would arrive
And one more of our good Marines
Would not go home alive

June was hot and dusty
As we fought from town to town
But this month we were lucky
For no man had gone down

A painful blow was dealt again
On a foot patrol in Hit
We tried to save the Corpsman
But he died within a week

In Cycla there would be more pain
While knocking on a door
A team leader and radioman
Would soon lay on the floor

In the heat of early August
Another blow was dealt
An amtrack would lie twisted
As more pain and grief was felt

Eleven was the number
On that day of August 3rd
When in our column's file
An eruption had occurred

The number twenty-three would stand
From then until October
Then Lima did come shuffling home
Their mission it was over

But none in rank or column
On that gray October day
Would ever forget their brothers
Or the price that they had paid.

CHAPTER 66

Skin in the Game

I don't know how long it took Mike to finally decide what he wanted on his tattoo. I know he has been thinking about getting one since he returned from Iraq. Many who serve, Soldiers and Marines, choose to emblazon on their bodies a memento of their combat experience.

In the winter of 2009 Mike told us he got a tattoo. He sent a picture on the cell phone to show us. It appeared large. I could make out the Marine symbol of the eagle, globe and anchor. He didn't say much about it. I asked him if it hurt and he said, "Just a little". Of course, a mom would ask such a question. It seems he wanted it before spring break and I said "yeah so you can walk a beach somewhere and have all the girls look." He chuckled.

Then, in the summer of 2009 while I am asking Mike about pictures for this book, the image of the tattoo comes up. Mike is showing me pictures on the computer that I might use for the book. One is a picture of a Blackhawk helicopter that he says is the medevac. Another picture is of the "trac" burning after being hit by an IED. I am not aware that he is talking about the medevac that airlifted the injured from the "trac" explosion of May 2005 so I am still just looking for pictures. Then Mike says, "These are the pictures the artist used to design my tattoo."

"What?"

"These pictures of the medevac and the 'trac' are on my tattoo."

"Oh Mike. No, I didn't know that."

"Yeah," he says as he lifts his shirt to show me. There on the left side of his body is the picture of the medevac and the burning trac.

I realize how out of touch I feel once again. He has had the tattoo for several months and this is the first I understand what it is.

"Here is the Blackhawk that came in for the rescue." Then he points to another part of his tattoo. "The rising smoke is from the burning 'trac.'"

"Mike, is this the "trac" you were in?"

"Yeah."

"Oh wow". I swallow back my emotion. "Honey, I didn't realize this is your tattoo. I thought it was just the Marine symbol."

"That is just part of it."

I look more carefully at his tattoo. This is the first time I really see it. I see the words forming a circle around his tattoo. "All gave some. Some gave all." I touch it and want to feel it. I want to feel what Mike feels. He is not going to talk about it.

He continues scrolling through pictures and talking about them but I am lost in this revelation.

I don't say anymore. I just listen and try to hear him.

Afterward I think how meaningful that tattoo is to Mike and how meaningful that event in 2005 is to him. It is

Operation Matador. Mike is in the "trac". His platoon leader calls him out. While watching from a following "trac" in over watch, he sees the "trac" explode some thirty seconds after he evacuates it.

The close call for Mike is also a close call for us. I realize how different my life would be if Mike was in that "trac." He has that day emblazoned on his side. But he says to me, "No, not just that day, it symbolizes every day of the whole deployment." He won't forget.

Mike will always have "skin in the game."

MIKE'S THOUGHTS

My first battle was fought at seventeen years old. It was with my parents. They were really concerned about their "little boy" becoming a Marine. Honestly, they should've seen this day coming ever since I was four or five and playing in the bushes (starting fires) in my camouflage clothes/ cast (broken arm). I was a little boy as all teenagers are but, I had decided for myself and my country that I wanted to give my time and my service. If I could not do this as an able bodied young male, then who will? The country needed me and will always need capable defenders. I did believe I could normally follow my plan for college and both would be accomplished. I was only going to Marine boot camp, "earning" the title of Marine along side of many others. However, as every young adult will learn, plans are always changing. Life can never be perfectly planned. As a Combat Veteran, at nineteen, the Marines taught me more in two years than most people in five or ten years. I will always appreciate that and those that serve. I had fought with my parents at seventeen. They wanted to protect me. I wanted something more, to be part of the best, only in the Marines. While we were in Iraq and at times in the most dangerous place on earth, I felt great knowing I had Marines fighting along my side. We were ready for anything and we would destroy anything that crossed us. We "earned" it over there.

Our Fallen Warriors; they are never forgotten, they are my brothers in arms. I'm honored to have fought along their side. They died for us, they died a Warriors death. (Mike)

"Please never forget why Marines, soldiers, sailors and airmen go forward and that's to push the cause of freedom." Gunnery Sergeant Delgado

Thank you, John and Crista and my brother in-law Jeff for everything during and after the deployment.

I owe a great thanks to all the family and friends, who kept my friends and me in their thoughts.

Jerry and Peggy Logue are two amazing parents, I'm glad I had the opportunity to show them the Marines and all the positives of our great military. I will say we have had disagreements dating back to the Peace Corps/ Marine Corps talk. During that deployment, I can't fathom what emotions they must have felt. Looking back, I wish I could have prepared my family better, protected them more from the experience. There are some things that people just don't need to know. I've never questioned their level of support or patriotism. Our ability to have disagreements is one of the freedoms of the many that I love about Our Country. God Bless America. (Mike, Nov.11,2009)

CLOSING THOUGHTS

It has taken a long time to get this book together and ready to publish. During all of that time, thoughts and feelings have had time to simmer. And that has been good. And at times I thought that there is no way I will ever publish this book. But it kept after me. It seems to have its' own legs.

One thing I realize is how important it is for me to know that Mike appreciates the book. I feel it is a story to be shared but how Mike feels about it is more important to me that anything else. It has been encouraging to me when I could get Mike to slow down enough to listen as I would read, or get him to read part and then get his reaction. His response has been positive.

As I near the end of writing I ask Mike if he would like to write something for the book, sharing some of his thoughts. I am pleased to hear that he wants to do that. I send him a copy of the book and ask him to read through it and add or make suggestions. One night he spends three hours reading and adding comments that he says he will send to me. Weeks go by and I hear nothing. I am also waiting for some pictures from him to use in the book. Finally, I tell him I am sending it to the publisher the next Monday and I will do with what I have. That spurs him into action. He comes home and spends eight hours reading and writing. This is when he writes *Mike's Thoughts*. Before he leaves to go back to school, I ask him how he likes the book. "It's good," he says. "Thanks Mama."

Wow! Those words "thanks Mama" fill my heart in a way that leaves me speechless. It says more than, "yeah the book is worth reading…" or "yeah, you did a good job." He knows I wrote out of my love for him and his Marines. We have a different experience about this war. He is the warrior in combat. I am the anti-war at home Mom desperate for his safety. He accepts my thoughts and convictions, my anger and frustration. He sees through to the love I have for him. And he says, "Thanks mama." Wow!

Mike is running high on adrenaline when he comes home from Iraq in 2005. It takes a long time for that to subside. He is on edge and unnerved often. Fight or flight is a common existence. He takes nothing from anyone. His brother has to subdue him at a Bengals game when he almost throws fists at a supporter of the challenging team. Often he has more to drink than he should. But maybe this is part of the process of coming out of combat. We don't have a place or a plan for our warriors to heal. And even warriors suffer the pain and grief of killing and being killed. Mike does make good, positive choices. He takes the money he earned, his combat pay, and buys a house in Athens, Ohio. It is a house that needs extensive hard work. And he has put that into it. He lives there while going to school and rents the other rooms to students. Often it is to other Marines. Another good choice Mike makes is to get a dog. This is against our wishes because we feel we will be responsible for its care. We beg him not to. But the truth is that dog helps Mike get in touch with his feelings and begin healing. In Iraq the combat Soldiers and Marines operate with two emotions, fear and anger. Mike finds comfort from and love for his dog Max, a black lab, chow, shepherd mix. And now he has another dog, Bailey, a pure bred white Siberian Husky. Mike's life now clearly has some black and white.

I cannot explain how humbling it is to know that more than once Mike is almost among the KIA. He starts counting the close calls for me that he remembers. After ten, he stops counting: RPGs, IEDs, mortars, sniper fire, and machine gun rounds. He saw the affect of these close calls on walls behind where he was standing. He heard bullets whiz by. On one occasion when sniper fire whizzed by his head, he said to himself, "I can't die on Mom's birthday." And he seems untouched. He has no visible wounds or scars. He looks healthy and intact. He looks like a very beautiful, young American male. But he knows and we know it could have been different. And this is humbling.

I don't know if he could articulate his thoughts as clearly about his decision to become a Marine as he made it five years ago, but he certainly is clear now. I don't feel that we were in "battle" as we challenged the recruiter and Mike about his joining but we definitely wanted to protect and guide Mike.

He is a man now. He is a Marine. He still has idealism and a desire to serve and that is admirable. I still want to cry and do cry. I just finished reading, *Where Men Win Glory*, by Jon Krakauer. This is the story of Pat Tillman. Part Two begins with an epigraph which I read over and over. It describes part of my struggle as I watched my son go to war. "*War is always about betrayal, betrayal of the young by the old, of idealists by cynics and troops by politicians.*" (Chris Hedges, "A Culture of Atrocity")

Jerry and I are very proud of Mike. Would we feel differently about his deployment if he were in combat now, even though he is four years older? I don't think so. It isn't just that he was so young that we were so traumatized while he was in combat. It is because we love him so much. Age makes no difference when speaking about loved ones going to war. Dying from illness, accident or natural causes though difficult, is very different than dying from combat. We choose combat. We allow our national leaders to send our loved ones to combat. We best do that only as a last resort. Not for reasons less than that.

Mike is on a solid road now. He is studying aviation at Ohio University. He has his pilot license and worked this summer as an intern at Net Jets. He started an organization recognized on campus for veterans. They meet regularly and have brought recognition and honor to Ohio University students who are Iraqi veterans that have returned from war.

And yes, we harbor fear and pride because warriors are not stopped when others hesitate. They respond. And we know whenever called or inspired, Mike will respond, as the best, as a Marine.

Life is sacred for everyone. It is all we have and we have it in common. We bring our individual gifts and talents, strengths and weaknesses. Initially I titled this book with the narrow concept of the military and their families having *skin in the game*. And this is true. It is a small percentage of American families that are engaged at this level. And I don't want to diminish that reality. But now I speak in a larger context. A warrior willingly puts his *skin in the game* as he serves and follows orders. A Marine or Soldier does not go to battle by himself. He has been ordered to do so by a society that believes in what is ordered.

We are not all warriors on the battlefield. But maybe we can reduce the number of battlefields and the number of warriors on the battlefield by choosing to use our gifts to bring peace. I realize the potential for violence is in each of us and maybe this is where we start to end war by quelling our own personal violence, our own personal anger, intolerance and hatred. We can become warriors for peace.

Our country is still at war and engaged in combat. We, at home, struggle to decide if we should be. I can only hope we make this decision with the utmost diligence because the decision to be at war is a final decision for some.

We have the power to choose the order given the Marine or Soldier. We decide to be apathetic or involved. We choose to use our gifts or deny them. We choose how to be in this world. We choose life or death. We all bring what we choose to the game because we are here right now, and in this way we have *skin in the game.*

Love Peace.

About the Author

Peggy Logue is the mother of three children. Her youngest became a Marine and at age 19 was in some of the fiercest combat in Iraq with Lima 3/25th. Peggy has a Master's in Education and has been writing for many years. She has several articles published in books and journals. Peggy lives in Lebanon, Ohio with her husband, Jerry.

APPENDIX

Deployment Statistics

Although they suffered many losses, Lima 3/25th Marines will be remembered for what they accomplished while serving in Iraq. Here are some facts:

During their deployment the 3/25th Marines:
-conducted 185 days of combat operations
-conducted 11 Battalion/regimental Combat Team operations (25 company operations)
-conducted 150,000 miles' worth of motorized patrols
-participated in the following operations:
River Bridge
Outer Banks (1 April- 3 May)
Matador (7-14 May)
New Market (23-29 May)
Cache sweep (30 May -1 June)
Spear (16 -18 June)

Sword (27 June -5 July)
Saber (23 July - 1 August)
Quick Strike (2-9 August)
Toll Booth (12 - 18 August)
Detour (30 August - 3 September)
Toll Booth II 92-8 September)

-captured the following: 387 AK-47's, 34 SKS, 27 Rpks, 51 pistols, 36 rifles, 31 shotguns, 5 sterling submachine guns, 7 medium machine guns, 1 heavy machine gun, 31 RPS launchers, 5 Al Jaleel 60mm mortar systems, 2 120mm systems, 2 base plates/bipods, 6 pellet/b guns, 67 RPG grenades, 16 rifle/hand grenades, 5 82 mm mortar systems, 25 flak jackets, 7 gas masks, -captured literally thousands of enemy artillery, mortar, tank and ammo rounds and also rockets -3/25 is the only unit serving with the 2nd Marine Division to clear and liberate an Iraqi city Area of Operations Atlanta

- found and destroyed 161 IEDs and mines and an additional 107 IED kits

- sent 119 detainees to Abu Gharab

- In the city of Hit, under 40 Iraqis voted in the January 05 elections; now an estimated 35,000 Iraqis in Hit sat they plan to vote this month (October 10, 2005)

THIS INFORMATION WAS SENT VIA EMAIL FROM Isolde Zierk, our Key Volunteer Network Coordinator. It was forwarded to her from Bob and Marla Derga with this note: *The following was forwarded from our CACO officer and summarizes 3/25th's efforts in Iraq.*

RESOURCES

Web sites
www.afsc.org
www.codepink4peace.org
www.crawfordpeacehouse.org
www.fofchange.org
www.gsfp.org
www.icasualties.org
www.ivaw.org
www.mfso.org
www.truthout.org
www.veteransforpeace.org
www.icasualties.org

Organizations:
American Friends
Code Pink
Families of the Fallen
Gold Star Families for Peace

Iraq Vets Against the War
Military Families Speak Out
Veterans For Peace

Videos:
Combat Diary – The Marines of Lima Company (A&E Channel)
America's Secret Shame (Channel 4 Dispatches UK)

BIBLIOGRAPHY

Deis, Michelle, *The Lima Company Memorial, A Remembrance of Spirit and Choice.* Columbus, Ohio: Hopkins Printing, 2008.

Krakauer,Jon, *Where Men Win Glory, The odyssey of Pat Tillman,* New York: Doubleday, 2009.

Thibault, Captain MD Glenn, *Sword in the Lion's Den, Navy Doc with 3/25th Marines in Iraq,* Baltimore: Publish America,2008.

Tick,PH.D.Edward, *War and the Soul, Healing Our Nation's Veterans from Post-traumatic Stress Disorder,* Wheaton, Illinois: Quest Books.